ADDITIONAL PRAISE FOR *TYRANNY COMES HOME*

"Coyne and Hall brilliantly reveal that a fatal coarsening comes with the rise of an empire. One can only respond with the cant phrase, heard often in these latter days, which would be better applied to peaceful, intellectual exchanges than to the corrupting enterprise of foreign intervention: 'Thank you for your service.'"
—Deirdre Nansen McCloskey, University of Illinois at Chicago

"An old German saying claims that losing a war is bad, but winning a war is worse. Coyne and Hall document one way in which that is the case: the architecture of social control created by militarism is easily adapted to domestic life. *Tyranny Comes Home* illustrates this phenomena in the United States, while offering a path to reclaiming the 'Great Republic.'"
—Michael Munger, Duke University

"*Tyranny Comes Home* argues that a nation cannot act brutally in the world and still respect the rights and liberties of its own people. It is a wonderfully insightful look at the connections between the violence of American foreign policy and our shrinking democracy at home."
—Stephen Kinzer, Watson Institute, Brown University, Columnist, *The Boston Globe*, and author of *The True Flag*

"Christopher J. Coyne and Abigail R. Hall have built a highly original and penetrating argument on a neglected topic that demands attention in the age of endless war. Their thorough analysis, understanding of history, and fresh correlations are insightful and a pleasure to read. We need more of this kind of creative bridge-building."
—John Tirman, MIT Center for International Studies

"This is an important and provocative exploration of an overlooked cost of militaristic foreign policy: domestic freedom. This well-researched and lively book is a must read for those concerned with the preservation of individual liberty and the perils of permanent war."
—Daniel Ellsberg, author of *Secrets: A Memoir of Vietnam and the Pentagon Papers* and *The Doomsday Machine: Confessions of a Nuclear War Planner*

"An adept and engaging examination of the processes by which militaristic policy abroad can lead to the loss of civil liberties at home."
—John Mueller, Ohio State University and Cato Institute

"Many people believe that U.S. 'peacekeeping' efforts abroad help to protect American civil liberties at home. Coyne and Hall show just how mistaken that view is. I know of no other work that makes such a clear connection between foreign intervention and the erosion of domestic civil liberties."
—Randall Holcombe, Florida State University

"Clearly and boldly argued, this is an excellent contribution to our understanding of the economics of interventionism."
—Joshua Hall, West Virginia University, and coauthor of *Economic Freedom of the World Report*

"A number of America's founding fathers expressed the view that foreign military ventures would come at a high cost. In *Tyranny Comes Home*, Christopher J. Coyne and Abigail R. Hall put this warning to the test: How have America's wars of choice and its colonial experiments affected the homeland and the power of the presidency? And what does economic theory have to say about the transformation from state to empire? Their analysis makes for an engrossing read, a remarkable demonstration of the foresight that went into the Constitution, and a stark depiction of the dangers that it faces today."
—Scott Horton, Contributing Editor, *Harper's Magazine*

TYRANNY COMES HOME

TYRANNY COMES HOME

HOME

THE DOMESTIC FATE
OF U.S. MILITARISM

Christopher J. Coyne and Abigail R. Hall

Stanford University Press
Stanford, California

Stanford University Press
Stanford, California

Printed in the United States of America on acid-free, archival-quality paper

Library of Congress Cataloging-in-Publication Data

Names: Coyne, Christopher J., author. | Hall, Abigail R., author.
Title: Tyranny comes home : the domestic fate of U.S. militarism
Christopher J. Coyne and Abigail R. Hall.
Description: Stanford, California : Stanford University Press, 2018. |
Includes bibliographical references and index.
Identifiers: LCCN 2017034112 (print) | LCCN 2017035625 (ebook) |
ISBN 9781503605282 | ISBN 9780804798471 (cloth : alk. paper) | ISBN
9781503605275 (pbk. : alk. paper)
Subjects: LCSH: Militarism—United States. | United States—Military
policy | Civil rights—United States. | Social control—United States. |
Authoritarianism—United States. | United States—Politics and government |
United States—Foreign relations.
Classification: LCC UA23 (ebook) | LCC UA23 .C685 2018 (print) | DDC
306.2/70973—dc23
LC record available at https://lccn.loc.gov/2017034112

To Robert Higgs—
Scholar, Teacher, Champion of Liberty

Contents

"The means of defence against foreign danger have been always the instruments of tyranny at home."   —James Madison, 1787

"It is a much easier thing to unloose the demon war than to chain him up again." —Moncure D. Conway, 1884

"War makes men barbarous because, to take part in it, one must harden oneself against all regret, all appreciation of delicacy and sensitive values. One must live *as if those values did not exist*, and when the war is over one has lost the resilience to return to those values."   —Cesare Pavese, 1961

"It is especially important that we, who wield such massive force across the globe, see within ourselves the seeds of our own obliteration."   —Chris Hedges, 2002

Acknowledgments

The development of this book has benefited from detailed comments from Josh Hall, Randy Holcombe, and Sheldon Richman. We are grateful to our editor at Stanford University Press, Margo Beth Fleming, for her encouragement, guidance, and support throughout this project.

Parts of this book were presented at the Center for Public Choice and Market Process, Charleston College, Charleston Southern University, and the Free Market Institute at Texas Tech University. Portions of this manuscript were also presented at the Association for Private Enterprise Education Annual Conference, the Southern Economic Association Conference, and the Applied Research in the PPE Framework Colloquium at the Mercatus Center at George Mason University. We are grateful to organizers and to the participants for their comments and suggestions.

The Mercatus Center at George Mason University also convened participants to discuss the manuscript in its entirety. We are grateful to Peter Boettke, Don Boudreaux, Anne Rathbone Bradley, Ted Galen Carpenter, Jesse Kirkpatrick, Jayme Lemke, Phil Magness, Claire Morgan, Chris Preble, Hilton Root, William Ruger, and Trevor Thrall for taking the time to carefully read the manuscript and participate in that close reading. The manuscript is vastly better because of their input.

The F.A. Hayek Program for Advanced Study in Philosophy, Politics, and Economics at George Mason University's Mercatus Center, the Charles Koch Foundation, and the Earhart Foundation provided financial support that allowed us to focus on, and complete, this project. We are grateful for their generosity.

Chris would like to thank his wife, Rachel, and daughter, Charlotte, for their love and support.

Abby would like to thank her parents, Chet and Mary, for always encouraging her writing and for being her first and most influential editors. She would also like to thank her husband, Edgar, for his support and encouragement.

Preface: Tyranny Comes Home

In August 2014 a police officer in Ferguson, Missouri, shot and killed teenager Michael Brown, leading to widespread protests throughout the city. The response from the local police to the protests drew national attention to the equipment and tactics employed. Officers dressed in full military garb, including camouflage uniforms, body armor, helmets, and gas masks, confronted the protestors. The officer's vehicles included Ballistic Engineered Armored Response Counter Attack Trucks (BearCats), a mine-resistant variant of which is used abroad by the military. In addition to their dress and vehicles, police were armed with military-grade rifles capable of hitting long-distance targets. Who can forget the picture of a sniper in full military gear perched atop a tactical operations vehicle pointing his rifle with a high-powered scope at the protestors?

These and other images from Ferguson could easily have come from U.S. military operations in Afghanistan or Iraq. Police officers tasked with protecting and serving the local community looked much more like soldiers tasked with finding and destroying an enemy in a war zone. The police response shined a spotlight on the militarization of domestic policing, a national phenomenon that had been unfolding quietly for decades.

More broadly, the events in Ferguson illustrate how the mentality, methods, and gear of war can return from abroad and affect domestic life. The purpose of this book is to provide insight into this phenomenon. We offer a general framework for *how* approaches and tools that have been developed for and deployed in foreign interventions return home and, in the process, threaten domestic liberties. This helps explain not just the militarization of police but also the domestic use of surveillance, drones, and torture. In doing so it sheds light on an overlooked cost of a proactive, interventionist foreign policy.

PART I

Losing the Great Republic

CHAPTER I

Mark Twain's Ominous Warning

Mark Twain, most celebrated as the author of *The Adventures of Tom Sawyer* and its sequel, *Adventures of Huckleberry Finn*, was also an astute political commentator. One issue that particularly concerned Twain was the U.S. government's foreign intervention and imperialism.[1] He worried that U.S. military adventures were unjust because they significantly and often brutally harmed innocent people abroad. But Twain also emphasized that foreign intervention had real effects on the social fabric of America as the intervening country. These concerns are apparent in two fictional essays from the early twentieth century written in response to the U.S. government's occupation of the Philippines.[2] The essays discuss a hypothetical "Great Republic" that had adopted an aggressive foreign policy of intervening in distant societies. Twain warned that the methods associated with this policy would return home and destroy the Great Republic:

But it was impossible to save the Great Republic. She was rotten to the heart. Lust of conquest had long ago done its work; trampling upon the helpless abroad had taught her, by a natural process, to endure with apathy the like at home; multitudes who had applauded the crushing of other people's liberties, lived to suffer for their mistake in their own persons.[3]

What if Twain's scenario was not fictional but real? What if foreign intervention undermines liberties at home? The purpose of this book is to answer these questions by exploring how both preparation for intervention abroad and intervention itself affect domestic institutions in ways that threaten or reduce the freedoms of individuals living in the intervening country. Many believe that interventions overseas by the U.S. government protect domestic liberties. This book shows that this view is incomplete, if not entirely mistaken. When a society adopts the values of an aggressive empire, it runs the risk of adopting imperial characteristics at home.

To explain why, we develop a theory of the "boomerang effect" to understand Twain's "natural process" through which foreign intervention increases the scope of domestic government and erodes citizens' liberties from state coercion.[4] The underlying logic of the boomerang effect is as follows. Preparing for and engaging in foreign intervention provide a testing ground for intervening governments to experiment with new forms of social control over distant populations.[5] Under certain conditions, these innovations in social control are then imported back to the intervening country through several channels that expand the scope of domestic government activities. The result is that the intervening government becomes more effective at controlling not only foreign populations but the domestic population as well. Under this scenario, the preparation and execution of foreign intervention changes domestic political institutions and the relationship between citizen and government. Domestic freedom from interference and coercion by others erodes or is lost altogether as the state gains power over citizens.

THE UNITED STATES AS THE GREAT REPUBLIC

Although our analysis is generalizable, we focus on one specific "Great Republic"—the United States. We do so for several reasons. First, when writing about the hypothetical Great Republic, Twain was referring to America and the government's decision to invade and occupy the Philippines. We thus address Twain's concerns about the domestic implications of the U.S. government's activist foreign policy, which has persisted since his time. In doing so, we offer a systematic study of the effects of foreign intervention on domestic freedoms in the United States.

In addition, we are both U.S. citizens and are concerned about the current, and future, state of our country. The deaths of Michael Brown in Ferguson, Missouri, and Eric Garner in New York City in 2014 provoked public debate about the militarization of domestic policing. As we will argue, foreign intervention has been a contributing factor in domestic militarization. At the same time, in the wake of Edward Snowden's revelations about the scope of U.S. government surveillance, debates rage about the appropriate role of the national security state as it relates to control over the private lives of U.S. citizens.[6] As all these debates take place at home, the U.S. government continues to embrace a militaristic foreign policy, which entails intervening around the globe and attempting to shape world affairs according to the wishes of those with political power.

It has recently been noted that "[t]oday US military operations are involved in scores of countries across . . . five continents. The US military is the world's largest tenant landlord, with significant military facilities in nations around the world with a significant presence in Bahrain, Djibouti, Turkey, Qatar, Saudi Arabia, Kuwait, Iraq, Afghanistan, Kosovo, and Kyrgyzstan, in addition to long-established bases in Germany, Japan, South Korea, Italy, and the UK."[7] The U.S. Central Command (CENTCOM) is also currently carrying out various military-related activities in at least twenty countries in the Middle East and Central and South Asia, meaning that "the US has some kind of military presence in Afghanistan, Bahrain, Egypt, Iran, Iraq, Jordan, Kazakhstan, Kuwait, Kyrgyzstan, Lebanon, Oman, Pakistan, Qatar, Saudi Arabia, Syria, Tajikistan, Turkmenistan, U.A.E., Uzbekistan, and Yemen."[8] This presence is not a recent phenomenon, as the U.S. government has been actively engaged in military intervention in the Middle East for over three decades with no end in sight.[9]

The list of countries subject to U.S. military influence becomes even longer when one moves beyond the Middle East and Asia and considers that "the US Africa Command (AFRICOM) supports military-to-military relationships with 54 African nations."[10] A recent review of the global use of U.S. special ops forces concludes that "[d]uring the fiscal year that ended on September 30, 2014, U.S. Special Operations Forces (SOF) deployed to 133 countries—roughly 70% of the nations on the planet."[11] Only a minority of countries are immune from direct U.S. military influence.

Another indicator of the reach of the U.S. military is the prevalence of American bases as cataloged in the Department of Defense's (DoD's) annual *Base Structure Report*. For FY 2014 the DoD operated over 570 bases in foreign countries with an additional 4,200 bases in the United States and its territories.[12] The agency's total real estate portfolio is significant, consisting of "more than 562,000 facilities (buildings, structures, and linear structures), located on over 4,800 sites worldwide, and covering over 24.7 million acres" both domestically and internationally.[13] Anthropologist David Vine estimates a higher total number of U.S. bases on foreign soil. According to his calculations, "today there are around eight hundred U.S. bases in foreign countries, occupied by hundreds of thousands of U.S. troops."[14]

In addition to its direct global military presence, the U.S. government indirectly influences foreign affairs through a variety of mechanisms, including international arms-transfer agreements with other governments. "In 2015, the United States ranked first in arms transfer agreements with developing nations with $26.7 billion or 41% of these agreements. In second place was France with $15.2 billion or 23.3% of such agreements."[15] The United States also ranked first in the actual delivery of arms to developing nations, controlling $11.9 billion, or 35.4 percent, of the arms market.[16] Adding developed countries to the account, "the United States was predominant, ranking first with $40.2 billion in such agreements or 50.29% of all such agreements."[17] France ranked second with $15.3 billion, or 19.2 percent, of global agreements. As this makes clear, the U.S. government is the world's largest arms dealer.

The U.S. government's global boot print is no post-9/11 phenomenon. The United States has been in a state of permanent war for decades, and the U.S. government has intervened in global affairs for centuries.[18] No consensus exists on how many times the U.S. government has employed military force throughout the country's history; nevertheless, attempts to catalog historical foreign interventions, beginning in the 1790s, have documented hundreds of cases.[19] Each list varies depending on the relevant time frame under consideration and how the author defines foreign intervention. An exact number, however, is not important for our purposes. What is important is that no matter how one cuts the data, the U.S. government has used military force abroad a significant number of times. The historical prevalence of the U.S. government's activist foreign policy is captured by economist Deepak Lal, who concludes that "[t]he United States is indubitably an empire. It is more than a hegemon, as it seeks control over not only foreign but also aspects of domestic policy in other countries."[20]

The militarism that characterizes U.S. foreign policy is a central tenet of the country's national identity. As historian Andrew Bacevich notes, "[t]oday as never before in their history Americans are enthralled with military power. The global military supremacy that the United States presently enjoys—and is bent on perpetuating—has become central to our national identity. More than America's matchless material abundance or even the effusions of its pop culture, the nation's arsenal of high tech weaponry and the soldiers who employ that arsenal have come to signify who we are and what we stand for."[21] Given the ubiquity of the U.S. government's foreign interventions across time and place, and the associated militarism that is synonymous with U.S. foreign policy, it makes sense to focus on the United States.

That the United States is the dominant economic and military force in international affairs grants significant scope for U.S. government officials to use their discretionary power to intervene in the affairs of others. As Barry Posen, a political scientist, writes, "The United States is a wealthy and capable state. It can afford more security than most states. But the United States has extended the boundaries of its political and military defense perimeter very far."[22] He concludes that this expansive foreign policy results in "an embedded system of ambitious and costly excess" due to attempts by the U.S. government to influence global outcomes.[23]

Many scholars and writers argue that, given this power, the U.S. government and its citizens should embrace the status of global empire.[24] For these authors, and for many politicians in both major political parties, an activist foreign policy does not threaten institutions and policies at home. If anything, it is argued, an interventionist foreign policy enhances domestic institutions by fostering global stability, peace, and freedom. For reasons we will discuss throughout this book, we are skeptical of this claim and believe that the proponents of *Pax Americana* neglect significant costs of foreign intervention that threaten the individual liberties which make America exceptional.

As Chalmers Johnson, a political scientist, warned, "[a]s militarism, the arrogance of power, and the euphemisms required to justify imperialism inevitably conflict with America's democratic structure of government and distort its culture and basic values, I fear that we will lose our country."[25] As we will argue, coercive foreign intervention fosters an environment in which constraints on government are loosened, accountability is diminished, and domestic citizens, whether willingly or unwillingly, become more accepting of increases in the scope of government power. Given the prominence—both historical and current—of the U.S. government in the shaping of international affairs, as well as the calls for it to embrace, if not expand, its role abroad, it makes sense for us to focus exclusively on the United States.

WHAT CONSTITUTES FOREIGN INTERVENTION?

The term *foreign intervention* is broad and has many different meanings. We use this term to refer to the use of the discretionary power held by government officials to achieve some desired end in another society.[26] We limit our focus to what we call "coercive foreign intervention," which has three notable characteristics. First, the intervening government seeks to shape outcomes—political, economic, social, legal, and so on—to achieve an end different from what would have emerged absent the intervention. Second, the intervention is unwelcome by a portion of the target population. Third, to achieve its objectives the intervening government invests resources to deter and suppress resistance from foreign governments or populations.

Our notion of coercive foreign intervention is purposefully broad to incorporate a wide range of interventions in other societies. Under our definition intervention may be direct or indirect. Examples of the former would be traditional war and military occupation such as the U.S. government's occupations of Japan and Germany after World War II, or of Afghanistan and Iraq more recently. Examples of the latter would include the provision of various types of aid to key government and non-state persons so that the intervening government can indirectly influence affairs in another society. For example, the U.S. Central Intelligence Agency (CIA) orchestrated the 1954 coup to overthrow Guatemala's democratically elected president Jacobo Árbenz in favor of Carlos Castillo Armas, a military dictator aligned with the goals of those in control of the U.S. government.[27] There are many other examples of the U.S. government indirectly intervening in societies to change the status quo toward goals sought by U.S. leaders.[28]

Our analysis applies both to preparations for coercive foreign intervention—actual or potential—and to the act of intervening itself. Throughout its history the U.S. government has invested significant resources in innovating and honing techniques of social control in preparation for future foreign intervention. At the same time the U.S. government has developed, implemented, and refined techniques of social control while intervening in distant societies. In many instances these two aspects occur simultaneously as the government invests resources in preparing for future intervention while already engaged in intervention abroad. The key point is that both aspects—preparation and intervention—affect domestic political institutions and threaten the liberties of domestic citizens.

For our purposes the stated goal of a foreign intervention is irrelevant. It does not matter whether the intervening government is motivated by humanitarian concerns, the desire to retaliate against a group or government, national security concerns, or regime change. Instead, what matters for our analysis are the methods employed in the intervention and how these tools of social control ultimately affect domestic institutions and life in the intervening country. Also unimportant for our analysis is the degree of success or failure in individual instances of coercive foreign intervention. As the historical record shows, some foreign interventions have succeeded in achieving the goals of interveners, while many others have not.

Instead of being a judgment on the efficacy of individual instances of intervention, our analysis should be read as a warning against neglecting a key aspect of foreign intervention in general—its perverse effects on domestic political institutions and the lives of domestic persons. These effects are often long in developing and variable, requiring careful analysis to identify and appreciate. This is precisely why as economists we have something to contribute to this area of study. As economic journalist Henry Hazlitt noted, "The art of economics consists in looking not merely at the immediate but at the longer effects of any act or policy; it consists in tracing the consequences of that policy not merely for one group but for all groups."[29]

SITUATING OUR CONTRIBUTION

There is a deep tradition of well-known thinkers who expressed concern that coercive foreign intervention and war threaten domestic negative liberties. Writing in 1795, James Madison noted,

Of all the enemies to public liberty, war is perhaps the most to be dreaded, because it comprises and develops the germ of every other. War is the parent of armies; from these proceed debts and taxes; and armies, and debts, and taxes are the known instruments for bringing the many under the domination of the few. In war, too, the discretionary power of the Executive is extended; its influence in dealing out offices, honors, and emoluments is multiplied; and all the means of seducing the minds, are added to those of subduing the force, of the people. . . . No nation could preserve its freedom in the midst of continual warfare.[30]

A year later, in his 1796 farewell address, President George Washington cautioned about "overgrown military establishments which, under any form of government, are inauspicious to liberty, and which are to be regarded as particularly hostile to republican liberty."[31] John Quincy Adams's declaration in 1821 that America does not go abroad "in search of monsters to destroy" is well known. Less discussed is his reasoning, which is that otherwise "[t]he fundamental maxims of her policy would insensibly change from *liberty* to *force*. . . . She might become the dictatress of the world. She would be no longer the ruler of her own spirit."[32]

In discussing the relationship between democracy and war, Alexis de Tocqueville indicated,

War does not always give over democratic communities to military government, but it must invariably and immeasurably increase the powers of civil government; it must almost compulsorily concentrate the direction of all men and the management of all things in the hands of the administration. If it does not lead to despotism by sudden violence, it prepares men for it more gently by their habits. All those who seek to destroy the liberties of a democratic nation ought to know that war is the surest and the shortest means to accomplish it.[33]

Finally, writing in 1918 the journalist Randolph Bourne warned,

War is the health of the State. It automatically sets in motion throughout society those irresistible forces for uniformity, for passionate cooperation with the Government in coercing into obedience the minority groups and individuals which lack the larger herd sense. The machinery of government sets and enforces the drastic penalties; the minorities are either intimidated into silence, or brought slowly around by a subtle process of persuasion which may seem to them really to be converting them. . . . [I]n general, the nation in wartime attains a uniformity of feeling, a hierarchy of values culminating at the undisputed apex of the State ideal, which could not possibly be produced through any other agency than war.[34]

While these authors held diverse views regarding the role of government in domestic and foreign affairs, they all recognized that foreign policy is not distinct from domestic life. They also recognized that foreign intervention poses a genuine threat to domestic political institutions by increasing not only the scale but also the scope of government over its citizens. Our analysis is motivated by these warnings. We build on these thinkers' insights by delineating specific channels and mechanisms through which foreign intervention leads to the loss of freedom from interference and coercion at home.

In addition to contributing to this tradition of skepticism regarding the net benefits of foreign intervention, we engage three broad categories of academic literature. The first category is scholarship on constitutional political economy. This research explores the role, design, and enforcement of rules as constraints on government and private behavior.[35] We advance this literature by emphasizing that the domestic political structure is not invariant with respect to intervention abroad. We demonstrate how preparing for and carrying out coercive foreign intervention can expand the scope of domestic government power, resulting in a loss of negative liberty at home.

Second, we offer an addition to the literature focused on the costs and consequences of war and foreign intervention—monetary and nonmonetary, seen and unseen.[36] Our analysis advances this literature by emphasizing that the costs of foreign intervention are typically understated because they tend to neglect the associated changes in the scope of domestic government power, which refers to the ability of political actors to influence and control the lives of inhabitants. Increases in government power reduce the freedoms of the domestic populace to control their own lives free from the interference of others.

Finally, we contribute to the scholarship on theories of government growth. These theories fall into several different categories. Political science and public choice scholars have developed two types of theories of government growth. "Citizen over state" theories argue that government growth results from increased citizen demand (through individual voters or organized special interests) for government programs. In contrast "state over citizen" theories posit that political actors seek to expand the size, or supply, of government irrespective of citizen demand. There is an array of empirical evidence with mixed results for both sets of theories.[37] These two theories are not necessarily at odds, however. Aspects of each potentially could operate simultaneously under certain conditions.

Another category of explanations for the growth of government emphasizes the role of crises. Economist Robert Higgs proposes a "ratchet effect" theory whereby government grows during crises.[38] A crisis leads to calls for the government to do something. This can result in an increase in both the scale (size) and scope (range of activities) of government. Retrenchment typically takes place following a crisis, but the government's scale and scope often remain greater than they were before the crisis.

Other scholars engaging this category of literature, along with Higgs, focus on how crisis and war-making have furthered the centralization of state power.[39] Those at the political center have the resources and incentives to fund and control military technologies that further centralize and strengthen political power. One consequence is that peripheral political units, which serve as important external checks on the central government, tend to become entangled with the center in order to receive funding, privileges, and protection. Another strand of literature in this category documents a variety of ways in which government has expanded due to war, including an array of new regulations to control resources and production, and taxes to finance further foreign intervention.[40]

Yet another explanation for government growth focuses on how technological advances enable government to better coordinate and communicate in expanding its reach over its citizens.[41] Consider, for example, that with advances in technology governments can more easily collect taxes, communicate with dispersed agencies over a broader area, and monitor their citizens.

We advance the literature on the growth of government in two ways. First, we demonstrate how foreign interventions can lead to the growth of domestic government. Second, our analysis stresses the different margins of government growth. Growth can take place in the scale, as typically emphasized in the literature, as well as in the scope of government activities. These two margins are often reinforcing, but not necessarily so. The scope of existing government activities may change, for example, even though the overall scale may remain the same. In other words, the fiscal dimension of the state—that is, its scale—may stay constant, but the range of activities undertaken with that constant budget—that is, its scope—may change.

In this regard our analysis is closest to the aforementioned work of Robert Higgs, whose treatment of the growth of what he calls "Big Government" appreciates the interrelation between scale and scope.[42] He has argued that government growth during crises can and often does occur both in the scale of traditional state activities and in "widening the scope of its effective authority over economic decision making."[43] Higgs's ratchet model of government growth does not imply or require that increases in the size of government are a neat and linear process. Instead, government can evolve on a variety of margins depending on the broader context and conditions surrounding changes in government, as well as the specifics of the interventions undertaken. We build on Higgs's ratchet effect framework for understanding the growth of government by stressing that coercive foreign intervention often increases the scope of domestic government power, resulting in the erosion of negative liberties domestically. We discuss specific mechanisms underpinning this process that can be seen as contributing to the broader ratchet effect.

At the same time, we do not neglect the insights of the other theories of government growth. For example, as noted, we draw on the technological theory of government growth by emphasizing how coercive foreign intervention creates opportunities to develop and refine methods and technologies of social control. These innovations are often brought back to the intervening country, where the scope of domestic government power expands. Unfortunately, economists have generally neglected the scope aspect of government growth. Our analysis can be seen as an effort to correct this situation. To begin, we need to understand why economists have neglected the scope of government activity.

WHY DO ECONOMISTS NEGLECT SCOPE?

Economists have largely focused their studies on the scale of government. As noted, scope refers to the range of government activities, while scale refers to the size of the state.[44] Scale typically is measured by focusing on aggregate quantitative variables, such as state expenditures. Some examples of standard measures of scale include (1) annual total budget, (2) annual budget by component (health care, defense, and other government functions), (3) annual budget per capita, (4) annual expenditures—total or by component—on final goods and services as a percentage of Gross Domestic Product (GDP) or Gross National Product (GNP), (5) total number of government employees, and (6) government employees as a percentage of the total labor force. These measures of scale can be and are applied to local, state, and national governments. They provide an aggregate measure of government size for a given period. In doing so, however, they provide no insight into the microlevel activities undertaken or how those activities evolve.

For example, comparing overall expenditures on "defense" over time does not tell us what specific defense-related activities were undertaken or how "defense" has changed. Instead, these measures of scale consist of broad categories intended to amalgamate government activities into a single measure comparable across time. However, as Higgs notes, a "modern government is not a single, simple thing. It consists of many institutions, agencies, and activities and includes many separate actors—legislators, administrators, judges, and various ordinary employees. . . . Because government is complex, no single measure suffices to capture its true 'size'."[45] This suggests that focusing exclusively on aggregate quantitative measures of scale will overlook important issues of scope and whether government activities enhance or undermine citizens' freedoms.

Nobel laureate economist James Buchanan recognized the important distinction between scale and scope when he noted that "[a]n interfering federal judiciary, along with an irresponsible executive, could exist even when budget sizes remain relatively small."[46] This highlights that while the scale of government is indeed important, so too is the scope. Even a relatively small-scale government bureau can wreak havoc on the freedoms of citizens if the scope of its activities is not appropriately constrained. Scope is difficult to quantify in a uniform aggregate measure because the devil is in the details when it comes to understanding the range of activities that the state is able to undertake.

Some scholars have attempted to measure the scope of government activities using alternatives to the list of measures that opened this section. For instance, they have developed a variety of indicators to measure government's regulatory burden.[47] These alternatives provide insight into the growth of government on certain margins, but they fail to capture the true scope of government activities.

For example, one indicator is the number of pages added annually to the *Federal Register*. Compiled by the Office of the Federal Register, the *Federal Register* serves as the official record of the rules, proposed rules, and public notices of the U.S. government.[48] While the *Federal Register* records changes in such things, it does not indicate the nature of the changes. One can envision a situation in which a significant number of small changes in rules and policies—that is, a large number of pages in the *Federal Register*—have little impact on the scope of government activities and the liberties of citizens. In contrast, a small number of new rules and policies, which significantly broaden the scope of government power, could severely infringe on negative liberties. This suggests that appreciating the scope of government activities requires going beyond an aggregate measure and instead looking at the specifics of how government activities evolve, with a particular focus on how they affect the liberties of citizens.

To provide some concrete examples of the types of changes in the scope of government power we have in mind, Table 1.1 lists a sample of select government activities in the period following the September 11 attacks. These activities are broken down into categories (listed in the first column) that relate to individual liberties.

In each instance the range and nature of domestic activities undertaken by the government expanded. These expansions may not be captured by standard measures of the scale of government since they do not necessarily require an increase in expenditures. For example, the government's budget might stay relatively flat over time, but state actors can use the same amount of resources to intrude into the lives of its citizens in new and

Table 1.1. A Sample of Select Violations of Freedom in the Post-9/11 Period.

Individual Liberty	Government Activity
Due Process	Authorization of trial by military commission for violations of the law of war and other offenses. The Military Commissions Act of 2006 defines "unlawful enemy combatants" so broadly that it is possible for U.S. citizens to be included. It also expands the power of the executive to determine who is an unlawful enemy combatant. At least two U.S. citizens were arrested and designated as "enemy combatants" meaning they were not entitled to a civilian trial.
Freedom of Movement	Creation of a "no fly list," which lists people, including U.S. citizens, prohibited from boarding a commercial aircraft to travel in or out of the United States. The number of people on the list has increased from 10,000 in 2011 to over 45,000 in 2013. Numerous U.S. citizens have been inaccurately included on the list and prevented from freely traveling into or out of the United States. The National Security Entry/Exit Registration System requires noncitizen males from twenty-five countries to report to INS facilities for "special registration," including fingerprints, photographs, and questioning. Over 82,000 have been registered.
Freedom of Speech	Denial of local permits to protestors of U.S. foreign policy. Arrest of protestors in New York City who were detained and questioned (with their answers recorded) regarding their political affiliations and past activities. Mass arrest of 400 protestors in Pershing Park for "failing to obey a police order" to disperse. Police later admitted that no order was given and charges were dropped.
Press Freedom	Increased use of the Espionage Act to prosecute sources and journalists who print leaked national security information. Months of journalists' phone records have been subpoenaed and charges of co-conspiracy were brought against one journalist. The Pentagon operated a public affairs program using retired military officers employed as "objective" media analysts on war and security as "message force multipliers" to broadcast the Bush administration's talking points regarding the war on terror (Afghanistan, Iraq).
Privacy	Warrantless wiretapping of phone calls and monitoring of emails of U.S. citizens without a warrant by the National Security Agency (NSA). Expansion of data collection, storage, tracking, and mining by the NSA, FBI, and CIA. Abuse of National Security Letters (NSLs) by the FBI to collect information on citizens. The FBI and Department of Defense spied on domestic organizations including the ACLU, Quakers, People for the Ethical Treatment of Animals, Greenpeace, and the American-Arab Anti-Discrimination Committee. Implementation of the Terrorism Information and Prevention System (TIPS) program for domestic citizens to report suspicious activities to the government.
Private Property	Increased use of asset forfeiture by domestic law enforcement, which allows the state to confiscate cash and property without pressing criminal charges. The onus is on citizens to prove their innocence. It is estimated that since 9/11 there have been over 62,000 cash seizures from private citizens and $2.5 billion worth of assets confiscated under the Equitable Sharing Program between federal and state authorities.
Writ of Habeas Corpus	The writ of habeas corpus for individuals unilaterally designated as "enemy combatants" by the president was eliminated under the Detainee Treatment Act (2005) and the Military Commissions Act (2006).

Source: Text for table compiled by the authors. For expansions in the scope of government power during other, historical periods of war, see Dorsen 1989; Linfield 1990; Rehnquist 1998; Cole and Dempsey 2006; Cole and Lobel 2009; Herman 2011; Hummel 2012; and Coyne 2015.

novel ways that curtail their freedom from external interference. This is especially likely as the real cost of producing the goods and services associated with social control falls because of technological advances over time. Similarly, government toleration of and complacency toward rights violations of certain groups would not show up in indicators of new policies or regulations.

There are three potential reasons why so few economists have bothered to look at the scope of government activities. First, many economists assume that scale and scope are correlated. If it is true that scale and scope move together, then focusing on the former would effectively capture the latter. For example, in his analysis of the growth of government economist Sam Peltzman stated that he was "going to equate government's role in economic life with the size of its budget" and that "[m]y operating assumption has to be that large and growing budgets imply a large and growing substitution of collective for private decision in allocating resources."[49] Peltzman was fully aware that his assumption was not reflective of the actual workings of government when he indicated that "[t]his is obviously wrong since many government activities (for example, statutes and administrative rules) redirect resources just as surely as taxation and spending."[50] However, his preoccupation with quantitative measures of government scale necessitated his simplifying assumption.

Scale and scope could be correlated, but at any time, the scope of state activities could expand (or shrink) for a given scale of expenditures. Further, even if one assumes that scale and scope are correlated, focusing solely on the former adds little insight into the specific changes in the latter. For example, if scale increases, one might say that scope increases. But what does that mean in concrete terms of what the state can and cannot do in relation to citizens? Only by focusing on the details of changes in allowable government actions can one hope to understand the implications of changes in the scope of government.

As for the second reason for the neglect of scope, James Buchanan writes, "It is more difficult to measure the growth of Leviathan in these [scope] dimensions than in the quantifiable budgetary [scale] dimensions of the productive state."[51] This further explains, returning to the previous point, why many economists assume that scale and scope are correlated.

There is no simple and readily available aggregative quantitative measure of the scope of government activities.

An alternative, however, is not to ignore issues of scope or assume correlation with scale, but rather to trace the history of and relationship between foreign intervention and changes in the scope of domestic government activities. This necessarily means that any attempt to discuss issues of scope will be less quantitative and fall outside the comfort zone of most of our fellow economists, who often associate rigor with measurement and testing. In our view, however, the scope of government activities is too important to ignore simply because it does not lend itself to quantitative analysis. Empirical evidence still exists in the form of history that enables us to understand how foreign intervention shapes the scope of domestic government activities. Ignoring issues of scope altogether is unsatisfactory, since our goal as social scientists is to understand the actual world. In this world the range of activities that governments undertake is just as important as, if not more important than, the amount of resources the state consumes.

Third, the dominant model of state-provided defense that economists employ renders scope irrelevant. Economists tend to use the term *defense* in a simplistic and broad sense to include all military and security expenditures and activities, including foreign intervention. They then proceed to model this overbroad notion of defense as a "public good," which is provided in optimal quantities and qualities by an omniscient and benevolent government.[52] J. Paul Dunne, an economist, noted that the standard economic approach to military provision "is based on the notion of a state with a well defined social welfare function, reflecting some form of social democratic consensus, recognizing some well defined national interest, and threatened by some real or apparent potential enemy."[53] Under this view the government is assumed to be doing exactly what is necessary to maximize social welfare, nothing more and nothing less. Given these simplifying assumptions, there is no need to be concerned with the scope of government activities since by assumption there is no room for the abuse of power by state officials.

Our position is that the standard treatment of defense by our fellow economists is naive and simplistic. The typical approach fails to recognize that state activities undertaken in the name of "defense" and "national security" not only may fail to be welfare-enhancing, but may undermine and erode the very domestic institutions they supposedly protect. The framework we develop appreciates how existing rules constrain, or often fail to constrain, those who exercise government power. It also recognizes that one cannot neatly separate foreign policy from domestic institutions. Foreign intervention can—and does—have real effects on domestic life, often for the worse.

A ROAD MAP

The rest of this book proceeds as follows. The rest of Part I consists of two chapters that provide the underlying framework for our analysis. These chapters provide insight into what Twain referred to as the "natural process" of losing liberty at home. Chapter 2 discusses how coercive foreign intervention requires state-produced social control over the target population. It also develops the boomerang effect framework, which explains how the tools of social control associated with coercive foreign intervention can infiltrate domestic life in the intervening country. This process can result in changes to domestic political institutions that affect the lives and liberties of American residents. Among other things, we discuss the channels through which the tools of control intended for foreign populations bleed into domestic life. Finally, we provide several caveats to clarify the boomerang effect framework and delineate the boundaries of its applicability and explanatory capabilities.

Chapter 3 explores why America is susceptible to the boomerang effect. We consider the weak formal constraints, both domestically and internationally, on U.S. government officials in matters of foreign policy. The result is that preparing for and carrying out foreign intervention present a largely unconstrained opportunity for government officials to develop, test, and hone methods of social control. The significant slack in domestic constraints creates an environment conducive to the return of these methods as per the boomerang effect.

Part II, which contains four chapters, applies our framework to a variety of cases to demonstrate the operation and applicability of the boomerang effect. The topics of these chapters—surveillance, the militarization of police, drones, and torture—were selected because of their contemporary relevance. According to a recent Gallup poll, half of Americans believe that their federal government poses "an immediate threat to the rights and freedoms of ordinary citizens."[54] Each case study details a current threat to domestic liberties that has come to light following the September 11 attacks on American soil. Each threat can be traced to past foreign interventions. Therefore, these events can be interpreted and understood in terms of the boomerang effect.

The cases are not intended to be theory testing, but rather illustrative and interpretive. Further, their purpose is not to provide a comprehensive history of each subject under consideration but rather to illuminate the operation of the boomerang effect and the unseen costs of coercive foreign intervention. For some of the cases, such as drones, detailed information is limited due to the covert nature of the activities and the lack of transparency on the part of the U.S. government. Although we lack access to classified information surrounding these operations, enough information is available to discuss these cases in the context of the boomerang effect.

A common theme that emerges through these chapters is that the unseen costs associated with the boomerang effect are not the consequence of a single discrete choice, but rather are an emergent and cumulative outcome of government actions driven by an interventionist and militarist mentality. This mentality holds that the U.S. government must not only intervene around the world to shape global affairs but also invest significant resources in preparing for such intervention. One overlooked consequence of this mentality is that it creates an array of possibilities, both in the present and in the future, for expansion in domestic state power that threatens to erode the negative liberties of the populace.

The Conclusion discusses key implications. Among other things we consider some of the conditions necessary to reclaim and protect the Great Republic that is America. We contend that limiting the boomerang effect ultimately requires curtailing the American empire, which requires that citizens possess an antimilitarist ideology.

CHAPTER 2

The Boomerang Effect

How Social Control Comes Home

In 1953 the U.S. Central Intelligence Agency (CIA), with assistance from the government of the United Kingdom, organized a coup to overthrow Mohammad Mossadegh, the democratically elected prime minister of Iran. The operation was multifaceted: it included a propaganda campaign against Mossadegh, the bribing of politicians, the coordination and funding of demonstrators, and the securing of the Shah's willingness to assume power.[1] The CIA-led coup was an exercise in state control over a distant population. The U.S. and U.K. governments determined that the status quo in Iran was unacceptable and took steps to intervene and implement their own vision for Iran. The Iranian coup, however, was far from unique.

Following the 2003 U.S. invasion of Iraq, journalist Stephen Kinzer studied past efforts by the U.S. government to engage in foreign regime change. He found that the Iraq occupation "was the culmination of a 110-year period during which Americans overthrew fourteen governments that displeased them for various ideological, political, and economic reasons."[2] And these are just instances of direct or indirect regime change. As discussed in the previous chapter, in hundreds of additional cases the U.S. government employed military force to manipulate and shape social, political, and economic outcomes around the world. Appreciating the nature of coercive foreign intervention, which entails exerting control over others, is the first step in understanding how these activities threaten the domestic liberties of the American populace.

FOREIGN INTERVENTION AS EXTERNAL, STATE-PRODUCED SOCIAL CONTROL

Social interaction requires rules governing the behavior of individuals. Rules can be formal, such as private contracts and legislation, or informal, such as social norms and religious beliefs.[3] Rules place limits on people's behavior by influencing the payoff or penalty for certain activities. For example, a rule against a type of behavior can be seen as raising the cost of engaging in it. These payoffs and penalties in turn influence economic, legal, social, and political outcomes. Social cooperation requires rules that increase the payoff to peaceful interaction relative to conflict.

Rules by themselves, however, are not enough to ensure social cooperation. Also important are mechanisms of enforcement to ensure that rules are followed and that violations are punished. Together the rules and mechanisms of enforcement constitute a system of social control that facilitates social order by limiting what people can do.

There are three potential mechanisms of social control.[4] One entails individuals limiting their own behaviors through internalized norms of right or wrong. Alternatively, parties may voluntarily agree to rules and mechanisms to resolve potential conflicts. For example, two parties may voluntarily enter into a contract that stipulates how each party is supposed to behave toward the other and how conflicts are to be resolved, such as through arbitration. Finally, rules can be coercively imposed and enforced by a third party, such as the state.

Coercive foreign intervention falls under the third category, since it relies on external state imposition and enforcement. A third party, the intervening government, attempts to achieve its ends in another society. This requires the imposition and enforcement of rules aimed at changing the behavior of the target group to align with the preferences of the intervening government. By its very nature foreign intervention is at odds with the status quo in the target society. If it were not, the coercive intervention would not have been necessary. Because of the difference between the status quo and the state of affairs sought by the interveners, the social control imposed through foreign intervention requires force in order to raise the cost of resistance.

The idea that the state is a mechanism for implementing and enforcing social control over a population is not new. Max Weber famously recognized the state as an instrument of coercive social control when he noted that "[t]he modern state is a compulsory association which organizes domination"[5] and that "[t]he right to use physical force is ascribed to other institutions or to individuals only to the extent to which the state permits it."[6] Weber emphasized that the state's monopoly on force existed over a specific geographic territory. Foreign intervention introduces an additional component, since the government projects power beyond its territory to exert social control over people in a different territory.

As the example of the militarization of domestic police that opened this book illustrates, the methods and tools of social control used abroad can return home. How is this possible? To answer this question we need a general framework for how methods of social control that have been developed as part of foreign interventions boomerang. We begin by discussing two conditions that create a favorable setting for state-produced social control to return home. We then consider three channels through which the methods and tools of social control used abroad can return to the intervening country.

SETTING THE STAGE FOR SOCIAL CONTROL AT HOME

Certain domestic conditions create an environment that is conducive to the boomerang effect. They create space for government to expand the scope of its powers and adopt the techniques of state-produced social control that it has developed and honed abroad. Let's examine these conditions.

Citizens' Fear

Fear is an emotional state caused by some real or perceived threat. Public fear involves "people's felt apprehension of some harm to their collective well-being—the fear of terrorism, panic over crime, anxiety about moral decay—or the intimidation wielded over men and women by governments or groups."[7] When citizens fear some threat and demand government protection, it enables those in power to increase the scope of their oversight and control over domestic and international life.

The idea that citizens' fear creates opportunities for expansions in the scale and scope of state power is not novel.[8] Writing in 1776, Adam Smith noted how anxiety associated with national security and foreign intervention could result in increases in the scale of government. He wrote that "[w]hen a nation is already overburdened with taxes, nothing but the necessities of a new war, nothing but either the animosity of national vengeance, or the anxiety for national security, can induce the people to submit, with tolerable patience, to a new tax."[9] Over two centuries later, Nobel laureate economist F. A. Hayek warned that fear of real or perceived threats can lead to increases in the scope of government power. In the face of national emergencies, he noted, citizens often act "[l]ike an animal in flight from mortal danger" and grant government additional powers to address the threat.[10] However, great caution must be exercised, Hayek warned, because emergencies "have always been the pretext on which the safeguards of individual liberty have been eroded."[11]

Fear can emerge as a genuine response to threats and actual events. But it can also be intentionally manufactured and fostered by those in government. Robert Higgs argues that the sustainability and growth of government requires citizens to fear threats that it seems only the government can thwart. The result, he argues, is that governments "exploit it [fear], and they cultivate it. Whether they compose a warfare state or a welfare state, they depend on fear to secure popular submission, compliance with official dictates, affirmative cooperation with the state's enterprises and adventures."[12]

There are two related ways in which fear enables expansions in the scope of state power. First, citizens' fear can have a disarming effect, leading them to tolerate and even actively demand expansions in state control over their lives that, under other circumstances, they would not accept. For example, many U.S. citizens tolerate and justify the sweeping surveillance activities of their government by reasoning that "if you have nothing to hide, you have nothing to fear." This assumes that expansive government powers will be employed in a constrained and effective manner to combat precise threats to citizens. What is neglected is that these powers can be abused, both in the present and also in the future, in ways that threaten freedom instead of protecting it.

Fear of immediate threats can lead to decisions with significant long-term costs. As philosopher Bertrand Russell indicated, "neither a man nor a crowd nor a nation can be trusted to act humanely or to think sanely under the influence of a great fear."[13] When citizens allow "great fear" to dominate their lives they run the risk of demanding and accepting expansions in state power that can become permanently entrenched. This may seem like a slippery slope, but it is a genuine concern, captured well by political scientist Corey Robin when he warns U.S. citizens that "one day, the war on terrorism will come to an end. All wars do. And when it does, we will find ourselves still living in fear: not of terrorism or radical Islam, but of the domestic rulers that fear has left behind."[14]

Here, he is referring to heads of state who are not serving people as citizens, but who see themselves as rulers in a more expansive sense of the term. Over time, extensions of state power that had been thought of as inappropriate and extreme become a normal part of life. In discussing the effects of foreign intervention at home, political scientist Thomas Dye found that those in the intervening country become conditioned "to tolerate major increases in government activity, and thus, after the war, government activity remains on a higher plateau than before the war."[15]

A complicating factor is that the expansion in government power is often not readily observable to citizens in its entirety. For example, U.S. citizens who wish to become informed about the extent of government domestic surveillance have an extremely limited ability to do so since it is shrouded in the secrecy of national security.

Second, those associated with the state and security complex—either as government employees or as contractors—will foster fear and exploit it once it exists. Legal scholar David Cole argues that "[a]s history demonstrates, fear tends to lead the populace to seek reassurance from the authorities, and as a result there is always a risk that authorities will exploit fear to their advantage."[16] It is naive and simplistic to assume that the national security state is composed of passive personnel who sit idly by waiting to respond in a public-spirited manner to only genuine external threats to domestic citizens. Instead, those who work for the security state have an incentive to intentionally foster it.

General Douglas MacArthur recognized this exact dynamic in 1957, when at the peak of McCarthyism he noted that "[o]ur government has kept us in a perpetual state of fear, kept us in a continuous stampede of patriotic fervor—with the cry of grave national emergency. Always there has been some terrible evil—to gobble us up if we would not blindly rally behind it by furnishing the exuberant funds demanded. Yet in retrospect, those disasters seem never to have happened, seem never to have been quite real."[17] In other words, fear can be an instrument of social control proactively used by those with political power to manipulate and regulate citizens to encourage community solidarity in support of the activities and goals of those in power.

Consider the thriving terrorism industry that has blossomed post-9/11 to create, perpetuate, and benefit from American citizens' fears.[18] This industry consists of elected officials, bureaucrats, and members of the military, as well as private contractors and consultants, who all gain from expansions in government power couched in terms of protecting citizens from terrorist threats. The result has been intense competition among these various parties to secure as large a piece of the terror-related pie as possible while simultaneously advocating for the expansion of the pie itself. As economist James Bennett writes, "[t]he vicious circle gets even more vicious: lobbyists vie for homeland security grants and contracts; corporations and state and local governments become more dependent on federal subsidies; the vested interest in prolonging and intensifying the homeland security 'crisis' increases; and lobbyists press for even more money."[19] This results in increased government control, massive waste, and little additional genuine security.[20]

Once the forces of fear lead to expansion of government, newly vested power tends to be self-perpetuating and self-extending due to four factors. First is the ideological change discussed earlier, according to which the new normal among citizens consists of expanded government powers to combat the objects of fear. Second is political inertia, whereby major changes to the structure of government are hard to reverse because of "lock in" effects. For example, following the end of the Cold War the U.S. government's nuclear weapons policy was extremely slow to change due to bureaucratic resistance, political infighting, and institutionalized ways of thinking.[21] Political scientist Paul Pierson captured these first two factors when he wrote, "[o]nce established, patterns of political mobilization, the institutional 'rules of the game,' and even citizens' basic ways of thinking about the political world will often generate self-reinforcing dynamics."[22]

Third, new agencies, positions, and funding create vested interests with an incentive to perpetuate and expand their power. One example of this is the Department of Homeland Security (DHS), created in 2002. The agency's budget has doubled since its founding, while the number of people employed has increased from 180,000 to 240,000.[23] Because of an ill-defined notion of what constitutes "homeland security," the agency is characterized by mission creep such that it is now involved in investigating mundane activities including pirated movies, counterfeit sports merchandise, and pickpocket crimes.[24] Altering this situation is difficult precisely because the benefits from the status quo are concentrated in the hands of narrow interests, while the benefits of change are dispersed among millions of citizens such that voters have little incentive to seek change through the political process.[25] The result is that the status quo tends to be sticky and resistant to alteration.

Fourth, and related, the ideology of those with vested interests changes as the expansion creates "opportunities for many people both within and without government to do well for themselves and hence to look more favorably on the new order."[26] This shift in ideology reinforces the status quo and makes change much more difficult to generate. As more and more people are subsumed into the government ambit, they become part of the machinery and, as such, are more likely to accept the expanded activities of the state as they view what is personally beneficial to them as being aligned with the "national interest."

In sum, fear sets the stage for the boomerang effect because distressed citizens are more likely to accept expansions in the scope of government activity over their lives. Those in positions of power leverage this fear to entrench and enlarge their power. Fear, however, is not the only factor that makes domestic life conducive to the boomerang effect. The balance of power within domestic political institutions also shifts away from local governments and toward the national government.

The Consolidation of State Power

A militaristic foreign policy can change the composition of domestic government by centralizing decision making and power. The national government increases its power and control at the expense of state and local governments. This consolidation makes sense when one appreciates that national governments and their agencies are responsible for planning, implementing, and overseeing foreign policy. Foreign intervention requires resources and the ability to make decisions about how to use them. So, naturally, a proactive, militarist foreign policy would be linked with the greater centralization of control. As political scientist Bruce Porter noted, "a government at war is a juggernaut of centralization determined to crush any internal opposition that impedes the mobilization of militarily vital resources. This centralizing tendency of war has made the rise of the state throughout much of history a disaster for human liberty and rights."[27] These dynamics are likely to be especially relevant during larger-scale government interventions, such as the two world wars, which required significant coordination and mobilization, and open-ended global wars, such as the War on Terror or the War on Drugs, in which the entire world, including America, constitutes the battlefield and there is no clear definition of victory.

There are two main mechanisms through which the consolidation of control and power at the national level takes place. The first is bureaucratization, whereby government agencies gain more power and resources while new ones may be created, staffed, and resourced. To achieve the goals of foreign intervention, specific forms of bureaucratic organization and regimentation are required. The result is that resources and the routines of citizens are increasingly brought under state control, sometimes willingly and sometimes not, in a regimented, rigid, and centralized manner as "the nation" seeks to achieve a unification against an external enemy. Historically, Porter notes, the "organizational challenge of modern war compels the rationalization of state administrations—the replacement of personal, traditional, and arbitrary methods of rule by impersonal, hierarchical, and bureaucratic methods."[28]

In some cases this bureaucratization is directly observable—take, for example, the socialization of investment and production during World War II. In other cases it is less observable and transparent—such as today's covert expansion in the state's surveillance apparatus. But in any case, these types of moves in the name of defense lead to a political alignment within the government—as opposed to pluralism—and the extension of the government's reach into our lives.

Second, foreign intervention provides a focal point to rally citizens around a common external cause.[29] This diverts their attention from the fundamental tension between state power and individual liberty, drawing their attention to external matters. Just as the government becomes more unified, citizens and the government become unified in the common effort against an external threat, real or imagined. The result is that government activities that previously would have been intolerable become acceptable sacrifices necessary to achieve "the country's" foreign policy goals.

Playwrights, philosophers, and social scientists have long recognized this dynamic. In William Shakespeare's *Henry IV, Part 2*, the dying king offers the following wisdom to his son: "[b]e it thy course to busy giddy minds with foreign quarrels, that action, hence borne out, may waste the memory of the former days."[30] The sixteenth-century political philosopher Jean Bodin wrote that "the best way of preserving a state, and guaranteeing it against sedition, rebellion, and civil war is to keep the subjects in amity one with another, and to this end, to find an enemy against whom they can make common cause."[31] More recently, political scientist Nelson Polsby argued that "[i]nvariably, the popular response to a [U.S.] President during international crises is favorable, regardless of the wisdom of policies he pursues."[32] As these writers highlight, international affairs are often a means of unifying domestic citizens in support of the activities of the state. Unquestioning support due to distraction from an external threat allows government to consolidate its power relatively unchecked. And such is the case in today's world, where we are told that threats are but a heartbeat away.

At some point, the preparation for conflict and use of force abroad become so normalized that citizens expect and often endorse foreign intervention as a solution to a widening array of real and perceived problems.[33] This culture of militarization has existed in the United States for decades.[34] Colonel James Donovan noted that "[t]he American people had come to accept, with no little pride prior to Vietnam, the idea of being responsible for the 'freedom' of all nations requesting aid and have created the military power needed to help to provide the benefits of the American system to the less privileged—and to provide an American solution to every world problem."[35]

Similarly, historian Andrew Bacevich has traced the growing propensity of the U.S. government to use military force abroad with endorsement from citizens. He argues that the "American public's ready acceptance of the prospect of war without foreseeable end and of a policy that abandons even the pretense of the United States fighting defensively or viewing war as a last resort show clearly how far the process of militarization has advanced."[36] This environment is especially conducive to the consolidation of power in the national government, since permanent war serves as a stable and consistent rallying point, allowing bureaucratization to churn ahead vigorously.

Coercive foreign intervention can thus erode federalist checks on power. Federalism divides power between a central political unit and subunits. Specifically, federal governments are characterized by the existence of "at least two levels of government that have independent constitutional existence."[37] In the United States federalism refers to the relationship between the national and state governments. A main benefit of federalism is the dispersion of power. In principle, it serves as a constraint on the power of the political center. The underlying idea is that by distributing some decision-making power to the political periphery, the national government is limited in what it can do. Federalism thus offers one potential solution to the paradox of government, according to which, if all power ostensibly to protect citizens is given to the central government, the citizens' liberty could be undermined.

The pro-liberty benefits of federalism are not, however, guaranteed. As economist Richard Wagner argues, "[w]hether federalism is favorable or hostile to liberty depends on whether the governments within the system must compete with one another for citizen support or whether those governments are able to collude with one another, and thus expand political power relative to citizen liberty."[38] As the central government assumes additional power, lower levels of government are less able to provide the intended checks on the national government.

Two present-day examples will illustrate this logic. The first is the militarization of domestic policing, as discussed at the opening of this book. Section 1208 of the National Defense Authorization Act of 1990 authorized the Department of Defense to transfer military equipment to federal, state, and local agencies. This linked lower-level governments to the central government through resource flows, increasing their connection to and dependence on the political center. Further weaponized, these lower-level authorities are poised to exert more control over citizens at the local level, as we have now seen numerous times.

A second example involves the "fusion centers" that emerged after the 9/11 attacks. Fusion centers are partnerships between various national and local government agencies intended to facilitate coordination and information sharing. As of 2012, over seventy state and local fusion centers had been created or expanded using funding from the federal government. This direct partnership led to an integration of the activities across state and national governments, eroding their separation while creating real threats to the freedoms of U.S. citizens. For example, a report on federal government involvement in the fusion centers by the Senate Permanent Subcommittee on Investigations found that in numerous instances "reviewers raised concerns the documents [produced by fusion centers] potentially endangered the civil liberties or legal privacy protections of the U.S. persons they mentioned."[39]

These two programs are part of two broader open-ended "wars"— the War on Drugs and the War on Terror—which are carried out by the federal government both domestically and internationally. In each case, political subunits have become subservient to top-down control by the political center, which oversees the provision of resources and benefits associated with these war efforts.

While often neglected in today's discussion of foreign intervention, concern for the loss of freedom through the consolidation of power was once common. Writing in 1816, Thomas Jefferson asked, "[w]hat has destroyed liberty and the rights of man in every government which has ever existed under the sun?" His answer was that it was "[t]he generalizing and concentrating all cares and powers into one body, no matter whether of the autocrats of Russia or France, or of the aristocrats of a Venetian Senate."[40] Five years later Jefferson returned to this theme when he wrote, "[w]hen all government, domestic and foreign, in little as in great things, shall be drawn to Washington as the center of all power, it will render powerless the checks provided of one government on another and will become as venal and oppressive as the government from which we separated."[41] Together, these warnings suggest that centralizing power is dangerous because of the real possibility that this power will be abused at the expense of citizens.

A militaristic foreign policy is especially dangerous in this regard since it efficiently facilitates the consolidation of power.

This results in a fundamental tension regarding coercive foreign intervention. Preparing for and engaging in it typically is justified on the grounds that it is necessary to protect the freedoms of domestic citizens. As a result, however, power is consolidated, and the checks and balances on the use of domestic government power change drastically, and often for the worse.

HOW SOCIAL CONTROL BOOMERANGS

With the door open for the expansion of government power, the methods of social control originally developed for use abroad are able to be imported for domestic use. This takes place through three related channels.

The Human-Capital Channel

Human capital refers to the knowledge, skills, and characteristics that contribute to individual productivity. All organizations have goals, the achievement of which requires managers and employees with certain types of human capital. The numerous government agencies involved in designing and carrying out coercive foreign intervention are no different. While the objectives of intervention vary, the important point is that, to succeed, every intervention requires social control to ensure that people's actions align with the goals of the interveners. This requires that those involved in the operation either possess or develop certain types of human capital.

For example, among other activities, those executing an intervention must be ready to implement directives against an often unwilling foreign populace. Success also requires a willingness to use various techniques—monitoring, curfews, segregation, bribery, censorship, suppression, imprisonment, torture, violence, and so on—to control those who resist foreign governments or their goals. More broadly, successful coercive foreign intervention requires a certain mind-set consisting of some mix of the following five characteristics.

1. *Extreme confidence regarding the interventionist's ability to solve complex problems in other societies through a massive, bureaucratic public-private apparatus.* Foreign intervention requires the belief that an elite can

redesign societies according to a grand blueprint. Moreover, intervention requires the belief that this blueprint can be followed in the desired manner. According to this logic, all issues are to be treated as technical engineering problems that can be resolved with appropriate resources in the hands of the intelligentsia. The unquestioning confidence in the intelligence of elites neglects the severely limited knowledge possessed by even the most gifted analysts and bureaucrats.[42] The very idea of externally driven "nation building" perfectly captures this extreme confidence, since it assumes that entire nations, including all of the complex institutions necessary for a well-functioning society, can be designed and built by outsiders.

In addition to implicit assumptions about the capabilities of elite planners, there are also embedded assumptions about the operations of government bureaucracy. Foreign intervention is implemented by numerous overlapping government bureaucracies. This massive bureaucratic network partners with the private sector to produce goods and deliver services abroad.[43] The unwavering confidence in this far-reaching public-private complex to carry out foreign intervention neglects the perverse incentives that contribute to waste, fraud, and corruption.[44] These include spending on easily observable and measurable outputs to demonstrate progress, the spending down of budgets to demonstrate activity even if these expenditures are not value-added, and mission creep to justify expansions in budget and staff requests.[45]

2. *A sense of superiority regarding scientific knowledge, preferences, and righteousness.* Interventionists believe that their vision is superior to the status quo or else they would not have the urge to intervene in the first place.[46] This sense of supremacy is multifaceted and entails the interventionists' belief that they possess technological knowledge superior to that of foreigners, preferences that are better than those of the targeted population, and the moral right and duty to spread their superior knowledge and preferences. Together, this overarching sense of superiority reflects a condemnation of the preferences, choices, and ways of life of others, which are necessarily viewed as inferior if not outright savage.

3. *Comfort with the use of a wide range of often repugnant means to impose ends on others.* Interventionists are so confident in their vision for other societies that they are comfortable using a variety of means to real-

ize them. In some cases, this entails extreme forms of hard power, such as torture, long-term incarceration without due process, and the killing of innocent civilians, which is dismissed as "collateral damage."[47] When such extreme tactics are employed, the interventionists fail to appreciate that they have adopted the most vicious methods and characteristics of those they condemn and combat.

In addition to directly adopting ruthless techniques of social control, intervening governments often partner with brutal authoritarian regimes to achieve short-term foreign policy goals.[48] In doing so the intervening government seems indifferent, if not oblivious, to the significant costs imposed on innocent people through human-rights violations. In general, to succeed, the interventionist must be willing to consider employing any and all means available in the belief that the ends justify the means.

4. *Limited compassion and sympathy toward the target populace.* Intervention typically is complex and motivated by a variety of goals. These may include humanitarian goals to the extent they align with the interventionists' broader aims. Even where humanitarian motives and outcomes exist, however, the interventionists' compassion and sympathy toward the target populace are limited.

Consider the U.S. interventions in Afghanistan and Iraq. Part of the justification was to improve the well-being of the citizens in each country. And on some margins intervention has indeed improved life for certain groups. This is not surprising given the significant sums of money spent by the U.S. government on the occupations, which included an array of humanitarian programs. Despite these benefits, however, concern for the well-being of Afghans and Iraqis is limited. As U.S. General Tommy Franks once remarked when discussing the number of people killed by U.S. forces in Afghanistan, "[w]e don't do body counts."[49] This indifference toward deaths caused by intervention suggests a neglect of the fact that while enemies can be killed during foreign intervention, so too can innocent civilians.[50] In addition to fatalities, foreign intervention can also impose other, nonlethal costs on innocent civilians, including displacement, disease, and psychological harm. These costs run counter to any humanitarian benefits generated by interveners.

Limited compassion is also evident when those in the intervening country, when discussing the costs of war, narrowly focus on the lives lost and monetary costs incurred by their own country. Excluded are these same costs for the intervention's target population.[51] This approach not only severely underestimates the total costs of intervention but also reinforces a moral apathy toward harms imposed on human beings in the target country.

5. *The association of order with state control.* Absent government control and planning, the interventionist sees disorder and chaos in the world. Moreover, it is not just control by any government that is required for order, but control by the "right" government as determined by the preferences of the interventionist. This mentality has a long history in the United States and can be traced back to at least 1904, when President Theodore Roosevelt declared that "[c]hronic wrongdoing, or an impotence which results in a general loosening of the ties of civilized society, may in America, as elsewhere, ultimately require intervention by some civilized nation, and in the Western Hemisphere the adherence of the United States to the Monroe Doctrine may force the United States, however reluctantly, in flagrant cases of such wrongdoing or impotence, to the exercise of an international police power."[52] Over time, the U.S. government has extended its reach well beyond the Western Hemisphere in the name of promoting global order and stability.

The entrenched belief that order is contingent on government design and control neglects the importance of spontaneous order—order that emerges through people pursuing their diverse ends rather than through conscious central planning. Instead of viewing societies as complex, constantly evolving entities consisting of numerous emergent phenomena, the interventionist treats society as a grand science project that can be rationalized and improved on by enlightened and well-intentioned engineers. This disposition neglects the long tradition of spontaneous-order thinkers who emphasized that crucial parts of the world—that is, economic, legal, and social arrangements—are not the result of human design, but rather emerge from the actions of dispersed individuals. These organic orders cannot be designed because they do not fit a single general form regardless of time and context.[53]

These five characteristics are fundamental to the mental schema associated with a proactive, interventionist foreign policy that seeks to reshape other societies. It is a general mind-set, and not all of the constituent characteristics will necessarily be possessed by each and every individual involved in the numerous aspects of foreign interventions.

The interventionist mind-set is reinforced through five mechanisms which ensure that those involved in coercive foreign interventions will either already possess elements of this mentality or will acquire them.[54] First, those in government bureaus are often actively indoctrinated with an unquestioning attitude toward the orders provided from above. For example, Colonel James Donovan noted that U.S. military training "stresses the fundamental obligation to serve the nation loyally and without question to carry out the policies and orders of the President, who is Commander in Chief, and the orders of his appointed officers."[55] Historian Jack Conrad Willers emphasized that those entering bureaus quickly realize that "[s]uccess within bureaucracy requires not only skill and expertise and knowledge but also above all, an apparent devotion to the bureaucracy and unquestioning loyalty to its goals."[56] In other words, success requires adopting and perpetuating the mind-set necessary to succeed. Under the U.S. government's militaristic foreign policy strategy this mind-set aligns with the characteristics described above.

The second mechanism is the desire for personal advancement within government bureaucracy. As in any organization, those employed in government agencies advance their careers by developing the appropriate skills and reputation, and signaling these abilities to key decision makers. General David Shoup, who was awarded the Medal of Honor in World War II, noted that in the U.S. military establishment, "[p]romotions and the choice job opportunities are attained by constantly performing well, conforming to the expected patterns, and pleasing the senior officers."[57] Similarly, Colonel Donovan emphasized that in order to advance, the bureaucrat "must become known as a faithful disciple of his service. In order to promote the organization and its success, he has to compete for goals other than dollar profits, within the fields of operational doctrines, service doctrines, roles and missions, defense appropriations, new weapons programs, and service prestige."[58] This incentive generates peculiar, and often undesirable, outcomes in the context of foreign interventions.

In for-profit markets, professional competition is desirable precisely because it yields beneficial outcomes from the perspective of consumers. That is, competition tends to generate new and better products at lower prices as entrepreneurs and producers compete to develop skills that are conducive to earning profits by satisfying customer wants. But in coercive foreign intervention the nature of professional competition is dramatically different. In this setting, the "customers" are those in positions of power in the intervening government. The people tasked with carrying out the intervention will strive to satisfy their customers by going above and be-yond minimum requirements to achieve the goals of the operation. This entails embracing the interventionist mind-set and efficiently controlling foreign populations to secure cooperation and dampen, suppress, or erad-icate any resistance. Facing these incentives, interveners have reason to act entrepreneurially to develop, implement, and refine a range of social-control techniques.[59]

These dynamics were evident in the Abu Ghraib torture scandal in Iraq, when members of the CIA and U.S. Army committed human rights abuses against prisoners. Loose bureaucratic guidelines and mandates com-bined with unclear rules about what constitutes torture led to the abuse of detainees to secure "actionable intelligence"—which itself is a general and undefined goal set by those higher up the hierarchy.[60] More broadly, the incentives surrounding coercive foreign intervention result in a "nar-row professionalism," whereby a fierce competition to efficiently and ef-fectively regulate the target population leads to a willingness to engage in otherwise unthinkable acts of social control to achieve the ends of those in the intervening government.[61]

Finally, there are three sorting mechanisms, beyond the aforementioned indoctrination techniques, to ensure widespread conformity. First, part of what initially attracts people to an organization is its goals and val-ues, meaning there will tend to be self-selection aligning individual mind-sets and the broader organizational culture. Second, there are selection mechanisms—such as applications and interviews—to filter out people who do not align with the organization's goals and ethos. Third, people will tend to exit organizations where they do not fit because of either poor performance or a lack of personal satisfaction. In the context of the U.S. government's proactive foreign policy, these mechanisms lead to the selection of people who conform to the mentality necessary for successful interventionism.

The human capital associated with state-produced social control can also be imported from outside the country preparing for and engaging in foreign intervention. For example, in the aftermath of World War II the U.S. government implemented Operation Paperclip, which recruited Nazi scientists to work for the U.S. government.[62] Among other things, these scientists assisted the U.S. government with experiments related to psychological control, interrogation, and behavior modification. Operation Paperclip was the precursor to Project MKUltra, which continued similar experiments on unknowing human subjects, some of whom were citizens of the United States and Canada. The findings from these various operations served as the basis for the torture techniques employed at Abu Ghraib decades later, which demonstrates how past efforts to develop tools of social control create knowledge and methods that can lay dormant, only to be employed decades later.[63]

In other instances U.S. government officials traveled abroad to study how other governments engage in social control. For example, in early 1941, when establishing the foundations of what would later become the Office of Censorship during World War II, the U.S. Army sent a captain to Bermuda to study the British government's censorship methods with the intention of incorporating these insights into censorship operations at home.[64]

No matter the specifics, the unique human capital gained through preparations for and the execution of coercive foreign intervention does not simply disappear at the conclusion of the intervention, assuming there is a clear end. Instead, it becomes a permanent part of the skills of the people involved. From those who prepare for potential future interventions, to those who design and manage the various aspects of the intervention, to those who have their boots on the ground, intervening abroad provides a learning environment in which participants obtain a unique set of skills for coercively controlling fellow human beings. Those possessing these skills and experiences eventually shift their focus from abroad to home and influence the fabric of domestic institutions through their participation in private and public life.

The Organizational Dynamics Channel

The innovators and implementers of intervention—both civilian and military—participate in the various private and public organizations that constitute domestic life. Some of the participants return to normal civilian life and, although their mentality and worldview regarding the appropriate role of the state are shaped by their experiences abroad, they no longer actively participate in the domestic security sector. Still others involved in foreign interventions reallocate their unique human capital and experiences to the public or private organizations constituting the domestic defense sector.

In some cases the careers of specialists in state-produced social control span both the public and private aspects of this sector. To illustrate this overlap, consider the finding of one recent report that, of the 108 three- and four-star generals and admirals who retired between 2009 and 2011, 70 percent accepted jobs with private defense contractors or consultants.[65] This is one illustration of the "revolving door," the back-and-forth movement of personnel between the government and private sectors based on an intricate network of overlapping relationships and influence.[66]

Those who develop a comparative advantage in innovating and implementing state-produced social control via foreign intervention will benefit, through better career prospects and higher wages, by employing their unique human capital domestically. They can act entrepreneurially by suggesting and implementing new organizational forms and techniques for controlling the domestic populace on the basis of their experience at doing the same to distant populations. Because of their skills and reputations for success in foreign intervention, some of these specialists can rise to positions of leadership from which they can influence an organization's objectives.

In the public sector, positions of management and leadership allow these individuals to influence domestic and foreign policy. Those in leadership positions in the private sector are also able to influence public agencies, since the U.S. security and defense industry is a unique blend of public funding and private provision by civilian contractors and consultants.[67] The result is that domestic activities, whether in the public or private sector, are influenced by the experiences and skills gained during coercive foreign intervention. As this process unfolds, the distinction between state-produced social control conducted abroad and domestically begins to blur.

In some cases a person's skills in state-produced social control are explicit, that is, he or she becomes known as an expert in a certain type of control—for example, monitoring and surveillance, military strategy and tactics, or psychological techniques—and the person is rewarded for effectively implementing and administering those techniques at home. Specialists with explicit human capital in state-produced social control may be employed within an existing government agency, or they may be involved in the creation of an entirely new state agency or group within one.

Alternatively, the specialist may be hired by or might found a private firm that receives government contracts associated with the production of domestic social control. For example, L-3 Communications is an American-based company that produces equipment and technology for the military as well as for domestic police. The company's website boasts that "L-3 is proud to employ more than 15,000 veterans of the U.S. military, helping them use their unique training and skills to meet our customers' needs." According to the firm, "Many of L-3's top business leaders are former military personnel who provide critical insight and support for using L-3's advanced technology and services to protect our country's freedoms."[68]

In other cases the human capital acquired through coercive foreign intervention is implicit; that is, past experiences unconsciously shape the person's view of the appropriate role of the state and the methods employed. That an organization's culture and goals influence employee personalities was recognized by Nobel laureate Herbert Simon, who noted that "[o]ne does not live for months or years in a particular position in an organization, exposed to some streams of communication, shielded from others, without the most profound effects upon what one knows, believes, attends to, hopes, wishes, emphasizes, fears, and proposes."[69] Simon's point is that one cannot help but be shaped by the context within which he or she is embedded. Similarly, Colonel Donovan noted that "[i]t takes only a matter of months for each of the services to remold the average young American and turn him into a skilled, indoctrinated and motivated member of the armed forces."[70]

As discussed earlier, this indoctrination might be effective in ensuring that those involved in coercive foreign intervention are oriented to the necessary interventionist mind-set. However, we must acknowledge that these experiences become part of the people involved, irrespective of how they reintegrate into domestic life. Activities that would have previously been thought of as unacceptable, extreme, or outright repugnant can become normalized and natural to those carrying them out. Instead of state-produced social control being seen as a threat to domestic liberty, it is seen as standard government procedure. And this view is diffused into our culture as participants in foreign intervention reassimilate into the array of diverse organizations in American life.

Historian and journalist Godfrey Hodgson captured these dynamics in his discussion of the effects of foreign intervention on U.S. society:

Government service in World War II—in the War Department or other civilian departments for the slightly older men, in the Office of Strategic Services or elite military units for the younger ones—gave a whole generation of ambitious and educated Americans a taste for power, as opposed to business success, and an orientation toward government service which they never lost. When they went back to their law offices or their classrooms, they took with them contacts, attitudes and beliefs they had learned in war services.[71]

Similarly, General Shoup noted that in the postwar period

[D]istinguished military leaders from the war years filled many top positions in government. . . . [M]ilitary minds offered the benefits of firm views and problem-solving experience to the management of the nation's affairs. Military procedures—including the general staff system, briefings, estimates of the situation, and the organizational and operational techniques of the highly schooled, confident military professionals—spread throughout American culture.[72]

Colonel Donovan also emphasized that World War II military experience shaped the character of the homeland. He wrote that "[t]he indoctrination with military codes and creeds experienced by millions of men and women who move in and out of the services has a continuing and prolonged and even regenerative effect upon the ideas, attitudes, and martial fiber of the nation as whole."[73] He went on to note that "[t]he lives, the attitudes, and the beliefs of America's war veterans have been influenced by their military service; and because they represent such a large share of the adult male population their degree of militarism creates a strong imprint on the national character."[74]

As these passages make clear, foreign policy and foreign intervention have real effects on domestic political and social life by affecting the attitudes, beliefs, and skills of those staffing and shaping those organizations. The cumulative effect is that domestic life can begin to reflect the characteristics of coercive interventions abroad. These effects are further enhanced by the domestic use of physical capital initially designed and developed to carry out foreign interventions abroad.

The Physical-Capital Channel

Coercive foreign intervention leads to innovations in physical tools associated with social control. This lowers the cost of projecting government power over people both abroad and at home. The logic behind the physical-capital channel is an extension of the argument advanced by economist Tyler Cowen, who suggests that the growth, or scale, of government is linked to technological advances that lower the cost of operating a larger government.[75]

Similar reasoning can be applied to the scope of government activities. Technological innovations allow governments to use lower-cost methods of social control with a greater reach, not only over foreign populations but also over domestic citizens. Examples of such methods include but are not limited to surveillance and monitoring technologies, equipment for maintaining control of citizens, and weapons for efficiently controlling and killing potential and actual resistors.

The U.S. government invests a significant amount of money annually in defense-related R&D and procurement. In FY 2016, for example, the Department of Defense spent $64.8 billion on R&D and $102.7 billion on procurement.[76] This combined expenditure buys a variety of military capabilities that, among other things, serve as inputs into the preparation and execution of control over distant populations. Even if advances in this physical capital are initially undertaken solely for interventions abroad, they can end up being used domestically. For example, it was recently reported that an aerial surveillance system initially developed for use in the Iraq War has been adapted by the Baltimore Police Department for domestic use in its routine operations.[77]

Further, there is a synergy between human capital and physical capital. Those involved in coercive foreign intervention develop unique skills at using certain types of physical capital to produce effective social control. At the same time advances in physical capital allow these specialists to be even more productive in carrying out activities related to social control over both foreign and domestic populations.

Once physical capital is available domestically, it reduces the cost of behavior conducive to aggressive social control. A literature in psychology identifies a "weapons effect" whereby tools of force can prime bellicose behavior on the part of those controlling them.[78] This suggests that when tools of social control are made available to domestic government agents, they will be more likely to use them. Aggressive behavior can manifest itself through violence or through the willingness of state personnel to proactively use technologies of social control to increase regulation of citizens. For example, in the post-9/11 world the U.S. government has proactively used surveillance technologies to monitor U.S. citizens en masse.

The issue is not necessarily unprofessional conduct but rather the perception of what constitutes professional conduct by those empowered to exercise authority over others.[79] What it means to be a professional depends on the context. Protecting the lives and property of domestic citizens is different from seeking out and destroying an enemy during war. When the equipment and techniques used to coercively control distant populations seep into domestic life, so too does the associated notion of professionalism.

Together, the three channels discussed here explain how the methods of social control used abroad can return home and influence domestic life. A militaristic foreign policy requires and fosters a certain set of skills among those involved. The human capital gained by the personnel in interventions does not simply disappear following the intervention. Instead, it returns home as those involved participate in domestic life. In the process, the private and public organizations within which these people work and live are influenced by their experiences controlling others. These effects are complemented by the return of physical capital used to control foreign populations. The three channels redirect state-produced social control from foreign populations to domestic citizens and threaten the very liberties that the government purports to protect through its foreign policy.

POINTS OF CLARIFICATION

Before we move on, the following seven points will ensure clarity and delineate the boundaries of what the boomerang effect framework does, and does not, include.

1. *The boomerang effect is one of numerous factors affecting political and social systems in the intervening country.* The theory of the boomerang effect does not maintain that expansions in the scope of domestic government activities arise *solely* from coercive foreign intervention. The world is a complex place, with numerous factors influencing political institutions and outcomes. It would be naive to suggest a monocausal explanation for the growth in the scope of government activities. We can envision numerous reasons and contexts that may contribute to increases in this scope.

For example, domestic emergencies—such as a financial crisis or natural disaster—might also lead to an expansion in the scope of state control.[80] Citizens' ideology might be such that they demand further expansions in scope.[81] And special-interest groups might maneuver to expand government's scope in the interests of their members. Each of these possibilities may be entirely unrelated to interventions abroad.

Likewise, not all expansions of state power over the lives of the domestic populace during times of war are necessarily due to the boomerang effect. For example, the U.S. government relied on conscription during World War I and World War II for military manpower. The implementation of compulsory enlistment for military service, which dramatically expanded state power over the lives of private citizens, was not the result of the boomerang effect. That said, coercive foreign intervention and the boomerang effect often play an important and neglected role in the expansion of domestic state power.

2. *The boomerang effect is not the same as blowback.* Blowback refers to the negative consequences of clandestine operations incurred by the intervening society.[82] These unintended consequences typically take the form of violent revenge by foreigners against the citizens and interests of the co-

vertly acting government. For example, the U.S. Central Intelligence Agency covertly funded Afghan "freedom fighters" during the Soviet-Afghan War, which lasted from 1979 to 1989, in order to thwart the military efforts of the Soviet Union. In the wake of the war some of the U.S.-funded rebels founded al-Qaeda, which was the organization at the center of the 1998 U.S. embassy bombings in two East African countries and the September 11 attacks on the World Trade Center in New York City.

While the boomerang effect can also include the unintended consequences of coercive foreign intervention, it is not the same as blowback. The boomerang effect does not require covert operations by the intervening government, and it is not about violent acts of revenge by foreign groups against the citizens and interests of the intervening government. Instead, the theory of the boomerang effect is focused on how foreign interventions influence domestic institutions and the relationship between the domestic government and its citizens through the innovation and refinement of methods and tools of state-produced social control.

3. *The boomerang effect does not imply that coercive foreign interventions produce no benefits.* The theory of the boomerang effect in no way implies that coercive foreign intervention has no benefits. On the contrary, intervention can benefit a variety of private and public parties. Foreign intervention may very well achieve the ends stated by the interveners, which will generate benefits from their perspective. Historically, there are instances when war has led to the acquisition of territory, increased state capacity, unification, and a variety of social reforms, among other changes which clearly yield benefits for some.[83] What the boomerang effect does suggest is that the net benefits of intervention will tend to be overstated. That is, neglecting its adverse effects on domestic political institutions and hence on citizens' freedom means that the costs of intervention will be understated. These overlooked costs occur irrespective of the benefits and success of intervention.

4. *The magnitude and speed of the boomerang effect, as well as the importance of each foundational condition and channel, will vary.* Coercive foreign interventions are diverse in their purpose, execution, and setting. Therefore, the extent of innovations in state-produced social control, as well as the speed at which they return home, will vary. For some coercive

foreign interventions the boomerang effect may be significant, while for others it will be minimal or even nonexistent. Further, in some instances one or more of the foundational conditions and channels discussed may be more important than in others. The relevance of the foundational conditions and individual channels, as well as the magnitude and speed of the boomerang effect, will depend on four related factors and conditions.

The first factor is the formal constitution reflecting the principles and rules governing the activities of the state. In delineating what those in political positions can, and cannot, do with their power, constitutional rules place limits on the scale and scope of the state. This includes placing parameters on how those in government can exert social control both at home and abroad. Ideally, these limits will be enforced by checks and balances to disperse power and minimize abuses.

The relevance and influence of the foundational conditions and channels will be shaped by the specific constitutional rules in place. If, for example, constitutional rules limit the ability of those in government to intervene in other societies then opportunities for innovation in methods and tools of social control abroad will be limited. Likewise, effective constitutional rules will limit the consolidation effect as a foundational condition by firmly maintaining the separation of powers between political units and between those units and private individuals. These same constitutional rules may constrain the scope of domestic state powers—surveillance, the use of military equipment at home, and so on—limiting the ability of the government to import methods and tools of social control developed abroad. In contrast, where constitutional constraints are dysfunctional or absent those in government will have greater leeway in intervening abroad, developing new ways of engaging in social control, and importing those innovations domestically.

The second factor is domestic ideology, which can influence the magnitude and speed of the boomerang effect in a variety of ways. The ideology held by judges regarding the proper role of state power will influence the legal interpretation of domestic state activities.[84] An ideology consistent with a more limited role for the state will work against the boomerang effect by constraining the importation of foreign-produced social control. In contrast, an ideology supportive of a more expansive scope of state activities may increase the magnitude and speed of the boomerang effect.

In the context of national security, legal scholar Michael Glennon argues that a variety of factors are currently at play in the U.S. political system that result in the selection of judicial nominees who are often supportive of an active, unchecked, and expansive security state.[85] Judicial nominees, he notes, "often come from the ranks of prosecutors, law enforcement, and national security officials, and they have often participated in the same sorts of activities the lawfulness of which they will later be asked to adjudicate."[86] If this reasoning is correct, the current judicial ideology is conducive to expansions in the scope of domestic state power.

Of course the judiciary does not always passively endorse the activities of the state. In *Boumediene v. Bush* (2008), for example, the Supreme Court ruled that prisoners held at the Guantánamo Bay prison camp had a right to *habeas corpus* under the U.S. Constitution. This illustrates how the beliefs of the judiciary, in this case regarding the extent of the constitutional right to *habeas corpus*, matter for constraining state powers.

The ideology of domestic citizens likewise matters in terms of determining the range of acceptable domestic policies.[87] If, for example, an expansion in the scope of domestic government activities is unacceptable to a significant number of citizens, this will limit the magnitude and slow the speed of the boomerang effect. The reverse will occur when citizens are more accepting of militarism and associated expansions in the scope of domestic government activities.

Of course, this mechanism requires that citizens care about constraining the activities of their government as they relate to domestic social control. It also requires that citizens can observe state-produced social control. Technological advances enable governments to oppress citizens in more indirect and covert ways. For example, it is extremely difficult for American citizens today to observe the surveillance activities of their government due to the covert nature of these operations. In general, when citizens are indifferent to or supportive of expansions in the scope of domestic government power, or when they cannot easily observe the methods and tools used by their government for social control, innovations in control are more likely to boomerang.

The third factor includes the methods and technologies of oppression used abroad. Some are more easily imported to the intervening country than others. Consider the apparatus of social control that King Leopold of Belgium established in the Congo Free State in the 1880s. Based on brute force—including mutilation and murder—it was one of the most notorious and repugnant instances of tyrannical control of a distant population. Yet these extreme methods were not imported to Belgium.

To understand why, it is important to appreciate that the methods involved institutional changes in the Congo backed by rudimentary violence.[88] The Belgians had no drones, electronic surveillance, or other stealth technologies that could be easily transferred to a different context. Instead Leopold established an exploitative institutional structure that involved enslavement, direct monitoring of output by slaves, and punishment for failure to meet quotas. The punishment, which typically involved machetes and guns, was brutal, efficient, and public. Journalist Adam Hochschild writes, "[w]hen a village or district failed to supply its quota of rubber or fought back against the regime, Force Publique soldiers or rubber company 'sentries' often killed everyone they could find."[89]

Thus the method of social control was context-specific and not easily imported home, since doing so would have required Leopold to make wholesale changes to Belgium's domestic political institutions to mimic the repressive colonial system in the Congo. This would have made little sense: Leopold and Belgians saw themselves and their society as highly civilized, leaving little reason for self-colonization. In general, where techniques and technologies of social control are context-specific, they are less likely to boomerang to the intervening country.[90]

Similarly, the U.S. government was the first country to develop nuclear weapons and, to date, is the only government to use them during war, with the bombings of Hiroshima and Nagasaki during World War II. These weapons are a brutally efficient means of conquering and controlling foreign territories. However, this method of control is not easily imported back to the United States as it would require massacring significant numbers of citizens while generating widespread destruction, including posing direct threats to those in positions of political power.

The final factor is the nature of the group or population targeted by the intervention. The "in group" of the intervening government seeks to control an "out group," the targeted foreign population in another territory. The distinction between the in-group and the out-group, however, is not always neatly demarcated by national boundaries.

For example, sometimes the target "out group" is not readily identifiable or some members may live in the intervening country. Japanese Americans were interned in 1942 because their possible sympathy for the Japanese government was said to present a potential security threat to Americans. As another example, consider that post-9/11 a central concern of the U.S. government has been terrorism on American soil by both foreign and homegrown jihadists. The result is that the War on Terror is not purely a foreign intervention, but also a domestic intervention as well. Given the absence of a uniform profile of potential terrorists, all—including U.S. citizens—are seen as potential threats whom the state must control.

In general, when the target of intervention includes people who may be on domestic soil, the state-produced social control typically associated with foreign intervention is more likely to be employed domestically. As David Cole notes, "[n]othing unifies more than an enemy. But that means that those who are identified as associated with the 'enemy'—often on grounds of race, religion, ethnicity, or nationality—are especially vulnerable when emergencies arise. The divisive and dangerous politics of 'us-them,' while an ever-present danger in democracies, are dramatically intensified when the nation feels threatened from without (and from 'foreign' elements within)."[91] This logic was at work in the United States during the first and second Red Scares and during the aforementioned internment of Japanese Americans, as well as post-9/11. In some cases specific groups were viewed as part of the enemy "out group," while in others significant parts of the population were viewed as threats that needed to be controlled by the state. In each case this dynamic allowed for expansions in the scope of domestic state power over citizens' lives.

5. *The theory of the boomerang effect does not preclude reversibility.* The theory of the boomerang effect does not mean that a broadening scope of domestic government is irreversible. Rather, it suggests that reversals are often extremely costly due to fundamental changes in how government carries out its domestic activities. The theory is about stickiness and

not necessarily permanence. David Cole captures this point when he notes that the history of the United States "demonstrates that it is far easier for government officials to declare emergencies and take on new powers than to declare the emergency over and give up those powers."[92]

We can envision different ways that an expansion of the scope of government could reverse course. One possibility is that the ideology of judges, elected officials, or citizens may support more limited state activities relative to the status quo. Consider the case of the judiciary. Although the courts have often granted the security state great leeway, in some instances they have pushed back against expansions in government power.

For example, in *Ex parte Milligan* (1866) the Supreme Court held that it was unconstitutional to try civilians in military tribunals when civilian courts were operating. In *New York Times Co. vs. United States* (1971) the Supreme Court upheld the right of media outlets to publish the classified Pentagon Papers without government censorship. As mentioned earlier, in *Boumediene v. Bush* (2008) the Supreme Court found that it is constitutional for federal courts to review *habeas corpus* petitions by those declared "enemy combatants." Although these examples are exceptions rather than the norm, they indicate that the beliefs of judicial personnel matter in decisions regarding the lawful scope of government activities. Similar logic can be applied to elected officials and the citizenry.

The broader point is that the United States need not be on an inevitable path toward an authoritarian garrison state.[93] Though much damage has been done to the liberties and freedoms of citizens due to a militaristic foreign policy, it is possible for that damage to be reversed.

6. *The true costs of the boomerang effect are long and variable.* Intervention does not necessarily map neatly with immediate reductions in domestic liberty. James Madison captured the essence of this point when he warned that "[t]here are more instances of the abridgment of the freedom of the people by gradual and silent encroachments of those in power than by violent and sudden usurpations."[94] The implication is that while an intervention may have no discernible immediate effect on the scope of government, effects could emerge years or even decades later. For example, the origins of the current domestic surveillance state in the United States can be traced back to the intervention in the Philippines over a century ago.

Crucial for understanding these long and variable effects is an appreciation that actions undertaken at one point in time establish precedents and institutional possibilities for future government activities. This has two implications. First, interventions that initially seem harmless might generate unanticipated and unforeseen consequences in the future. Second, an expansion in government activities may initially seem to have a clear end only to reemerge in the future. The Committee on Public Information, also known as the Creel Committee, serves to illustrate this latter possibility.

The Creel Committee was established in April 1917 by President Woodrow Wilson to shape public opinion regarding World War I. It disbanded in June 1919. At first pass the termination of the agency would seem like a clear end to this expansion of the scope of government activities. However, as the journalism professor Michael Sweeney notes, "[b]efore the Creel Commission was dissolved in 1919, it laid the groundwork for censorship in the next war" by creating a plan that ultimately would influence the activities of the Office of Censorship during World War II.[95] As this illustrates, even what appears to be a short-term expansion in the scope of government power often has long-term consequences, which only become evident in the future.

As another example, consider the Espionage Act of 1917, which was passed shortly after the U.S. government entered World War I. The Act was intended to punish those who interfered with military recruitment or who supported enemies during times of war. Under the Obama administration, which lasted eight years, there were eight prosecutions under the Espionage Act. Importantly, the nature of these prosecutions differed from past notions of espionage and focused on whistleblowers and the journalists who received information. There was no way that those who originally designed the Espionage Act of 1917 could have anticipated its use a century later. Indeed, the Act was passed three decades before the notion of "classified information" was used by the government.[96] This illustrates how past actions create precedents and institutional possibilities that can be used in new and unanticipated ways in the future by those wielding power. Historical actors who are choosing within a certain context cannot possibly predict how their decisions will affect future precedent and decisions.

The broader implication is that the true costs of coercive foreign intervention may not appear until years or decades after it takes place. Further, these costs are not purely monetary but instead involve nuanced changes in the scope of domestic government powers, which alter the fundamental relationship between citizen and state. This has two important implications.

First, the long-developing and variable nature of these costs, combined with the difficulty in measuring them, means that the consequences of the boomerang effect will often be neglected in discussions of the costs and benefits of foreign intervention. Thus intervention will seem, on net, more beneficial and attractive than it is in reality. Second, precisely because these consequences are long and variable, they cannot be easily predicted. A coercive foreign intervention that initially appears innocuous may generate an array of possibilities for the expansion of the scope of state power that only become evident in future periods. The boomerang effect framework identifies the process through which innovations in social control may return home. Therefore it can offer insight into how an overlooked cost of foreign intervention may emerge. It cannot, however, offer point predictions regarding the specific effects and manifestations of current and future interventions on domestic life.

7. *The boomerang effect is not a simple "bad man" theory.* The boomerang effect highlights how state-produced social control can return home and perversely affect domestic institutions and life. While individual actors are central to this process, the boomerang effect is not a simple "bad man" theory. In other words, the central claim is not that unscrupulous people intervene abroad, engage in wicked behaviors, and then return home only to do more of the same.

Instead, the focus is on incentives and selection mechanisms within the context of existing political institutions and the U.S. government's militaristic foreign policy. Success in executing this foreign policy requires a certain mind-set and skill set to achieve. And there are certain mechanisms in place to ensure conformity around these requirements. Under certain conditions the skills, mentalities, and methods of social control honed abroad can return home. None of this assumes nefarious motivations on the part of actors. All that is required is the assumption that people respond to the incentives created by the institutions within which they act.

This is not meant to suggest that specific people do not matter at specific times in history. To understand the evolution of the scope of state power over time we need to focus on pivotal people at pivotal moments. Indeed, our illustrations in Part II highlight key actors who played a central role in bringing back methods and mentalities of social control from abroad. The central point is that the boomerang effect framework does not require any *ex ante* assumptions about agent type or motivation. From this standpoint the framework is entirely compatible with Justice Frank Murphy's insight that "[f]ew indeed have been the invasions upon essential liberties which have not been accompanied by pleas of urgent necessity advanced in good faith by responsible men."[97] What the boomerang effect framework suggests is that even well-intentioned interventions undertaken by responsible people can perversely affect domestic liberties.

THE BOOMERANG RETURNS TO THE THROWING NATION

A militaristic foreign policy allows members of an intervening government to experiment with new forms of state-produced social control. But domestic persons ruled by the intervening government are not immune from innovations that are hatched to control those overseas. The boomerang effect demonstrates why. Widespread fear of a threat, combined with consolidated power in the hands of the central government create an environment favorable to the importation of techniques and tools of social control first used abroad. Fear of enemies creates space for government to increase the scope of its activities at home in the name of "protecting the people." Consolidation weakens the checks created by political subunits and private individuals while empowering the national government to expand its broadcast of power over citizens.

The importation of innovations in social control takes place through three related channels. First, those involved in coercive foreign interventions accumulate unique human capital in designing and implementing social control over others. These experiences and skills become a part of the person and remain with them well after the intervention has ended. Second, this human capital leads to change in the organizational dynamics of domestic life. As those involved in coercive foreign interventions participate in domestic life, some are able to leverage their comparative advantage as specialists in state-produced social control. In doing so they can influence private and public institutions at home. Still others reassimilate into civilian life but with a changed view of the appropriate scope of state activities. Finally, the physical capital developed to control those abroad often returns home, enhancing the ability of the intervening government to engage in domestic control. In conjunction, the cumulative effect of these three channels is that the intervening government becomes increasingly efficient at controlling not only distant populations but also the domestic population as well.

Given that our focus is on the United States, the next chapter explains why America is susceptible to the boomerang effect. In principle, strong constitutional constraints on the activities of the government will limit its potential to engage in social control both abroad and at home. Effective constraints would limit the likelihood of innovations in social control returning home. However, when it comes to the activities of the national security state, the domestic and international constraints on the U.S. government are weak or nonexistent. These ineffective formal constraints set the stage for the process discussed here to come into its own.

CHAPTER 3

A Perfect Storm

Why America Is Susceptible

The U.S. national surveillance state is shrouded in secrecy. In rare instances, however, public revelations make clear the extent of its operations. For example, in 1931 Herbert Yardley wrote a tell-all book documenting his experiences as the head of the American Black Chamber, a cryptanalytic bureau which preceded the National Security Agency (NSA).[1] Yardley revealed to the public the Black Chamber's methods, techniques, structure, and budget. Four decades later, the *New York Times* published some content from the "Family Jewels," a collection of internally produced reports documenting the covert activities of the U.S. Central Intelligence Agency (CIA).[2] The reports documented the extensive domestic spying carried out by the CIA in violation of its charter. More recently, in 2013, Edward Snowden publicly leaked documents revealing the global reach of the mass surveillance activities of the NSA.[3]

Each of these revelations shed light on the awesome powers possessed by those controlling America's surveillance apparatus and the potential for abuse. In doing so each highlights the "paradox of government," which refers to the inherent tension in granting government significant coercive power.[4] Again, the issue is that any government strong enough to protect its citizens is also strong enough to abuse them. James Madison captured the essence of this paradox in "Federalist No. 51," when he wrote that "[i]n framing a government which is to be administered by men over men, the great difficulty lies in this: you must first enable the government to control the governed; and in the next place oblige it to control itself."[5] More recently, political scientist Barry Weingast emphasized the importance of this paradox when noting that "[t]he fundamental political dilemma" is that a "government strong enough to protect property rights and enforce contracts is also strong enough to confiscate the wealth of its citizens."[6] The concern is that absent constraints, those in government can abuse their powers in order to achieve their own narrow ends.

This matters not just for domestic life but also for international relations because a government strong enough to intervene in another society is also strong enough to abuse its power in that intervention. Given this concern, the constraints on government, or their absence, are crucial because they will determine the types of social control that can be developed and employed against others through foreign intervention. For example, strong constraints on how government officials can treat people in other countries will limit what can be done abroad. For this reason it is important to understand the nature of constraints on the U.S. government in foreign affairs.

The reality is that when it comes to foreign intervention, formal domestic and international constraints on the members of the U.S. government are either weak or nonexistent. The result is that America is susceptible to the boomerang effect because the members of the U.S. government, pursing a militaristic foreign policy, have significant opportunity to engage in largely unconstrained experimentation in social control over distant populations. As per the previous chapter, domestic life is not immune to these innovations in state-produced social control, which often return home.

WEAK DOMESTIC CONSTRAINTS: THE DUAL GOVERNMENTS OF THE UNITED STATES

America is supposedly a constitutional republic with clear constraints on the government to prevent abuses of power. And the U.S. Constitution does include a variety of rules intended to restrain government, including checks and balances aimed at dispersing power. But when it comes to national security and defense, the constraints are significantly weaker than many might realize.

In studying the origins and evolution of the modern U.S. national security state, Michael Glennon, a legal scholar specializing in international law, has identified a "double government" with two distinct sets of institutions.[7] The first set of institutions consists of the "dignified institutions," the executive, legislative, and judicial branches. These are the institutions that most people have in mind when they think of the Founding Fathers or when they praise America for its constitutionally constrained government. The traditions and pomp and circumstance that surround many government activities—for example, the rituals surrounding election day, the ceremony of the presidential inauguration, and the president's annual State of the Union address—are associated with this category of institutions. Traditions foster and perpetuate feelings of loyalty, patriotism, and nationalism among citizens.

The origins of the dignified institutions can be found in the Madisonian structure of dispersed power across the three branches of government. In advocating the separation of powers, James Madison and the other founders intended to create an environment which recognized that the maintenance of liberty requires that "[a]mbition must be made to counteract ambition" within government.[8] This was necessary, they argued, so that if a branch sought to expand its power, it would be constrained by the others. However, over time the Madisonian checks and balances on the national security state were eroded and supplanted by a new set of government institutions—the "efficient institutions."

These efficient institutions consist of the complex network of government agencies and departments—military, intelligence, law enforcement, diplomatic—as well as the private contractors and consultants that constitute the national security state. This deep state falls outside of the electoral process and many of the checks and balances intended to resolve the paradox of government.[9] Those populating these institutions have significant, although by no means exclusive, influence over U.S. national security policy, including foreign intervention.

The efficient institutions can be traced to President Harry Truman's signing of the National Security Act of 1947 (and its subsequent 1949 amendments), which created the foundations of the modern security state. The context of the Act is as follows. During World War II the branches of the U.S. armed forces and the government's wartime agencies were only loosely coordinated. This led to tensions between the armed services—for example, the Army and Navy over the use of airpower—and piecemeal coordination among the agencies involved in mobilizing resources for the war effort. The result was a variety of frictions and tensions often making it difficult to formulate and implement a unified set of strategies and policies. Coordination mechanisms, which were informal and fragile during the war, began to unravel in its aftermath.[10] Policymakers viewed this as problematic given the significant postwar ideological shift that occurred after the war.

In the wake of World War II, the national security ideology in the United States was one of preparation for global total war driven by the perceived Soviet threat. As historian Michael Hogan noted, "the immediacy of the Soviet threat made preparedness a matter of urgency, the long term nature of that threat required a permanent program of preparedness, and the danger of total war dictated a comprehensive program that integrated civilian and military resources and obliterated the line between citizen and soldier, peace and war."[11] This ideology was shaped both by the members of the U.S. government, who fostered the idea that the United States was engaged in a never-ending struggle with the Soviet Union, and by the public, who accepted a shift in how government operated both domestically and internationally. In their comprehensive study of U.S. public opinion, political scientists Benjamin Page and Robert Shapiro documented the significance of World War II, noting that it "transformed American public opinion concerning virtually all aspects of foreign affairs," including the role of government.[12] The result was a marked shift from the prewar beliefs of the American people which, due to an enduring fear of standing armies and militarism, resulted in rapid demobilization at the end of prior conflicts.[13] The postwar ideology, characterized by support of permanent preparations for perpetual global war, set the stage for a massive reorganization of the U.S. government's military and intelligence agencies.

The resulting National Security Act of 1947 created the National Military Establishment (later the Department of Defense), unified the military under a new position—the secretary of defense—and established the CIA, the Joint Chiefs of Staff, the National Security Council, and the Armed Forces Security Agency (later the National Security Agency).[14] In doing so it changed the power structure of the U.S. government. The act "unified the armed forces, expanded the defense budget, harnessed science to military purposes, and forged new institutions, many of which, like the National Security Council and the Central Intelligence Agency, are among the best known and more powerful organs of government."[15] The reforms also created and elevated a new class of non-elected security bureaucrats, at the core of the efficient institutions, who "presided over the largest and fastest growing sector of the federal government."[16] The result was a massive expansion in the scope of the national security apparatus, which now had the autonomy and power to influence significant aspects of government policy both abroad and at home.

In making these changes, however, Truman's reforms necessarily moved away from the Madisonian structure of dispersed power across the three branches of government. By centralizing power and granting security agencies independence, previous checks were weakened, lowering the barriers to government expansion.[17] Ultimately, the Truman reforms created an environment for the national security institutions to grow and operate without the constraints envisioned by the founders.[18] The implications are counterintuitive to many and troubling for those who take the paradox of government seriously.

While those in the dignified institutions do exert some power, those in the efficient institutions also possess more influence than is commonly realized. This matters because the deep state is largely "removed from public view and from the constitutional restrictions that check America's dignified institutions."[19] To understand why the efficient institutions have influence over national security policy, it is important to understand the factors limiting the three branches of government constituting the dignified institutions.

The effectiveness of the executive branch is limited because the president's national security policies are heavily influenced and shaped by the national security state it is supposed to constrain.[20] "The reality is that when the President issues an 'order'" to those in the national security state, the members of the security establishment "themselves normally formulate the order."[21] The power of the national security state was evident in the recent debate over the expanded use of drones by the CIA. Some questioned why the president was allowing the development of what was essentially a second air force under CIA control. Others asked whether drones were causing more harm than good by creating additional terrorists and anti-American sentiment.[22] During one meeting President Barack Obama dismissed these concerns, saying, "The CIA gets what it wants."[23]

In addition, elected officials—both in the executive branch and in Congress—face four realities that limit their ability to monitor and constrain the efficient institutions. The first relates to the sheer volume of information. Foreign affairs are complex even for narrowly focused experts, let alone for political representatives who are expected to have knowledge of a wide range of domestic and foreign policy issues. Given this reality, politicians must prioritize a small number of policy issues, leaving the unprioritized aspects to be influenced by those in the efficient institutions.

Moreover, given the immense size of the national security apparatus, understanding the specifics of its operations is near impossible even for top government officials to grasp. For example, during a 2009 public relations event President Obama asked one government employee where he worked, to which he answered, "I work at NGA, National Geospatial-Intelligence Agency." President Obama responded, "So, explain to me exactly what this National Geospatial . . ." with his voice trailing off, unable to parrot the agency he had just learned of.[24] The employee went on to explain that the NGA works with satellite imagery. The broader implication is that the vast complexities of the security state leaves significant space for those in the efficient institutions to control and influence many aspects of foreign policy.

Second, those in the efficient institutions can control and shape the information available to elected officials. This allows for the possibility of relevant information being withheld or manipulated to serve the interests of the members of the security state. For example, in 2016 it was revealed that officials from the U.S. Central Command (CENTCOM) altered intelligence reports delivered to the president and his close advisors. These altered reports sought to portray a falsely optimistic assessment of Iraqi security forces and the ongoing war by the U.S. government against the Islamic State in Iraq and Syria.[25] In other instances crucial intelligence was concealed until after CENTCOM officials testified in front of Congress about the status of progress in Iraq while requesting additional funding for these operations.[26]

Third, even where oversight does occur, it is shaped by perverse incentives. For example, when discussing congressional oversight of the NSA, author James Bamford noted that "the intelligence committees are more dedicated to protecting the agencies from budget cuts than safeguarding the public from their transgressions. Hence their failure to discover the Bush administration's warrantless wiretapping activity and their failure to take action against the NSA's gathering of telephone and Internet records."[27]

Fourth, the electorate tends to be uninformed on the specifics of foreign affairs and the complexities of the security state. Citizens tend to be focused on the domestic policies that directly affect their lives on a regular basis. And even if they did wish to be informed, the aforementioned complexities of the security state structure and operations make it impossible to do so. The result is that people tend not to pressure their representatives to understand and check the activities of the national security state. This reinforces the ineffectiveness of oversight.

This lack of oversight by citizens is compounded by a deep-seated fear of attack from evil, external threats. This fear can be traced back to the end of World War II, when the "United States adopted the roles of the world's premier power *and* its supreme worrier" about the possibility of constant, significant threats to domestic security.[28] Even though America is the safest country in the history of the world, this pervasive fear among American citizens creates significant space for the efficient institutions to influence and implement a proactive, militaristic foreign policy.

The judiciary is also often limited as a check on the security state. In matters of national security the courts often lack "the foremost predicate needed for Madisonian equilibrium: 'a will of [their] own.'"[29] Edward Corwin, a constitutional scholar, argued that "in total war the [Supreme] Court necessarily loses some part of its normal freedom of decision and becomes assimilated, like the rest of society, to the mechanism of national defense."[30] This alignment and integration of the courts with the other branches of government weakens the checks created by the separation of powers. This creates space for those in the efficient institutions to exert a range of influence over security policy in an unchecked manner.

Recognizing these issues is not meant to suggest that those in the efficient institutions of the national security state have complete and unconstrained freedom to do as they please. Those in the dignified institutions are not helpless pawns passively responding to the wants of the members of the security state.[31] Instead, to varying degrees they possess power to shape foreign policy and limit the activities of the deep state. For example, the president can influence the country's grand strategy and ultimately determine whether the government engages in war or not. Elected representatives in Congress influence budget allocations, and congressional oversight committees can, on certain margins, monitor and limit the activities of the national security state. Further, there are historical instances of the courts rebuffing the security state, declaring its actions unconstitutional.

That said, those in the efficient institutions have significant power and influence for the reasons already discussed. This power is independent of the electoral process and not subject to close oversight, meaning there is substantial slack in the constraints facing those in the national security state, creating space for a wide range of unchecked behavior. This reality stands in stark contrast to the common romantic view of publicly spirited civil servants openly debating national security issues under a system of checks, balances, and oversight all in the name of advancing the "national interest." This romantic view is not just wrong, but also dangerous, as it gives citizens a false sense that their government is constrained to act only in their best interest regarding national security. Nothing could be further from the truth. The reality of the double government is that U.S. officials are often able to design, prepare for, and implement coercive foreign interventions with weak domestic constraints on their behavior.

WEAK NATIONAL CONSTRAINTS:

THE CONSTITUTION DOES NOT FOLLOW THE FLAG

What about constraints on the international activities of the U.S. government? To what extent does the U.S. Constitution "follow the flag" and limit the U.S. government when it intervenes abroad? These questions have been at the center of legal debate and deliberation for well over a century. The answer can be found in precedents set by several Supreme Court decisions in 1901, collectively known as the *Insular Cases*.

The impetus behind these rulings was the acquisition of new territories by the U.S. government, including the annexation of Hawaii in 1898, the control of Cuba by a U.S. military government until 1902, and the signing of the Treaty of Paris in 1898 marking the formal end to the Spanish-American War and facilitating transfer of control over the Philippines, Puerto Rico, and Guam to the U.S. government. These events raised legal questions regarding the rights of people living in those territories; specifically, did the U.S. Constitution apply to them?[32]

Of the nine *Insular Cases*, most legal scholars consider *Downes v. Bidwell* (1901) the most important and influential. At its core was the applicability of the Uniformity Clause (Article 1, Section 8) of the U.S. Constitution to newly acquired territories. The Uniformity Clause requires that "all Duties, Imposts and Excises [imposed by Congress] shall be uniform throughout the United States."[33] Samuel Downes, a merchant who owned and operated S.B. Downes & Company, had imported oranges from Puerto Rico and was charged duties at the New York port. Downes sued George Bidwell, the U.S. customs inspector for the port, to recover the duties, claiming that taxing trade with Puerto Rico, now a U.S. territory, violated the Uniformity Clause.

In a 5-4 vote the Supreme Court decided against Downes, ruling that Puerto Rico was, as Justice Edward White put it, "foreign to the United States in a domestic sense."[34] The overall effect of the ruling was, according to one legal scholar, that "the Court endorsed Congress's authority to govern Puerto Rico as a satellite colony, formally validating the territory's hybrid status somewhere between foreign nation and domestic state."[35] Summarizing the decision, then Secretary of War Elihu Root said, "The Constitution follows the flag—but doesn't quite catch up with it."[36]

Thus the Supreme Court's decision recognized Congress's power to determine the applicability of the Constitution to territories. Since Congress could determine whether a territory was to be "incorporated" into the United States, it could also decide when and where full constitutional rights applied.[37] This flexibility provided the U.S. government with a menu of options regarding how to deal with territories. In some cases, Congress might decide to extend constitutional rights to the subjects in a conquered territory. In other cases, Congress may decide, as described by one legal scholar, to "grant to the conquered a lesser set of rights, if the people conquered are considered savages."[38]

Interestingly, Justice Henry Brown, who cast the decisive vote against Downes, highlighted future foreign interventions by the U.S. government as one reason for his decision. Specifically, Brown argued that the future might "bring about conditions which would render the annexation of distant possessions desirable" and that a "false step at this time [on the part of the Supreme Court] might be fatal to the development of what Chief Justice Marshall called the 'American empire.'"[39] In other words, one of the purposes behind the Court's decision regarding Puerto Rico was to leave slack in the constraints on the U.S. government in future foreign interventions.

If the Court had decided that the Constitution extended to territories acquired by the United States, it would have placed firmer constraints on the government when intervening abroad. In deciding that constitutional rights do not automatically extend to areas under the control of the American government, however, the Court lowered the cost of an activist foreign policy characterized by coercive social control over foreign populations. As political scientist Bartholomew Sparrow notes, "the *Insular Cases'* endorsement of expansion marks the emergence of an American empire" because the U.S. government could intervene without the consent of inhabitants and with no obligation to extend them the rights specified in the Constitution. Moreover, the government could exit territories it invaded with no responsibility to the citizens living there.[40] This made future intervention more likely.

Since the Supreme Court's decisions in the *Insular Cases*, the nature of the U.S. empire has shifted. U.S. foreign policy is no longer focused on outright territorial acquisition, but rather on exerting power and control through a variety of formal and informal channels. Formal means of power projection include military intervention and occupation. Informal means of controlling other societies include supporting and installing client governments, establishing relationships with authoritarian regimes, and establishing a global network of military bases along with associated military personnel.[41]

The *Insular Cases* precedent combined with the double government that arose domestically in the 1940s makes clear that the U.S. national security apparatus has significant freedom to pursue its policies and goals abroad. This freedom is evident in the numerous interventions abroad over the past century and more recently in the treatment of "enemy combatants"; the use of torture, or what the U.S. government terms "enhanced interrogation techniques"; drone strikes on foreign soil; and the extensive use of surveillance of U.S. citizens and noncitizens alike. But that is not all. International constraints on the members of the U.S. government are also weak and fail to effectively constrain foreign interventions.

In principle, international norms and treaties limit what states can do to those in other countries. For example, the Geneva Conventions were intended to limit the behavior of governments during war. Another supposed constraint is the customary principle of "state sovereignty" dating back to the Treaty of Westphalia in 1648. Per this principle, each nation-state has ultimate authority over its territory, limiting the possibility of intervention from other states.

However, the effectiveness of these mechanisms as checks on the behavior of the U.S. government is typically limited, if they have any teeth at all. The international system is highly decentralized, meaning that there are numerous nation-states but no overarching authority to enforce rules and punish states that do not comply with treaties. International organizations exist, but they lack the ability to enforce rules against nation-states in a consistent manner. The reality is that nation-states, and especially relatively strong countries, such as the United States, not only establish international rules but also influence their enforcement. Absent effective global governance mechanisms, individual governments can and do circumvent constraints when it is in their interest.

Scholars writing in the areas of international law and international relations are well aware of this point. For example, legal scholar Jakob Katz Cogan writes that "the international system contains few legislative, judicial, or executive processes analogous to those of States, and, consequently, the system's ability to self-correct and self-enforce is much more limited, creating gaps between aspiration and authority, procedures and policy."[42] John Mearsheimer, an international relations scholar, concluded that international "institutions have minimal influence on state behavior and thus hold little promise for promoting stability" by constraining the actions of governments.[43] Legal scholar Eric Posner notes that "[i]nternational law is only as strong as the states with an interest in upholding it.

Ambitious schemes that seek to transcend countries' interests routinely fail."[44] Similarly, legal scholar Nico Krisch writes, "[e]ven as the United States has remained active in the development and enforcement of international law, paradoxically it has in many areas sought to avoid its subjection to such law." The implication, he argues, is that the U.S. government "has emerged as a leading obstacle to those phenomena that characterize 'modern' international law, notably universal treaties and strong enforcement mechanisms."[45] For these reasons the notions of state sovereignty and international law are not effective as hard constraints on the behavior of the U.S. government in international affairs.

The concept of sovereignty is based on respect for the self-determination of nation-states and the principle of legal equality. Given the relative strength of the U.S. government, however, the political elite can determine when to respect the sovereignty of other states with little fear of recourse or punishment when choosing to violate that independence. Historian Alfred McCoy writes that "[n]ot only did the US play a crucial role in writing the new [international] rules [following World War II], . . . but it almost immediately began breaking them. After all, despite the rise of the other superpower, the Soviet Union, Washington was by then the world sovereign and so could decide which should be the exceptions to its own rules, particularly to the foundational principle for all this global governance: sovereignty."[46] To provide a few examples, consider that the U.S. government has carried out numerous foreign interventions without United Nations (UN) authorization—such as the invasion of Vietnam in the 1960s, the 1983 invasion of Grenada, the 1989 invasion of Panama, missile strikes on Sudan and Afghanistan in 1998, and the 2003 invasion of Iraq—with no direct sanctions for failing to gain international approval and support.

Most recently, the U.S. government's ability and willingness to interpret international law as its leaders see fit has been evident in the transnational War on Terror.[47] The U.S. government has detained prisoners at various "black sites" throughout the world without following the basic dictates of international norms or treaties. Government officials have justified this behavior by stating that international law simply does not apply to the War on Terror. A January 9, 2002, memo from U.S. Deputy Assistant Attorney General John Yoo and Special Counsel Robert Delahunty concluded that "customary international law, whatever its source and content, does not bind the President, or restrict the actions of the United States military. . . ."[48] A memo from Attorney General Alberto Gonzales later that month argued that the War on Terror "renders obsolete Geneva's [the Geneva Conventions'] strict limitations on questioning of enemy prisoners and renders quaint some of its provisions. . . ."[49]

Whether one agrees or disagrees with the U.S. government's actions in the War on Terror is irrelevant to the central point, which is that political leaders can ignore international constraints by simply writing a short memo saying that international laws are not applicable to their actions. This is not to suggest that the U.S. government always ignores international law, but that its personnel can do so when convenient for their purposes.[50] As a recent article in *The Economist* noted, while the U.S. government sometimes follows international law, "the view that America makes its pitches to international order from within a glass house is also partly correct"; also, "America's approach to foreign policy has long enjoyed a strain of exceptionalism," as evidenced by those instances when it has ignored international treaties.[51] Legal scholar Michael Stokes Paulsen is even more blunt in concluding that "[t]he force of international law, as a body of law, upon the United States is thus largely an illusion. On matters of war, peace, human rights, and torture—some of the most valued matters on which international law speaks—its voice may be silenced by contrary U.S. law or shouted down by the exercise of U.S. constitutional powers that international law has no binding domestic-law power to constrain. International law, for the United States, is international policy and politics."[52]

The overarching implication is that there are few effective international constraints on the behavior of the U.S. government. Constraints exist in principle, but in practice they are subject to the interests, opinions, and whims of those whom they supposedly restrain. When the interests of those in power do not align with the dictates of international law, the law will tend to be ignored with little recourse. This is equivalent to having no constraints whatsoever since restrictions on certain behavior will appear to be effective only when they align with what U.S. political leaders would have done anyway in the absence of the constraints. This significant slack in the international system allows members of the U.S. government to engage in unconstrained experimentation and refinement of techniques and methods of social control over distant populations.

FOREIGN INTERVENTION AS
EXPERIMENTATION IN SOCIAL CONTROL

In the realm of foreign affairs, the political constraints on the U.S. government are exceedingly weak at best and nonexistent at worst. Domestically the national security apparatus consists of an interconnected web of agencies, bureaus, and private contractors that have significant space to operate outside the checks and balances set forth by the Constitution. The *Insular Cases* established a legal precedent that limits the reach of the Constitution when the U.S. government intervenes abroad. And given the selective respect for and enforcement of international law, it is not a consistent and effective protector of the rights of non-U.S. persons against the paradox of government.

From an economic perspective, political constraints are rules that create incentives influencing the behavior of those in power. Given the severe slack in constraints regarding national security and international affairs, we should expect U.S. government officials to act just as the paradox of government and basic reason would predict. That is, with centralized power and limited formal constraints on its use, the U.S. government, when preparing for and engaging in foreign interventions, will tend to behave more like a despotism than a constitutionally constrained republic grounded in a commitment to individual rights and liberties.

This is not intended to be a polemic. Rather, it is the recognition and appreciation that government power is ultimately grounded in the threat or use of bald coercion. As Max Weber noted, "[t]he decisive means for politics is violence."[53] The threat and use of violence is readily on display in coercive foreign interventions, where U.S. officials are largely unconstrained in what they can do to establish the social control necessary to achieve their objectives. As an example of unconstrained social control, consider the following findings in a report by the United Nations Human Rights Council:

"Through its extensive spying and surveillance system targeting individuals within the country . . . the Government engages in the systematic violation of the right to privacy."[54]

"As a result of this mass surveillance, [citizens] live in constant fear that their conduct is or may be monitored by security agents, and that information gathered may be used against them leading to arbitrary arrest, detention, torture, disappearance or death."[55]

"The Government strives to control strictly any human movement. . . ."[56]

"Freedom of the press is another casualty of the Government's effort to control society."[57]

"Violations of the right to fair trial and due process of law are particularly blatant."[58]

"The use of information collected by the Government through spying networks leads . . . to arbitrary arrest and detention."[59]

"The detention network . . . is vast . . . with many secret and unofficial facilities.[60]

"The harshest conditions and the strictest regimes of detention are deliberately employed in a number of situations, including to punish those suspected of being a threat to national security."[61]

"[O]fficials use a variety of forms of ill-treatment during interrogations and to punish detainees and conscripts. The common element of these forms of ill-treatment, such as extreme forms of restraint, beatings or rape, is that they are intended to inflict severe physical and psychological pain."[62]

One might easily conclude that this report refers to behavior of the U.S. government—both domestically and internationally—post-9/11.[63] It does not. Instead, the report is detailing the behavior of the government of Eritrea, a brutal totalitarian regime that engages in "systematic, widespread and gross human rights violations" with "no accountability" and "a total lack of rule of law."[64] This is not to suggest that the U.S. government is the equivalent of the Eritrean government in all regards. However, when it comes to coercive foreign intervention, any differences between the activities of the U.S. government and authoritarian regimes are matters of degree, not kind. The corresponding behaviors are entirely predictable since weak, if not altogether absent, political constraints on the U.S. government lower the cost of developing, employing, and refining the methods of state-produced social control necessary to achieve the objectives of coercive foreign intervention.

One might argue that the U.S. government's development and use of extreme forms of social control abroad are necessary to protect the American populace at home. This reasoning assumes that such behavior overseas can be neatly separated from domestic life within the United States. Indeed, foreign policy is often treated as if it were isolated from the evolution of domestic policies and institutions. What is often overlooked, however, is that a government's preparation for and engagement in coercive intervention can also impose significant costs on domestic citizens due to changes in government at home as per the logic of the boomerang effect.

The chapters to come will look at examples of the ways in which the boomerang effect has influenced life in the United States. We will take a tour through the origins and the evolution of the U.S. national surveillance state. We will also explore how past foreign interventions directly influenced the militarization of domestic policing and the use of drones within U.S. borders. Finally, we will discover how foreign interventions have enabled the U.S. government to refine torture techniques only to use them against American citizens. In each instance interventions by the U.S. government in the lives of others returned home, knocking down the liberties of domestic citizens just as Twain predicted.

PART II

Cases of Domestic Liberty Lost

CHAPTER 4

Surveillance

Beginning in June 2013 the *Guardian* and the *Washington Post* began to publish information leaked by Edward Snowden, a former National Security Agency (NSA) contractor, regarding the U.S. government's global surveillance operations.[1] Snowden's disclosures included numerous insights into the vast range of post-9/11 activities undertaken by the government as part of the broader War on Terror. Among the major revelations were the following:

— The government was engaged in the mass collection of the phone records of U.S. persons, and major U.S. telephone companies were providing it unlimited access to their customers' records as part of this process.[2]

— A government program—PRISM—was in place to request data and information from at least nine major technology companies—including Apple, Google, and Microsoft—that were legally required to comply and maintain secrecy.[3]

— The NSA tapped directly into the data centers of major technology companies—including Yahoo and Google—without their knowledge when the activities described above were not feasible, as determined by the government.[4]

— A rule change in 2011 allowed the NSA to search telephone and email communications of U.S. persons without a warrant if they were in contact with foreign targets; during this process, purely domestic communications may be incidentally collected and reviewed.[5]

— The Foreign Intelligence Surveillance Court (FISC) issued orders weakening the constraints on government agencies—the NSA, FBI, and CIA—which allowed them to share unfiltered personal information about U.S. persons.[6]

— The communications intercepted by the NSA were primarily those of innocent, nontargeted Internet users—U.S. persons and foreigners—

rather than those of foreign individuals who were intended legal targets; according to one investigation, the information of nine out of ten Internet users captured by the NSA was of nontargets.[7]

— A program—XKeyscore—allows NSA analysts to search through comprehensive databases of the metadata and online content—including emails, chats, documents, passwords, webcam photos, and browsing histories—of millions of private individuals with no prior authorization.[8]

— The NSA had spied or was spying on over 120 world leaders.[9]

— The NSA weakened Internet security, including requiring technology companies to install various "backdoors," to circumvent encryption and ensure widespread government access.[10]

— The NSA, in conjunction with the United Kingdom's Government Communications Headquarters, has a program in place—DISHFIRE—that collects over two hundred million text messages globally on a daily basis.[11]

In discussing the impact of the Snowden disclosures, Barton Gellman, who reported the revelations for the *Post*, concluded, "[t]aken together, the revelations have brought to light a global surveillance system that cast off many of its historical restraints after the attacks of Sept. 11, 2001. Secret legal authorities empowered the NSA to sweep in the telephone, Internet and location records of whole populations."[12] The Snowden revelations shined a global spotlight on the scope of the surveillance activities of the NSA and U.S. government more broadly. To truly understand the modern surveillance state, however, it is important to appreciate two things. First, the U.S. surveillance of citizens and foreigners is not new, but instead has a long history. Second, the evolution of the modern surveillance state is directly linked to earlier U.S. coercive foreign intervention.

EARLY SURVEILLANCE IN AMERICA

Government surveillance is as old as America itself. During the Revolutionary War the Continental Congress approved several broad categories of surveillance and spying to support the Continental Army.[13] In September 1775 the Congress resolved to create a "Secret Committee" charged with gathering and sharing domestic intelligence. The Secret Committee collected information on domestic Loyalists and the location of their armaments and ammunition. The members of the Committee were also responsible for securing and allocating military supplies in secret to avoid detection by the British forces.[14]

Two months later the Congress created the Committee of Secret Correspondence to oversee foreign intelligence. This new organization engaged in a variety of activities, including spying and conducting covert operations on foreign soil, cultivating and maintaining connections with foreigners who supported America's effort to achieve independence, designing and funding propaganda campaigns, and monitoring private citizens' mail for any information related to the war effort.[15]

The third and final aspect of surveillance during the American Revolutionary War was the Committee on Spies, created by the Congress in June 1776. The Committee was founded in response to the arrest of Dr. Benjamin Church as a British spy. Since no espionage law existed, the Committee was formed to develop one, which imposed the death penalty.[16]

Surveillance was also a key part of the Civil War for both the Union and the Confederacy.[17] No formal intelligence agencies existed before the war, so intelligence activities emerged and evolved informally on both sides. In the early 1860s the Confederacy established a network of spies in Washington, D.C., with the assistance of Virginia governor John Letcher, who had an intricate knowledge of the city and helped to recruit agents to assist the Confederate cause. Also established was a Secret Service Bureau, which was housed in the Confederate States Army Signal Corps.[18] The Bureau managed a constantly changing network of couriers—the "Secret Line"—who facilitated the flow of information between Richmond, the North, and Canada. The methods used were largely rudimentary and included intercepting hard copies of communications, securing Northern newspapers that contained relevant information, and hanging certain colored clothing in visible areas when Union troops were either nearby or expected to arrive shortly.

Initially the Union also relied on a decentralized system of surveillance, with each general responsible for his own intelligence operations. For example, General George B. McClellan, commander of the Union's

Army of the Potomac, hired Allan Pinkerton, a detective from Chicago, to collect intelligence. While Pinkerton referred to himself as the "Chief of the United States Secret Service," he worked solely for McClellan since no central agency or formal position with that title existed at the time.[19] Absent a formal agency, Pinkerton and similar private hires created spying and information-sharing networks to assist the Union cause.

In 1863 these decentralized efforts were consolidated with the Union's creation of the Bureau of Military Information (BMI), the first formal American military intelligence agency. The BMI was tasked with gathering information, which it accomplished through spying, interrogating prisoners, and collecting Southern newspapers. Perhaps the best indication of the Union's effort to centralize intelligence gathering was that Commanding General Ulysses S. Grant incorporated the BMI into his headquarters' operations to ensure that information was communicated to him in a timely and efficient manner. The BMI was officially disbanded at the conclusion of the war in 1865.[20]

Although government surveillance has existed throughout America's history, its nature, scale, and scope have changed radically. Early efforts were ad hoc. Most of them were not undertaken through permanent centralized bureaus. Instead, they were short-term efforts associated with specific war efforts. And, as the BMI illustrates, even when formal centralization began, it was temporary and was discontinued at the conclusion of the war. This would change in the early twentieth century when the foundations of the modern U.S. surveillance state were established. To understand these foundations, it is important to start with the U.S. government's intervention in the Philippines in the late nineteenth century.

THE U.S. OCCUPATION OF THE PHILIPPINES

Today it is common to associate U.S. surveillance with the NSA. This association makes sense given the Snowden revelations, which exposed the extent of the NSA's operations. But the story begins over a hundred years earlier.

In December 1898 Spain formally ceded the archipelago known as the Philippine Islands to the United States following the Spanish-American War.[21] Filipino rebels, working with the United States, sought to end some three hundred years of Spanish rule. Hopes for an independent Philippines were quickly dashed, however, when the United States formally annexed the island chain. Almost immediately Filipino citizens found themselves subjugated to their supposed liberators. On January 23, 1899, the First Philippine Republic, or the Malolos Republic, declared independence from the United States and claimed to be the legitimate governing body of the islands.[22] The Philippine-American War ensued. Filipino resistance staged a full revolt against the American occupiers. The U.S. Congress responded by deploying some sixty-five thousand troops to the country by the end of 1899. By 1902 the formal insurrection was officially over, and the U.S. government claimed control of the country.[23] Despite this formal declaration of victory, rebel groups, which threatened U.S. control, operated throughout the country for the next decade.[24]

The modern U.S. surveillance state emerged in the context of this resistance to U.S. occupiers. As historian Alfred McCoy details, the U.S. government, using state-of-the-art technology, established a multitiered organizational structure of surveillance and social control.[25] This surveillance apparatus, in conjunction with brute force, suppressed dissent by rebels, local political players, and Filipino citizens.

Two main factors allowed the U.S. government to experiment with new forms of social control in the Philippines. The first was a lack of constraints on the interveners, who viewed themselves as shapers of the political, social, and cultural landscapes of the country in order to align it with the vision held by U.S. political leaders. The authoritarian-paternalist mentality that governed the occupation was evident in the U.S. legislation regarding the status of the country at the conclusion of the Philippine-American War. In 1902 Congress passed the Philippine Organic Act, which organized the Insular Government under the authority of the U.S. Bureau of Insular Affairs. The act also established the laws governing the Insular Government's operation, including creation of the office of governor-general, who was appointed by the U.S. president. Over a decade later, in 1916, Congress passed the Philippine Autonomy Act, which expanded domestic elections and formally indicated the U.S. government's intention to grant full independence—but only when a stable government was established, as determined by the Americans. Despite the formal U.S. commitment to independence, it wasn't until 1934, with the passage of the Philippine Independence Act, that the U.S. government established a clear plan for granting independence after a subsequent ten-year transition period.

Taken together, the timing and content of these three pieces of legislation capture the mentality of the U.S. government toward the Philippines. As historian Richard Millett writes, a defining characteristic of the situation was "the total control the United States, as the ruling colonial power, had over the islands and the expectation that such control would continue for an indefinite period."[26] There was no doubt that the Philippine Islands were to be controlled and shaped according to the desires of the U.S. political elite, with few if any constraints on the scope, scale, and duration of the occupation.

The second factor that allowed the U.S. government to experiment with a national surveillance state was the significant infrastructural and technological advances that took place in America starting in the 1860s. The key innovations included the telegraph, the typewriter, the telephone, the adding machine, photoengraving, and roll film.[27] These technologies significantly increased the efficiency of recording, transferring, and cataloging information in previously unknown quality and quantity. These advances afforded a unique opportunity to the U.S. government by providing "the potential for mass surveillance, allowing for the first time an advance beyond punishment of the few to control over the many."[28] The occupation provided the U.S. government with the perfect opportunity to take advantage of this potential. In the Philippines the U.S. government set up a multipronged apparatus to establish control over actual and potential resistance to its occupation. This apparatus included the Manila Police, the Philippines Constabulary, and the U.S. Army's Division of Military Information, each of which engaged in surveillance.

The police force consisted of the Metropolitan Police force in Manila and municipal police forces outside the capital. The Metropolitan Police included a combination of U.S. Army veterans and native Filipinos, all under U.S. control. In addition to standard police patrols, the Metropolitan Police Force included a Secret Service Division responsible for surveillance and for documenting the written and photographic data—physical, political, professional, and so on—of actual and suspected criminals. By the mid-1920s the division bureau had accumulated some form of information on an estimated 70 percent of the city's population.[29] The data were then used by the occupiers to arrest and manipulate people and to maintain control over the population of the capital.

The Philippines Constabulary was a national militarized police force created in 1901 by the occupiers to combat insurgents throughout the islands.[30] The constabulary engaged in both combat operations and covert surveillance of potential insurgents through its Information Bureau. These two sets of activities were carried out simultaneously so that "[w]hile the constabulary's patrols pursued peasant rebels in the countryside, its Information Division monitored and manipulated radical intellectuals in the capital."[31] It is estimated that the Constabulary maintained a network of over four hundred telegraph offices with more than forty-two hundred miles of copper wire. These offices intercepted over 1.7 million messages annually.[32]

The third and perhaps most crucial element of the U.S. surveillance state was the Division of Military Information (DMI), created in 1900. The DMI was tasked with gathering actionable intelligence related to actual and potential insurgents. It relied on direct surveillance as well as information exchanges with the police, the constabulary, and a network of Filipino spies and prisoners to develop "what soon became encyclopedic information on every aspect of the Filipino resistance: active guerrillas, civilian supporters, finances, firearms, ideology, propaganda, communications, movement, and terrain."[33] The DMI's comprehensive database included not just objective facts but also records of people's perceived dispositions and attitudes toward the United States and the resistance movement in order to gauge each person's threat as an insurgent.

Together these three entities constituted a centralized, comprehensive, and scientific effort by the U.S. government to manage, control, and shape the Philippines. This unprecedented effort was not just for the sake of passive defense. The occupiers used the information to manipulate people, groups, and public opinion to advance the interests of people and groups whose agendas and beliefs aligned with the goals of the U.S. political elite. The resulting system, McCoy argues, "protected cooperative Filipino politicians by suppressing rumors that could damage their career and persecuted uncompromising nationalists by releasing information selected and timed to destroy their reputations."[34] The covert surveillance and manipulation of information were complemented by brute force where needed to maintain control of the Filipino population.

Undoubtedly the U.S. surveillance state heavily influenced the evolution of political and social institutions in the Philippines. But the scope of influence did not end there. The innovations in surveillance and social control "percolated homeward to implant both personnel and policies inside the [U.S.] Federal bureaucracy for the formation of a new internal security apparatus."[35] While the imprint of the U.S. occupation was readily observable on the Philippines, the effects on U.S. domestic political institutions were less obvious. These unseen domestic effects are, however, crucial for understanding the present-day national security state in the United States.

THE "FATHER OF U.S. MILITARY INTELLIGENCE" RETURNS HOME

The career of Captain Ralph Van Deman, who would earn the informal honorific of "father of U.S. military intelligence" and who would formally be enshrined in the U.S. Army's Military Intelligence Hall of Fame in 1989, illustrates many salient aspects of the boomerang effect. Van Deman began his career in the U.S. Army in 1891. During the Spanish-American War he played a crucial role in gathering information on the Spanish military. Following that conflict he was assigned to the Philippines, where he was promoted to captain and assigned to the Bureau of Insurgent Records in Manila. Under Van Deman's guidance the Bureau became the DMI. As discussed, the DMI meticulously collected massive amounts of counterintelligence on Filipino citizens, including information on physical appearances, attitudes, personal finances, property holdings, networks of families and friends, and political affiliations and associations.[36] These data were vital to U.S. government control of the Filipino population.

In 1902 Van Deman returned to the United States and held a number of positions, including one in the U.S. Army War College. To his disappointment he initially found little interest in his unique skills and experiences in social control from his time in the Philippines.[37] He set out to change this by writing a history of the rise and fall of U.S. intelligence from 1895 to 1903, with an emphasis on its importance for the army. His goal was to provide a convincing case to U.S. military leaders for an organization dedicated to gathering intelligence. When his written history failed to receive the attention Van Deman desired, he did not stop but rather pursued a more direct approach. According to his unpublished memoir, Van Deman noted that at this time he "felt responsible that a suitable organization for intelligence work be created and put to work at the earliest possible moment. . . . [I] decided to employ other means to accomplish the objective if possible."[38] A chance assignment as an escorting officer for a visitor with connections to Secretary of War Newton Baker provided the opportunity for Van Deman to share his vision for a stand-alone intelligence agency that would forever change the dynamics of the government's surveillance activities. In the wake of this assignment, and with the ongoing world war as a backdrop, his plan for such an agency gained momentum among military leaders. Eventually, in May 1917, the Military Intelligence Section (MIS) was formed with Van Deman at the helm.

Beginning with a modest staff and limited resources, he worked tirelessly to grow the organization. The core of Van Deman's effort was the introduction of negative, or counter, intelligence, which focused on gathering information to protect against espionage, sabotage, and other perceived and actual threats to the U.S. government.[39] He had become an expert at counterintelligence because of his experiences in the Philippines, where among other things he "synthesized reports, analyzed captured documents, and provided pictures and descriptions of known revolutionaries."[40] Now he brought that same expertise home and used it to survey both U.S. persons and foreigners.

A month after the MIS was formed Van Deman established a civilian force of investigators that drew from members of the New York City Police Department. The group worked secretly to screen both members of the military and various applicants for government positions. The government feared that German sympathizers were infiltrating the armed forces through the draft, and Van Deman saw his intelligence activities as a solution to the problem. He established a surveillance apparatus that became self-extending and self-reinforcing. As the historian John Finnegan writes, "[o]nce this system was in place, it produced a growing stream of incident reports that drove the relentless expansion of the War Department's counterintelligence organization."[41] This expansion led Van Deman to create his next government organization, the Corps of Intelligence Police (CIP).

The CIP built on the counterintelligence foundation that Van Deman had already established. It sought to recruit multilingual agents to help identify potential German sympathizers both at home and abroad who sought to undermine the American government. The CIP itself was nothing extraordinary compared to Van Deman's existing operations. Its importance lay in the fact that it allowed him to further entrench and expand the power of those operations, since as his "organization grew larger and more complex, it achieved a position of greater prominence within the War Department."[42] This dramatic growth was combined with a subsequent restructuring that included renaming the MIS the Military Intelligence Division (MID). The change in name reflected the fact that the MID was now one of the four central divisions of the War Department General Staff.[43] Finnegan notes that with these changes, "Military Intelligence had finally reached the position of institutional equality on the Army Staff that Van Deman had long advocated. In turn, this elevation in status permitted a more elaborate form of organization. . . ."[44] This new organization involved twelve new divisions: administration (MI-1), information (MI-2), counterespionage (MI-3), foreign influence (MI-4), military attachés (MI-5), translation (MI-6), maps and photographs (MI-7), codes and ciphers (MI-8), combat intelligence instruction (MI-9), news (censorship) (MI-10), travel (passport and port control) (MI-11), and fraud (MI-12).

The influence of the experiences with surveillance and social control in the Philippines was especially evident in the operations of the codes and ciphers division (MI-8). Also known as the American Black Chamber, MI-8 was run by Herbert Yardley, a State Department employee who had previously worked as a cryptologic officer with the American Expeditionary Forces in France during World War I.[45] The division acted covertly as a commercial business in New York City with the mission of breaking the codes and monitoring the communications of foreign governments. Among many other activities, MI-8 entered into a secret agreement with Western Union, the largest U.S. telegram company at the time, to allow members of the codes and ciphers division to monitor and review communications passed over American cables.[46] Other telegraph companies, such as Postal Telegraph and the All-American Cable Company, which oversaw communications between North and South America, also reached similar agreements, granting MI-8 unprecedented access to private communications.[47] As James Bamford, a journalist renowned for his writings on past and present intelligence activities of the U.S. government, wrote, "by the end of 1920 the Black Chamber had the secret and illegal cooperation of almost the entire American cable industry. American cryptology had lost its virginity."[48]

These covert activities were illegal because they explicitly violated regulation 19 of the Radio Communications Act of 1912, which stated that "[n]o person or persons engaged in or having knowledge of the operation of any station or stations, shall divulge or publish the contents of any messages transmitted or received by such station, except to the person or persons to whom the same may be directed, or their authorized agent, or to another station employed to forward such message to its destination, unless legally required so to do by the court of competent jurisdiction or other competent authority."[49] MI-8's extralegal methods reflected the same type of techniques the U.S. government had employed in the Philippines to gather information for social control and manipulation. And they foreshadowed the type of activities that would continue well into the future, as evidenced by the Snowden disclosures.

The subsequent multitiered surveillance structure that Van Deman established reflected his experiences in the Philippines, where the DMI relied on the constabulary and police forces as local partners in its surveillance activities. A decade later on U.S. soil the MI-4 partnered with the American Protective League (APL), an organization of private U.S. citizens who worked to identify antiwar advocates, radicals, and German sympathizers within American borders. Estimates of the APL's size range from sixty thousand to two hundred thousand members, and its top leaders "were commissioned as officers in the MI-4 to enhance military control over the league's activities."[50] To provide some context for the scope of this operation, it is estimated that the MID-APL partnership yielded over a million pages of surveillance on German-Americans and conducted over three million "investigations" for the government in slightly over a year.[51] In pursuing these alliances Van Deman established a nationwide surveillance network inside the United States to produce input into state-produced social control in order to address what he saw as the "the manifold domestic problems arising from the fact of our mixed population."[52]

The evolution and growth of the domestic surveillance state was not without criticism and backlash. For example, when the MID-APL partnership was made public in 1919, Secretary of War Newton Baker called for an end to the use of private citizens as spies.[53] Following President Woodrow Wilson's departure from office in 1921, a Republican backlash took place against what was deemed to be an over-intrusive surveillance apparatus. In 1929 Secretary of State Henry Stimson closed MI-8, noting, "[g]entleman do not read each other's mail."[54]

Despite these retrenchments, the efforts and vision of Van Deman, who retired in 1929, had firmly established the foundations of a large-scale centralized national surveillance state capable of monitoring and tracking both American persons and foreigners. While the MI-8 was officially closed, its cryptanalysis and cryptography activities continued in the newly created Signal Intelligence Service (SIS), which was established in 1930.[55] In response to changing intelligence demands associated with World War II, the SIS was reorganized as part of the U.S. Army's Signal Corps and renamed the Signal Security Agency (SSA) in 1943.

The SSA primarily focused on intercepting codes and communications from Germany and Japan. The SSA grew significantly during the war, employing an estimated twenty-five thousand soldiers and seven thousand civilians tasked with intercepting, collecting, and processing mostly foreign signal intelligence.[56] At the conclusion of World War II the intelligence activities of the U.S. government were reorganized yet again: the SSA was separated from the Signal Corps and reorganized as the Army Security Agency (ASA) with the intention of centralizing all signals-intelligence operations of the U.S. Army.[57]

The ASA lost resources and influence when, in May 1949, the secretary of defense established the Armed Forces Security Agency (AFSA) with the goal of achieving a "degree of unification of the [intelligence] services as well as 'efficiency and economy' in the management of the cryptologic structure."[58] The AFSA's central purpose was to oversee all intelligence and security operations within the Department of Defense in order to unify these activities across the armed forces. To achieve this goal the agency was placed under the control and command of the Joint Chiefs of Staff, which returned the agency to a mainly military orientation. The ASA continued to operate (until 1976), but a significant amount of its resources and operations were transferred to the AFSA.[59]

The AFSA ultimately failed to achieve the intended coordination and efficiency and was criticized for its ineffectiveness during the Korean War.[60] This resulted in President Harry Truman's appointing a review panel in 1951 to study government intelligence efforts and make recommendations for improvements. The subsequent Brownell Report detailed the operations and failures of the AFSA and recommended a new national effort to centralize and unify intelligence operations, including extending them beyond the armed forces to civilian agencies.[61] The Brownell Committee emphasized that intelligence was a resource that was crucial not just for the military but for civilian government agencies as well. Therefore, the committee recommended that the AFSA director be empowered to centralize and consolidate control over intelligence operations.[62] The result of these recommendations was the rebranding and reorganization of the AFSA as the National Security Agency in 1952.

THE MATURATION OF THE NATIONAL SURVEILLANCE STATE

The founding of the NSA coincided with an unprecedented expansion in the scope of government surveillance of the daily lives and activities of American persons. The prevalence of unconstrained government surveillance is evident in the four main concurrent operations undertaken at the time: Project SHAMROCK and Project MINARET, both operated by the NSA; COINTELPRO, implemented by the Federal Bureau of Investigations; and Operation CHAOS, which fell under the purview of the Central Intelligence Agency (CIA).

Project SHAMROCK began before the NSA's founding. During World War II the ASA and AFSA had implemented a surveillance program to monitor foreign telegraphs passing through the United States. Reminiscent of the earlier MI-8 operations, the government again developed relationships with the major international telegraph companies—RCA Global, ITT World Communications, and Western Union—allowing intelligence agencies access to copies of foreign telegraphs. These relationships were covert, with no court order or congressional oversight. When the war ended, however, the program did not. Operations not only continued but expanded under the newly formed NSA.

This expansion was driven by concern that the antiwar and civil rights movements were being infiltrated and funded by foreign governments that sought to weaken, if not overthrow, the U.S. government. However, absent firm constraints or oversight on intelligence activities, the surveillance machinery continued to expand aggressively and without limit, infiltrating the lives of millions of innocent Americans. According to the Church Committee, whose investigation and subsequent report in 1975 revealed the scope and scale of the NSA's surveillance activities, "Operation SHAMROCK, which began as an effort to acquire the telegrams of certain foreign targets, expanded so that the NSA obtained from at least two cable companies essentially all cables to or from the United States, including millions of the private communications of Americans."[63]

In 1956 the FBI implemented a counterintelligence program known as COINTELPRO. The program, which operated until 1971 when it was publicly exposed, targeted individuals deemed "subversive" by the FBI. These subversives included civil rights leaders, antiwar protestors, and those on the New Left, among others. The program "skirted the law by using undercover operatives, disinformation, break-ins, and warrantless wiretaps. . . ."[64] In addition to engaging in covert surveillance of citizens via wiretap, microphones, and breaking and entering, the FBI spread false information to attempt to destroy their targets' personal and professional relationships, disrupt meetings, and pit organizations against one another.[65]

COINTELPRO was overseen by FBI director J. Edgar Hoover, who had direct ties to Ralph Van Deman. In 1921 Hoover was named to deputy head the Bureau of Investigation, the precursor to the FBI. A year later, in 1922, Van Deman secured Hoover a reserve officer's commission in the Army's Military Intelligence Division, which Hoover would hold until 1942 when he resigned with the rank of lieutenant colonel in military intelligence. In 1924 Hoover took over as the director of the Bureau of Investigation, which became the FBI in 1935, where he would remain until he died in 1972.

Hoover and Van Deman "maintained a mutually beneficial relationship that continued until Van Deman's death in 1952."[66] Both were obsessed with gathering and maintaining enormous amounts of information on American persons. "Van Deman, like his pupil J. Edgar Hoover, had a mania for collecting and filing things."[67] This shared passion for intelligence gathering meant that Hoover would provide FBI intelligence to Van Deman and he, in turn, would provide information to Hoover from his personal surveillance records, which ultimately included over eighty-five thousand files.[68]

Meanwhile the CIA implemented its own domestic surveillance program in 1965. Project CHAOS was the result of a direct request from President Lyndon Johnson for the CIA to begin a program to monitor domestic dissent. Project CHAOS can be traced back to the late 1950s, when President Dwight Eisenhower tasked the CIA with vetting Cuban exiles as potential recruits to assist the U.S. government in activities against Fidel Castro's government.[69] This vetting involved domestic surveillance operations, as many of the Cuban exiles were part of dissident groups located on U.S. soil. In carrying out these operations the CIA developed its own capabilities—organizational and human capital—for domestic surveillance that allowed it to subsequently implement Project CHAOS with relative ease.

Project CHAOS was heavily influenced by the CIA's chief of counterintelligence, James Jesus Angleton, another excellent illustration of the logic of the boomerang effect. During World War II Angleton served in the counterintelligence branch of the U.S. Office of Strategic Services (OSS), the precursor to the CIA, first in London and then in Italy. By the war's end he oversaw all counterintelligence activities for Italy. On returning to the United States Angleton worked in various positions in the OSS and eventually became a founding officer in the CIA, where he was placed in charge of its Office of Special Operations. The Office was central in coordinating the CIA's foreign intelligence activities, both internally and with the CIA's counterparts in other countries.

Given his position of power in the CIA, coupled with his prior experience with surveillance activities, Angleton significantly influenced the agency's domestic intelligence activities.[70] He served under six different CIA directors, who "kept Angleton in key positions and valued his work."[71] As Richard Helms, director of central intelligence from 1966 to 1973 and Angelton's boss during this time, noted, "[i]n his day, Jim was recognized as the dominant counterintelligence figure in the non-communist world."[72] Angleton's past experiences, combined with his reputation and position within the CIA, made him a perfect candidate to oversee Project CHAOS, which was a "large scale intelligence program involving the gathering of data on thousands of Americans and domestic groups to determine if they had 'subversive connections.'"[73]

As Project CHAOS grew, two new subprograms were added. Project MERRIMAC focused on infiltrating and monitoring "radical" domestic organizations that were believed to pose a threat to CIA property and personnel. Project RESISTANCE also focused on identifying radicals and threats in the antiwar movement. However, instead of infiltrating organizations, these operations involved indirect monitoring through the development of relationships with local individuals—including police, political leaders, and college campus administrators—who served as informants for the CIA. Through these relationships the CIA empowered and encouraged these individuals to engage in a variety of illegal activities, from gathering private information about citizens, to illegal entry and burglary, to collecting intelligence on targets.[74] The result was that the CIA's national surveillance activities adversely influenced institutions at the most local levels of American society without the slightest apparent concern for the basic rights and freedoms of private persons. And in addition to these violations, the independence of local government institutions was eroded as they became entangled with and subservient to agencies at the political center.

As part of Project CHAOS, information on approximately three hundred thousand individuals was entered into a CIA computer index. In addition, detailed files for over seven thousand citizens and one hundred domestic groups were created. The CIA also illegally opened and photographed several hundred thousand pieces of first-class mail belonging to private U.S. persons. Absent any clear definition of what "subversive" meant in practice, the CIA cast an overly broad net that "resulted in the extension of intelligence investigations beyond their original 'subversive' or violent targets," including many "engaged in wholly non-violent law-ful political expression."[75]

In 1967 the NSA introduced Project MINARET, which further ex-panded its own surveillance activities while also expanding its relationship with other government agencies. Project MINARET, which ran parallel to Project SHAMROCK, involved the sharing of information gathered from intercepted telegraphs with other government agencies, including the FBI, the CIA, and the Bureau of Narcotics and Dangerous Drugs, which would later become the Drug Enforcement Agency (DEA). This information was used to compile watch lists of anti-Vietnam protestors, civil rights lead-ers, and others determined to engage in "activities which may result in civil disturbances or otherwise subvert the national security of the United States."[76] It is estimated that 1,650 American citizens were placed on watch lists over the six years that Project MINARET operated, subjecting their private communications, activities, movements, and travel to scrutiny.[77]

As with Project SHAMROCK, the activities that constituted Project MINARET were undertaken without warrants or oversight. In fact, the NSA took steps to keep its activities as clandestine as possible. For example, the "NSA's guidelines for its watch list activity provided that NSA's name should not be on any of the disseminated watch list material involving Americans," the goal being to "restrict the knowledge that such information is being collected and processed" by the NSA.[78] The absence of constraints on those in privileged political positions lowered the cost of using, and abusing, surveillance powers to violate the liberties of American persons.

Ralph Van Deman died in 1952, which was fitting, given that the NSA was founded that same year. Over the course of five decades comprehen-sive government surveillance had evolved from a mere idea advocated by Van Deman to a mature and sophisticated surveillance apparatus that per-meated every aspect of American life. The success of Van Deman's vision and influence would emerge in the 1970s, when the scale and scope of the national surveillance state, and the American government's abuse of the power derived from controlling that machinery, were publicly revealed.

THE CHURCH COMMITTEE AND
UNCONSTRAINED LEVIATHAN

On December 22, 1974, the headline in the *New York Times* read, "Huge C.I.A. Operation Reported in U.S. Against Antiwar Forces, Other Dissidents in Nixon Years."[79] The article's author, Seymour Hersh, opened his report by stating that "[t]he Central Intelligence Agency, directly violating its charter, conducted a massive, illegal domestic intelligence operation during the Nixon Administration against the antiwar movement and other dissident groups in the United States according to well-placed Government sources."[80] The article went on to detail what would become known as the "Family Jewels," referring to a number of covert activities undertaken by the CIA. These included not just domestic surveillance activities but also efforts by the CIA to assassinate foreign leaders and undermine foreign governments.

In response to Hersh's report the Senate launched the Select Committee to Study Governmental Operations with Respect to Intelligence Activities, also known as the Church Committee for its chairman, Sen. Frank Church, to investigate the surveillance activities of the CIA, FBI, and NSA. In 1975 and 1976 the Church Committee revealed the extent of the abuses by U.S. intelligence operations and how they undermined the liberty of American persons. The unchecked surveillance apparatus had unleashed an unconstrained leviathan, as "virtually every element of our society has been subjected to excessive government-ordered intelligence inquiries."[81] The committee concluded that "this extreme breadth of intelligence activity is inconsistent with the principles of our Constitution which protect the rights of speech, political activity, and privacy against unjustified governmental intrusion."[82]

The Church Committee also revealed the underlying nature of these programs as a facilitator of state-produced social control, noting, "[w]e have seen segments of our Government, in their attitudes and action, adopt tactics unworthy of a democracy, and occasionally reminiscent of the tactics of totalitarian regimes."[83] The initial justification for the surveillance programs was the widespread fear that the United States was being infiltrated by communist and totalitarian influences. What the Church Committee report revealed, however, was that the government's activities had made it the very thing people feared—a government that employed totalitarian methods to monitor, control, and manipulate private citizens to protect and expand the state machinery.

In response to the committee's findings, Congress passed the Foreign Intelligence Surveillance Act (FISA) of 1978, which was intended to oversee and place judicial constraints on the government's surveillance activities. The act created the secret Foreign Intelligence Surveillance Court (FISC), consisting of seven judges, appointed by the chief justice, who serve staggered, seven-year terms.[84] The FISC is tasked with issuing warrants for domestic wiretapping activities. To maintain secrecy all FISC proceedings are *ex parte* and nonadversarial, meaning the only people at the hearings are the judge and government attorneys.

The Kafkaesque nature of the FISC and its limitations on checking abuses of government power have been highlighted and critiqued by legal scholars. For example, Nancy Gertner, a former judge and currently a law professor, suggests that "[t]he judges that are assigned to this court are judges that are not likely to rock the boat. . . . All of the structural pressures that keep a judge independent are missing there. It's one-sided, secret, and the judges are chosen in a selection process by one man."[85] Similarly, legal scholar Michael Glennon notes, "[a]ll of its proceedings are closed to the public. The adversarial system integral to American jurisprudence is absent. Only government lawyers appear as counsel, unanswered by any real or potential adverse party."[86] While the details of particular cases are not made public, aggregate data on the number of warrants requested, issued, and rejected are available. Between 1979 and 2013 the FISC received 35,333 requests for surveillance warrants and denied only 12, raising questions as to whether the process of judicial review is an effective check or simply a rubber stamp.[87]

The tragic 9/11 attacks on the World Trade Center and Pentagon reinvigorated the expansion of the national surveillance state, with massive injections of federal funds for government agencies and private contractors purporting to provide national security.[88] Reporting on a two-year investigation in the *Washington Post*, Dana Priest and William M. Arkin concluded, "[t]he top-secret world of the government created in response to the terrorist attacks of Sept. 11, 2001, has become so large, so unwieldy and so secretive that no one knows how much money it costs, how many people it employees, how many programs exist within it or exactly how many agencies do the same work."[89] They went on to note that their investigation had uncovered "what amounts to an alternative geography of the United States, a Top Secret America hidden from public view and lacking in thorough oversight. After nine years of unprecedented spending and growth, the result is that the system put in place to keep the United States safe is so massive that its effectiveness is impossible to determine."[90]

In the wake of the attacks, Congress hastily passed the USA PATRIOT Act, which among other things expanded the power of the federal government to collect information subject to approval by the FISC (Section 215).[91] With already weak constraints further loosened, the NSA and other government agencies again increased their collection of domestic and international data. Reminiscent of the findings of the Church Committee, a series of revelations by whistleblowers, including Thomas Drake, William Binney, and Edward Snowden, as well as investigative reports by journalists such as Glenn Greenwald, Laura Poitras, and Barton Gellman, exposed the scale and scope of the government's post-9/11 domestic surveillance activities.

The weaknesses of the constraints implemented by the FISA are illustrated in the following examples. A 2005 report by the *New York Times* revealed that in a secret 2002 executive order, President George W. Bush declared that U.S. intelligence agencies did not need to obtain a warrant to monitor communications within U.S. borders as long as one of the parties was outside the United States and there was some reason to believe that this party was affiliated with al-Qaeda or a group that supports al-Qaeda.[92] Congress would later pass the FISA Amendments Act of 2008, which amended the original 1978 act to reflect the president's executive order.

Also in 2002, the FISC reinterpreted the law and its role in protecting the privacy of U.S. persons. Among the Snowden revelations was that the court issued two decrees—the "Raw Take" order and the "Large Content" order—which "weakened restrictions on [U.S. government agencies] sharing private information about Americans." According to Charlie Savage and Laura Poitras, who first reported on the two orders in the *New York Times*, "[t]he files help explain how the court evolved from its original task—approving wiretap requests—to engaging in complex analysis of the law to justify activities like the bulk collection of data about Americans' emails and phone calls."[93]

In 2008 a report by the Department of Justice's Office of the Inspector General noted that the FBI had at least twice issued a National Security Letter (NSL) "after the FISA Court, citing First Amendment concerns, had twice declined to sign Section 215 orders in the same investigation."[94] An NSL is an administrative subpoena issued by the FBI or other federal agencies compelling the disclosure of certain information—including bank information and telecommunications—relevant to national security investigations. By issuing the NSLs after the FISC had rejected warrants under Section 215 of the PATRIOT Act, the FBI simply circumvented the court. These abuses of NSLs are not outliers, according to the Office of the Inspector General, which found numerous instances of improper and illegal use of NSL authority.[95]

As discussed in previous chapters, the paradox of government is that an unconstrained government can abuse its power in order to harm the citizens it is tasked with protecting. The Church Committee recognized this fundamental paradox in the context of national intelligence when it noted that "power must be checked and balanced and that the preservation of liberty requires the restraint of laws, and not simply the good intentions of men."[96] However, the post-9/11 activities of the U.S. government illustrate the flimsiness of constraints on the national security state. The president can singlehandedly void any constraint in the name of national security. Similarly, the FISC can interpret the law to justify the activities of the surveillance state, eroding its purpose of checking abuses of power. Since the FISC operates in secret, it is only through the revelations of whistle-blowers that the public knows about new interpretations of the law which allow for new state activities. Moreover, even when the FISC constrains government power by denying agency requests, there are mechanisms in place, such as NSLs, allowing these agencies to proceed as if there were no constraints on their behavior. The sobering implications are as follows.

At best, many constraints on government surveillance are annoying speed bumps that impose minimal costs on those in power. Moreover, mechanisms intended to serve as constraints, such as the FISC, can evolve to aid in the legal justification and expansion of the very activities they are supposed to limit. Ultimately, establishing secret constraints simply pushes the paradox of government up a level. That is, who will watch the watchman to ensure he doesn't abuse the power that he wields over citizens? Resolving this question is central to determining if the expansive powers of the surveillance state can be limited. A satisfying answer does not currently exist within current U.S. political and legal institutions.

THE FLOURISHING U.S. NATIONAL
SURVEILLANCE STATE

The thriving U.S. surveillance state clearly illustrates the logic of the boomerang effect. The centralized apparatus of social control that the U.S. government first developed in the Philippines in the late nineteenth century has boomeranged to the United States, where it is flourishing over a century later. There are four main reasons to expect the national security state to continue to endure, if not expand, in the foreseeable future.

The first is the sheer size and scope of the current U.S. surveillance state, which is the largest and most powerful it is has ever been. As James Bamford notes, "[o]ver his two terms, Obama . . . created the most powerful surveillance state the world has ever seen. Although other leaders may have created more oppressive spying regimes, none has come close to constructing one of equivalent size, breadth, cost, and intrusiveness. From 22,300 miles in space, where seven Advanced Orion crafts now orbit; to a 1-million-square-foot building in the Utah desert that stores data intercepted from personal phones, emails, and social media accounts; to taps along the millions of miles of undersea cables that encircle the Earth like yarn, U.S. surveillance has expanded exponentially since Obama's inauguration on Jan. 20, 2009."[97] There are no signs of this growth slowing in the near future. And even if it did slow, or even stop, the status quo surveillance apparatus would remain so massive that it would continue to pervade significant aspects of the lives of private persons, both domestically and internationally.

The second is the aforementioned absence of firm constraints coupled with the lack of incentives for the political elite to change the status quo in any meaningful way. Politicians pay lip service to the reform of government surveillance to protect against abuses, but there is little reason to think they will actually change anything. The very nature of surveillance means that those in power can act outside of public scrutiny. As the FISC illustrates, mechanisms to check this covert activity are also characterized by secrecy, which not only fails to solve the problem but also adds additional layers of secrecy to the surveillance apparatus. Another factor preventing reform is the ignorance of voters regarding the details of their government's activities. This ignorance is due to a lack of available information and, far too often, to an indifference regarding government surveillance and the potential threat it poses to their freedom.

Surveillance is a means for the political elite to control the masses, and absent some significant incentive to yield that power, we should expect it to be maintained and strengthened in any and all ways possible. The claim is not that reforms will not be introduced, as they were with the FISA of 1978. Rather, reforms are likely to be marginal and leave significant room for the expansion of surveillance, just as the FISA failed to protect against post-9/11 abuses. The reality is that the cumulative history of state surveillance has created an array of institutional possibilities for expansion of government power. Some of these possibilities will only become evident in the future. But others are already being exploited.

In early 2016 the Obama administration granted expanded power for the NSA to share the contents of the private phone and email communications it collects with federal law enforcement agencies.[98] This would allow domestic law enforcement unprecedented access to private emails and phone calls—of citizens as well as foreigners—without a warrant. As journalist Charlie Savage writes,

Until now, National Security Agency analysts have filtered the surveillance information for the rest of the government. They search and evaluate the information and pass only the portions of phone calls or email that they decide is pertinent on to colleagues at the Central Intelligence Agency, the Federal Bureau of Investigation and other agencies. And before doing so, the N.S.A. takes steps to mask the names and any irrelevant information about innocent Americans. The new system would permit analysts at other intelligence agencies to obtain direct access to raw information from the N.S.A.'s surveillance to evaluate for themselves.[99]

One concern, according to the American Civil Liberties Union of Massachusetts, is that "information the NSA collects for purposes of so-called 'national security' will be used by police to lock up ordinary Americans for routine crimes."[100] In general, powers granted to government in the name of national security tend to expand and evolve, seeping into facets of ordinary domestic life that have nothing whatsoever to do with providing safety from foreign threats.

Third, technological advances will further reduce the cost of government monitoring and collecting increasing amounts of information about private persons without their knowledge. For example, it has been reported that the NSA has developed speech-recognition technology, allowing it to transcribe and search conversations.[101] If so, this technology would lower the cost of surveillance because instead of analysts spending time listening to individual phone conversations, they could search the text of multiple conversations.

Finally, the U.S. government is involved in two open-ended wars—the War on Drugs and the War on Terror—which are being carried out both internationally and on the home front. These wars are unique in that the members of the enemy "out group" are not easily identifiable or isolated in a single geographic area. Instead, from the perspective of the U.S. government, all people—citizens and noncitizens alike—are potentially members of the enemy who must be monitored and controlled in the name of protecting the freedom of the very people being surveilled. There is concrete evidence of how this dynamic plays out.

In January 2015 the Justice Department revealed that the DEA, in conjunction with the U.S. military, had been collecting data on billions of calls by U.S. persons to "designated countries" a decade before the 9/11 attacks and NSA surveillance. This attempt to accumulate intelligence on the international drug trade captured the phone calls of millions of Americans, irrespective of whether they were accused of a crime, and served as a blueprint for the NSA program that would be implemented following 9/11.[102]

Together, these four factors provide good reason to expect the continued erosion of Americans' freedoms. If this happens, the loss of liberty, ironically and sadly, will result from government actions undertaken, at least rhetorically, in the name of protecting liberty.

In addition to posing a direct threat to the freedoms of U.S. persons, there is some empirical evidence that the existence of a surveillance state has the indirect effect of fostering a culture of fear and conformity among the general populace.[103] This discourages people from seeking out certain information and engaging in critical expression due to concerns that they are being monitored by state actors who possess the power to impose significant costs on those they deem to be subversive. By cultivating fear and stifling free expression, the surveillance state undermines the ability of people to monitor and check their government, which contributes to an environment conducive to subsequent expansions in the scope of state power.

CHAPTER 5

The Militarization of Police

On May 28, 2014, a sheriff's office in a small Georgia town, with assistance from a Special Response Team, executed a no-knock raid on a local home, acting on a tip from an informant regarding drug activity. A no-knock raid, as the name implies, involves law enforcement entering a property without notifying residents of its presence or intention to enter. Although the suspect was not at the house, Alecia and Bounkham Phonesavanh and their four children were. The Phonesavanhs' primary residence in Wisconsin had been destroyed by fire, so the family was temporarily staying with Bounkham's sister.[1]

As part of the raid, police tossed a flashbang, or stun, grenade into the house, intending to temporarily blind and deafen the occupants as police executed their warrant. The grenade landed in a playpen where the Phonesavanhs' nineteen-month-old son, Bounkham Jr., or "Bou Bou," was sleeping.[2] According to the boy's mother, she ran toward her son's screams following the blast, only to be stopped by a police officer,[3] who informed Alecia that her baby was "fine" and had "just lost a tooth."[4]

Far from being fine, Bou Bou sustained life-threatening injuries as a result of the police tactics. His face and torso were burned, exposing muscle and bone. His lung collapsed, and part of his face was torn off. Even after multiple surgeries he remains permanently disfigured. The family incurred well over $1 million in medical bills, and the sheriff's office refused to accept any responsibility for the incident.[5] In response to a civil suit filed by the family, the officers involved claim that the "injuries and damages, if any, were caused by *the deliberate, criminal conduct of the plaintiffs*. . . . [S]uch criminal conduct supersedes any and all negligence or liability, if any, on the part of these defendants [the police]."[6] However, neither Alecia nor her husband were ever charged with any criminal offence. The officers involved were acquitted of any wrongdoing because the damage was deemed to be unintentional. The Phonesavanhs have received $3.6

million in settlements from government insurance policies with most of the award going to pay medical and legal bills.[7] Bou Bou, now aged four, has undergone some fifteen surgeries as a result of his injuries.[8]

While tragic, this is far from the only case in which innocent Americans have been seriously injured or killed as a result of military-style police raids. Journalist Radley Balko has documented numerous cases of botched no-knock raids throughout the United States. In some cases the police raided the wrong residence, while in other instances they injured or killed innocent civilians or nonviolent offenders. In addition, on numerous occasions police officers have been injured executing the raids.[9]

As was the case in the raid on the Phonesavanh home, the execution of no-knock raids often involves Special Weapons and Tactics (SWAT) teams or Police Paramilitary Units (PPUs), groups with highly specialized military equipment and training. Over the past three decades these have become prevalent in U.S. cities and towns. Criminologist Peter Kraska estimates that about 20 percent of small-town police departments employed a SWAT team or PPU in the mid-1980s. By 2000 almost 90 percent of police departments serving populations of fifty thousand or more people had some kind of PPU. Eighty percent of small-town police departments have a SWAT team.[10] Kraska estimates that approximately three thousand SWAT deployments occurred in 1980. By the early 2000s SWAT teams were seeing about forty-five thousand deployments a year.[11] Data from 2005 indicates that SWAT teams were deployed fifty thousand to sixty thousand times that year.[12] Current estimates place the number of deployments as high as eighty thousand annually.[13]

SWAT raids are hardly the only example of police behaving more like an occupying military force than peacekeepers upholding the law. In 1999 Seattle police shot protestors with rubber bullets and tear gas outside a World Trade Organization conference.[14] In 2011 police used similar methods to disperse protestors in Oakland, California, during Occupy Wall Street demonstrations. At one such event a former Marine and protestor, Scott Olsen, was hit in the head with a police projectile. He suffered a fractured skull, broken neck, and brain swelling. The first responders— his fellow protesters—were prevented from offering medical care as police detonated additional explosives.[15] Most recently, protests in Ferguson,

Missouri, following the death of Michael Brown; demonstrations in Baltimore, Maryland, following the death of Freddy Gray; and marches in New York City following the death of Eric Garner were all met with tear gas, smoke bombs, curfews, armored personnel carriers, and police with high-powered weapons.

These trends in modern policing and the potential consequences for Americans' civil liberties have raised concerns on both sides of the political aisle. For example, in response to the protests in Ferguson, President Obama stated that he wanted to ensure "that we're [the U.S. government] not building a militarized culture inside our local law enforcement."[16] Republican Senator Rand Paul (R-KY) stated that "the images and scenes we continue to see [of police activity] . . . resemble war more than traditional police action. . . . There is a systematic problem with today's law enforcement."[17]

These concerns raise important questions. How is it that military weapons and tactics have become so prevalent throughout the United States? How and why has the use of these techniques increased? The militarization of police throughout the country is one clear illustration of the boomerang effect of foreign intervention. Military-like weapons and techniques, once used in missions abroad, have been brought back into the United States and used on American citizens.

EARLY EFFORTS TO SEPARATE THE POLICE AND THE MILITARY

Although paramilitary units are now commonplace among police departments of all sizes, this was not always the case. American history reveals careful attempts to delineate and separate domestic law enforcement from the military. The founding fathers and those who followed them recognized the fundamental paradox of government. In the context of domestic policing the fear was that use of military force on American soil would open up the possibility of tyranny by providing the government with the means of controlling its citizens. Because of this concern the framers of the Constitution did not grant the president or the Congress the power to use the army for everyday domestic law enforcement. As the historian Robert Coakley notes, "[t]hat no power to use regular forces in domestic disorders was explicitly granted to either the president or Congress was testimony to the fear of standing armies that pervaded the meeting."[18]

With the potential for abuses of power in mind, lawmakers moved to clarify the authority of the president and the Congress soon after the Constitution was ratified in 1788. Recognizing that the government might need to protect its citizens from domestic threats, Congress passed a series of militia acts starting in 1792 to delineate the president's emergency powers.[19] However, some people noted that, in doing so, Congress risked initiating a permanent expansion of government power. The militia acts gave the president the authority to call forth state militias in response to a domestic insurgency or foreign invasion. However, to limit this power the law required the president to exhaust all other alternatives, including using the judiciary to resolve domestic disputes and, in the case of domestic insurrections, first ordering the insurgents to disperse before the president used military force. Moreover, the law specified that the president could call on the state militias directly only when Congress was not in session. Otherwise the president would need its authorization.[20]

Another important law, the Posse Comitatus Act, was adopted in 1867, following the Civil War. This act expressly forbade the use of the military as a "posse comitatus," or "force of the people," to implement domestic law.[21] The catalyst behind this act was the recognition that the military and civilian law enforcement agencies are intended to engage radically different populations and to achieve two very different goals. Local police are tasked with protecting the rights of Americans on domestic soil, while the military is tasked with exterminating threats.

This distinction is captured in mottos still used today. The well-known Los Angeles Police Department (LAPD) motto is "To Protect and to Serve." Local law enforcement agents are to uphold the rights of all, victims and offenders alike; the police are peacekeepers, ordered to use violence only as a last resort. In contrast, the U.S. Soldier's Creed expresses the ultimate goals of the military, including "stand ready to deploy, engage, and destroy the enemies of the United States of America in close combat."[22]

Despite these separate aims and early attempts to isolate the police and the military from one another, the distinction between police and military has eroded. And while the militarization of police is a relatively recent trend, its origins are not.

THE U.S. OCCUPATION OF THE PHILIPPINES

Although the most radical and evident militarization of the U.S. police has occurred over the past forty years, it is not the first time the U.S. government has blended military and civilian forces, trampling civil liberties in the process. Its first venture into police militarization dates back to the late 1800s during the occupation of the Philippines.

As discussed in the previous chapter, the official end of the Philippine-American War in 1902 did not mean the end of resistance and violence against the occupiers. Opposition by various rebel forces persisted for the next decade.[23] Because of this, the U.S. government expanded and strengthened its control over the population by militarizing police forces. In the Philippines and elsewhere outside the United States, the U.S. government was not subject to the same constraints as back home, where the law expressly forbade using the military to enforce domestic law. This created space for the U.S. government to experiment with different kinds of social control, including the use of military tactics as a central component of policing.

The previously discussed Philippine Constabulary (PC) was established in 1901 as a gendarmerie, or a military force charged with policing the civilian population. Following the war's official conclusion a year later, the Constabulary remained as a paramilitary force and was used to combat resistance to the occupation. Among its obligations was a mix of military and civil law enforcement duties, including the administration of tribal territories, supervision of municipal police, surveillance of political activists, and rural pacification.[24]

Over the next several decades, the PC would continue to be used as both a domestic police force and a military unit. In fact, police and military were practically indistinguishable. This convergence toward one body is seen clearly in Commonwealth Act No. 343 of 1938. This Act allowed former military officers and enlisted men to join the PC but "retain their identity and legal rights and obligations as officers and enlisted men of the army."[25] Furthermore, the Act allowed the president of the Philippines to transfer men from the Constabulary to the army and vice versa at his discretion. From a legal perspective, work in either group was viewed as military service.

The intervention in the Philippines, in which the U.S. government sought complete control over the population, served as a testing ground for various organizational forms that blended military strategies, techniques, and equipment with control and policing. Those engaged in these actions abroad soon returned home with their skills and experiences. In some cases these experiences were drawn on to violently subdue U.S. persons. More important, however, the experience of veterans of the Philippine occupation influenced policing and changed the structure of police departments. These changes would ultimately set the stage for widespread militarization.

THE "FATHER OF MODERN POLICING" AND HIS CONTEMPORARIES

The influence of the PC and the war in the Philippines had some immediate effects. Returning to the United States, many veterans sought careers in local law enforcement, using the social-control techniques acquired abroad. August Vollmer, who would later become known as "the father of modern policing," participated in the occupation of the Philippines.[26] Just as Captain Ralph Van Deman used his experience in the war to champion the creation of a larger intelligence apparatus in the United States (see Chapter 4), Vollmer used his experiences to shape U.S. policing.

At the outbreak of the Spanish-American War, Vollmer enlisted in the Army and was stationed in the Philippines. During this time he volunteered and was selected for numerous dangerous combat missions in which he engaged in hostilities against the indigenous population. Several years after returning to the United States, Vollmer was elected town marshal (akin to a sheriff) of Berkeley, California. He became Berkeley's first police chief, holding the position almost continuously from 1909 to 1932. From these positions, Vollmer worked his way into even higher positions of authority and status. In 1921 he was elected president of the International Association of Chiefs of Police (IACP) and was appointed chief of the LAPD in 1923 while on leave from Berkeley. Throughout his career he served as a consultant to police departments in Chicago, Kansas City, St. Paul, Portland, Dallas, and other cities.[27]

The influence of Vollmer's time in the Philippines is readily apparent in his domestic police work. According to one biographical account Vollmer "came to admire the organizational skills of the professional army corps, and frequently referred to his army experience years later when discussing the strategy of police operations."[28] Another stated that "there was the impression among many people that martial law was in effect under his direction, a rumor he felt worked in his favor."[29] Yet another account of Vollmer's police work stated that his "belief was that the police force should be run, operationally, like the Army and he set out to do just that."[30] In alignment with this vision Vollmer sought to "modernize" police departments throughout the country.

Just as the PC in the Philippines had worked to incorporate the latest technology and surveillance methods into its work, Vollmer quickly introduced similar measures in Berkeley and gained national notoriety for his efforts. While working as a marshal in Berkeley in 1905, he had a complex system of flashing lights and telephones installed throughout the city so that police officers on patrol could be summoned to headquarters and dispatched from the field.[31] He insisted on putting his officers on bicycles to patrol the streets. Later he again looked to incorporate new technologies by having his officers mounted on motorcycles and eventually in automobiles.[32] In 1919 he began placing radio receivers in patrol cars.[33] According to O. W. Wilson, one of Vollmer's most well-known students, "the Berkeley Police remained a center of attention during the entire career of August Vollmer, the result of his unique ideas, unusual methods, and brilliant accomplishments."[34]

In the Philippines, the PC gathered extensive data on citizens and rebels—actual and potential—as part of its efforts to control dissent. Vollmer likewise proposed a systematic, centralized system of recordkeeping among local police in the United States. As early as 1907 he urged the California state legislature to create a bureau of criminal identification. The idea was initially rejected, but Vollmer remained undeterred and continued to champion it for another decade. In 1917 the California State Bureau was created, developing one of the first extensive police record systems in the country.[35] Vollmer pushed for such a system at the national level and eventually succeeded. It was following his tenure as president of the

IACP that a nationwide system, which included fingerprint collection for criminals, was implemented.[36] In the 1930s Vollmer successfully lobbied for Berkeley to implement universal fingerprinting of *all* its citizens, an idea he unsuccessfully advocated on a national level, arguing that "communists [and] anarchists, may be followed from place to place and their activities noted."[37]

Vollmer had a particularly illustrious career, with many highlights that feature troublingly in today's policing. But his real significance is as a poster child of the veterans of the Philippine conflict who returned home, became police, and used their unique skills to work their way into the hierarchy of a variety of law enforcement organizations.

For example, Sergeant Jesse Garwood, a member of the PC, became known for his unorthodox and brutal police tactics in the Philippines. He was particularly renowned for offering bounties for enemies' severed ears.[38] On one occasion a Filipino asked to join Garwood's force. Garwood told the would-be recruit he would first have to bring him the head of a particular local criminal. The recruit would eventually succeed in his gruesome task, but only after bringing Garwood the wrong head—twice.[39] Garwood returned to the United States and helped develop the Pennsylvania Constabulary (PAC) along with fellow Philippine-American War veteran John C. Groome.

The PAC was modeled directly on the PC and became well-known for its repression of labor strikes involving mostly foreign workers.[40] Adopting military tactics, the PAC implemented a "platoon system" in which, like a military occupation, police are assigned to patrol particular areas at specific times in order to maintain constant coverage of a geographic territory.[41] Although the PAC was technically a civilian police force, nearly all its members were former or current members of the armed forces, including several veterans of the Philippine Constabulary.

Other examples of Philippine veterans applying their warrior skills in the United States are readily available. Lieutenant Colonel Harry Bandholtz, for example, served as PC chief while in the Philippines, and his experiences in combat would transfer directly to his work at home. According to the historian Alfred McCoy, Bandholtz "used psychological methods developed during his years combating Filipino radicals to quash a militant miners' revolt in West Virginia."[42] U.S. Marine Corps Major General Smedley Butler likewise saw combat during the Philippine occupation and afterward headed a constabulary force in Haiti. Butler was later appointed Philadelphia's police chief, tasked with cleaning up corruption and other illegal behavior. Using the same tactics he had employed abroad, Butler ordered his men to raid speakeasies and other "vice" enterprises. In his first week on the job, Butler's officers had raided nearly a thousand different establishments. By the end of his first year, this number would reach nearly five thousand.[43] Before the courts intervened, many of these raids included illegal searches and seizures of private citizens and their property.[44] The methods and tactics honed abroad were brought home and employed to combat black markets resulting from alcohol prohibition, with U.S. citizens as the primary enemy.

Police militarization, however, did not become widespread during this period. This can be attributed in large part to the nature of the groups targeted by police forces at the time. In each of the cases referenced, the "out group" targeted by the government was readily identifiable. Since organized labor; foreign-born workers; and establishments offering illegal liquor, gambling, and prostitution were relatively easy to identify, the tools of social control could be targeted. Moreover, police activities were largely local and confined to specific regions in towns and cities. Policing at the time was largely decentralized and not linked to the federal government, so the political center and peripheral units of government were largely separate. Finally, the use of most brutal tactics employed abroad would have been unacceptable to most judges and much of the public. Together these factors meant that while state-produced social-control techniques were employed domestically, their widespread and systematic use did not take hold. Such would not be the case in the future.

As noted in Chapter 2, the boomerang effect does not specify a certain time frame in which the social-control methods developed during a foreign intervention are employed domestically. Rather, the theory offers insight as to how intervention erodes critical checks on government officials, whether that happens quickly or slowly. Police militarization is one example of how the boomerang effect manifests over time. The Philippine war's greatest impact on police militarization was not the activities of

Vollmer, Garwood, Bandholtz, and Butler, but more subtle changes that would transform police departments around the country as ideological, judicial, and other factors changed.

At a minimum this prompted fundamental changes in the organizational dynamics of many police departments. These influences established precedents whereby military personnel and tactics not only would be considered legitimate policing tools but also would be welcomed by police administrations. The factors preventing widespread militarization would eventually fall away. "Out groups" would be increasingly difficult to define; police departments would have fewer qualms regarding the use of harsher techniques to collect information; and public opinion would shift dramatically. These changes, combined with the tools favored by Vollmer and his colleagues, would bring the rise of militarized police—starting just a few decades later.

THE FIRST SWAT TEAM

It should come as no surprise that the first SWAT team in the country was organized by the LAPD—one of Vollmer's former outposts—in 1967. World War II veteran Daryl Gates and officer and marine John Nelson were crucial to introducing that first team.[45]

In Vietnam, Nelson had served in an elite Force Recon unit. Highly trained, these units operated deep behind enemy lines. While originally intended solely to gather intelligence through reconnaissance missions, these teams engaged in combat and received a variety of accolades for their intelligence work and their use of accurate and stealthy lethal force. For example, the "kill ratio" for regular marine infantry was about 7.6 enemies killed per each marine killed during the conflict in Vietnam. The kill ratio for the Force Recon units was much higher: they killed some 34 enemies for every man lost in action.[46] Not only were the units much more lethal than regular marine units, they also engaged the enemy more frequently. Regular units were the aggressors in combat only 20 percent of the time, with the enemy engaging the marines the remaining 80 percent. A very different record, however, was observed with Force Recon teams. These groups were the aggressors in an astounding 95 percent of their operations.[47] Simply put, Force Recon teams were trained to engage and kill, and they did so efficiently.

These experiences were integral to developing Nelson's skills, knowledge, and abilities in controlling groups, gathering information, and aggressively eliminating enemy targets. When he returned to the United States after his experience in Vietnam, these were the skills Nelson brought to the LAPD. In the 1960s the opportunity arose for Nelson to put his human capital to use. The Watts riots in the summer of 1965 and general social unrest left the LAPD feeling unprepared and vulnerable. In response to the perceived crisis surrounding the riots, leaders of the department became eager to develop new ways to control the large crowds frequently in attendance at civil rights rallies.[48] Drawing on his Force Recon experience Nelson suggested the development of a similar unit within the LAPD. "A small squad of highly trained police officers armed with special weapons," he posited, "would be more effective in a riotous situation than a massive police response."[49]

Implementation of his idea required the involvement of the LAPD administration, so Nelson went to Inspector Daryl Gates, who would become chief in 1978. Gates had served aboard the USS *Ault* as a navy seaman during World War II. The *Ault* saw varied action in the Pacific theater, providing defense in the high-conflict areas of Okinawa and Iwo Jima.[50]

Much like Nelson, Gates returned from his deployment with unique human capital. By the time Nelson joined the force nearly twenty years later, individuals like Gates had worked their way into the upper echelon of the LAPD, fortifying the administrative and cultural openness to the military tactics championed by Vollmer decades earlier. According to investigative journalist Joe Domanick, Gates in particular worked to turn the LAPD into a department that was "aggressive, intimidating and confrontational by design. . . . Gates believed that he and the LAPD were doing the city's most important work and that they should be accountable to no one but themselves."[51] It was in this environment that Nelson proposed the Force Recon–style unit.

With Gates's full support Nelson's idea was quickly adopted. The link between the newly formed paramilitary unit and the war in Vietnam was readily apparent from the first name given to the force, "Special Weapons and Attack Team." But it was soon decided that labeling the unit an "attack" team would be politically unpalatable. So Gates changed the name to "Special Weapons and Tactics," and the first SWAT team was born.[52] The unit consisted of sixty of the LAPD's top marksmen. The group was divided into teams, each consisting of five men—a leader, marksman, observer, scout, and rearguard.[53]

The men selected for the first SWAT team further illustrate how the human capital developed during foreign interventions combined with the organizational dynamics of the LAPD to influence police operations. According to the LAPD each member of the original SWAT unit had specialized experience and prior military service.[54] Just as Vollmer had sought to incorporate the newest technological advances into his department, the SWAT team sought to do the same. According to Daryl Gates,

We watched with interest what was happening in Vietnam. We looked at military training, and in particular we studied what a group of marines, based at the Naval Armory in Chavez Ravine, were doing. They shared with us their knowledge of counter-insurgency and guerilla warfare. . . . John Nelson became our specialist in guerilla warfare. . . . [W]e attended several marine sessions on guerilla warfare. . . . We brought in military people to teach [the SWAT units].[55]

By 1971 the SWAT team had become a permanent fixture in the LAPD. As if the militaristic qualities of the unit were not already apparent, the SWAT team was referred to as "D platoon" within the organization, reflecting that it was viewed as a military unit.[56] It would not be long before the SWAT concept was expanded throughout the LAPD and other state and local police agencies around the country. To explain this nationwide expansion, however, one must appreciate two important subsequent "wars": the War on Drugs and the War on Terror.

THE EXPANSION AND MATURATION OF MILITARIZED DOMESTIC POLICING

The War on Drugs and the War on Terror are fundamentally different from other conflicts in U.S. history. Engagements such as the world wars, the Korean War, and the Vietnam War featured external enemies. But in the "wars" on drugs and terror the face of the enemy changed, and both have been carried out internationally and domestically. Although the War on Drugs has foreign enemies—Latin American drug cartels, for example—

and the War on Terror is directed at the Taliban, al-Qaeda, and the Islamic State, other enemies are closer to the home front. Domestic drug users and dealers and "homegrown terrorists"—both real and potential—are just as much targets as foreign adversaries.[57]

This is particularly important in the context of police militarization and the related expansion of government domestically. The presence of a hard-to-identify "enemy" on U.S. soil has provided the U.S. government both the opportunity and the incentive to expand the scope of its activities. The expansion, which in itself is of great concern, is magnified by the fact that both wars are open-ended, with no definable conclusion, fostering a sense of normalcy among the American populace.

The War on Drugs

As with many wars, in the War on Drugs, the U.S. government took advantage of a preexisting and profound fear among Americans in order to expand the scale and scope of its activities. Beginning in the 1970s Americans were bombarded with messages, many funded and produced by the government itself, that drugs threatened the very core of their civilization. Among the concerns were that drugs would erode civil society and morals, and that the "drug culture" would ensnare and destroy American youth. Television and radio ads, as well as other government propaganda, highlighted these supposed dangers and placed the "drug problem" in the consciousness of every American adult. Perceived crises such as the "epidemic of 'crack babies'" reinforced the fears and catapulted drugs to the forefront of American domestic policy.[58]

The impact of these campaigns is clear. In 1968 about 48 percent of Americans thought that illegal drugs were a problem in their community.[59] By the late 1980s some 61 percent felt illegal drugs were the primary problem facing the country.[60] As a result, not only was the American public open to a government response, but many demanded that government "do something." A 1989 report from the Bureau of Justice Statistics found that 65 percent of Americans believed the federal government could substantially curtail the drug trade. Further, a significant number of Americans—82 percent—were in favor of using the military to combat illegal drugs.[61]

This outcry opened the door for police to widely adopt military tools and tactics. Increased attention and spending by the federal government meant that if police departments could demonstrate they were integral to the War on Drugs, they could secure a greater share of the pie.

As the federal government clamped down on drugs, those participating in the market were pushed underground into black markets. Left without legal ways to settle conflicts—one doesn't call the police to report a bad drug deal—black-market participants were left to resolve their own disputes, often by violence. Also contributing to this violence was the fact that dealers who could secure market share could also secure the significant profits associated with illegal drugs. This led to brutal turf wars between those with a penchant for violence, facilitating the rise of gangs and powerful drug cartels with access to cash, large social networks, and high-powered weapons.[62] This violence resulted not from any physical effects of drug use, but from the incentives created by prohibition policies.[63]

These dynamics of the underground drug market are important for three reasons. First, in response to the drug war, police departments, now on the "front lines," could claim that military equipment, training, and tactics were not only helpful but also necessary to achieve the goals of the federal government. This provided a critical argument in favor of militarization.

Second and related, the presence of drug gangs and cartels with "bigger and badder" weaponry created rationale for existing paramilitary units—like SWAT teams—to further increase their prominence, funding, and equipment. For example, the case for more no-knock raids became much easier to make when police could point to dangerous and highly armed drug dealers.

Third, the linkage of local police to the War on Drugs permanently connected local law enforcement to the federal government. As the political periphery relied on federal funds for its drug-interdiction efforts, its missions became inextricably tied to the larger goals of the central government. This linkage not only cost autonomy, it also facilitated standardized and systematic militarization across the country.

With a green light from the American public and additional funding and equipment from the federal government for local police departments, the door to nationwide militarization was kicked wide open. Nowhere is this more apparent than in the Military Cooperation with Law Enforcement Act (MCLEA) of 1981. The MCLEA was intended to "enhance" the ability of law-enforcement agencies to enforce new drug laws. The final version of the law allowed the Department of Defense (DoD) to share information collected within the course of "normal operations" with state and local law enforcement. The DoD could provide information, advice, and weapons to local police so long as they used them to enforce drug laws.[64]

Other programs provided additional opportunities for police to adopt military tactics and obtain military equipment. For example, the National Defense Authorization Act of 1990 created the 1208 Program, which also authorized the DoD to transfer military equipment to state agencies to combat drugs. In 1997 it became the 1033 Program. This incarnation allowed the DoD to transfer military equipment such as aircraft, armor, riot gear, surveillance equipment, watercraft, and weapons to state and local police. Other equipment, such as armored vehicles, was also made available for police forces for "bona fide law enforcement purposes that assist in their arrest and apprehension mission."[65]

A related program, 1122, provides another illustration of how the War on Drugs allowed for the rapid expansion of systematic police militarization and further linked state and local agencies to the federal government. While the 1033 Program focused on used military weapons, Program 1122 provided exclusively for the purchase of new gear and parts.[66] Like 1033, 1122 began in the 1990s as a response to the War on Drugs.[67] According to the program manual, "The '1122 Program' affords state and local governments the opportunity to maximize their use of taxpayer dollars, by taking advantage of the purchasing power of the Federal Government." Any "unit of local government" is eligible, meaning that any "city, county, township, town, borough, parish, village, or other general purpose political subdivision of a State" could apply to receive the weapons.[68] This further intertwined states and municipalities with the federal government as local law enforcement came to rely on such programs for their equipment. These programs thus created rules that reduced the cost to police of acquiring tools of social control that were initially developed and secured by the U.S. government to carry out military intervention against foreign enemies.

The War on Terror

If the War on Drugs kicked the door to militarization wide open, the War on Terror blew it off its hinges. Like the scourge of drugs, which supposedly threatened to undermine the fabric of American society starting in the century before, the post-9/11 "terror threat" reinforced and expanded police militarization.

As with the fear of drugs, the fear of terrorism following the 9/11 attacks played a central role in creating space for expansion of the scope of government power. As political scientist John Mueller explains, in many instances this fear was manufactured and fanned by the "terrorism industry," which includes the array of public and private interests that benefit from expansions in government antiterrorism activities.[69] Fear prompted Americans to place greater trust in the often-unchecked activities of the federal government. Four days before the attacks on the Pentagon and World Trade Center, just 14 percent of Americans polled stated they trusted the government a "great deal" to handle foreign issues. A mere 6 percent stated they trusted the government to adequately handle domestic problems. Less than a month later, 36 percent said they trusted the federal government "a great deal" on foreign issues, while 24 percent "highly trusted" the government to handle domestic issues.[70] Seventy-seven percent maintained at least some confidence in the government to correct domestic problems.[71]

Moreover, Americans seemed content to allow the federal government to encroach on civil liberties in the name of "public safety." Some 63 percent, for example, thought it would be necessary to give up some civil liberties to combat the terror threat.[72] Eighty-six percent approved the use of facial-recognition software at public events in the name of stopping terrorism. Some 54 percent approved the monitoring of private cell-phone calls, emails, and Internet usage.[73] These results illustrate the unifying effect of war: citizens rally around their government when threatened by an enemy, potential or real. Unification, in turn, lowers the cost of government expanding the scope of its power.

Just as the War on Drugs continues against faceless domestic and international enemies, so too does the War on Terror. While the U.S. government remains concerned with threats from abroad, the threat of "homegrown terrorists" is cited as a major problem by many top officials. Between January 2009 and April 2011, 104 people were arrested in the United States on terrorism charges, approximately 60 percent of them American citizens.[74] These arrests, combined with regular warnings by political officials of the imminent threat of domestic terrorism, fuel fear among Americans. For example, consider this statement by Eric Holder, who was attorney general at that time: "[The threat of homegrown terrorists] keeps me up at night. . . . You didn't worry about this even two years ago—about individuals, about Americans, to the extent that we now do. . . . *The threat has changed from simply worrying about foreigners coming here, to worrying about people in the United States, American citizens. . . .*"[75]

With the blessing of the fearful American public, the government massively expanded the domestic use of tactics once used exclusively by the military. The introduction of the USA PATRIOT Act played a central role in this process.

Passed in October 2001, the PATRIOT Act was the largest restructuring of the federal government in recent U.S. history. Among other things, the Act allowed federal *and* state and local law enforcement to gather intelligence on civilians, as detailed in Chapter 4. The newly created Department of Homeland Security (DHS) was tasked with "preparing for, preventing, and responding to terror attacks."[76] The cabinet department is best understood as a domestic DoD, though it engages in activities beyond as well as within U.S. borders.

The DHS is a massive bureaucracy, the third largest department behind the DoD and Department of Veterans Affairs. Its creation merged twenty-two agencies into one bureaucratic hierarchy. They include the Coast Guard, Customs and Border Protection, Immigration and Customs Enforcement, Transportation Security Administration, and the Federal Emergency Management Agency. According to the political scientist Peter Andreas, "[t]he massive reorganization highlights the unprecedented prominence of law enforcement, including border control (by far the single largest DHS budget item), on the post–September 11 security agenda."[77] In other words the DHS created a central bureaucracy with expanded powers related to domestic law enforcement. While many see this as beneficial to combating terrorism, it is problematic because such an agency enhances the ability of the national government to efficiently control the lives of Americans in the name of thwarting terrorism.[78]

The aforementioned Program 1033 also experienced unprecedented growth as a result of the War on Terror. The program's mission was amended to give preference to agencies working to implement counterterrorism policies.[79] In 2010 it set a record by transferring some $212 million in military equipment to local agencies. This record was shattered the following year, with nearly $500 million in military weapons, gear, and other supplies transferred to state and local law enforcement.[80] Program 1033 provides no oversight of the use of this equipment, which practically ensures it will be used inappropriately. Per program guidelines, participants are *required* to use any transferred equipment within one year of receipt or return it.[81]

According to the DoD, over 11,500 agencies have taken part in the program.[82] Table 5.1 provides an accounting of some of the items transferred to state and local police during the War on Terror. This is not a comprehensive accounting of all the equipment transferred to departments through the program, however. The DoD does not report such data or require systematic recording of equipment use. Despite the lack of complete data, it is clear that many civilian agencies have acquired equipment designed and used for foreign combat.

The equipment does not seem to go to high-risk localities—major cities, states along the borders or coasts, and so on. Table 5.2 shows the number of guns per thousand citizens acquired by the top-ten recipient counties through the 1033 program from 2006 to April 2013. The 1033 program claimed to emphasize the fight against terrorism. So why were these counties the top recipients of guns? The top two counties do contain state capitals, but Frankfort, Kentucky, and Pierre, South Dakota, do not typically top the lists of high-risk targets in discussions of terrorism. Of course, these weapons may assist law enforcement in fighting crime.[83] But they can also put innocent civilians in danger, while contributing to a militarized culture among the police.[84]

Program 1122 also received renewed attention in the name of combating terrorism. The program was amended in 2009 to include not only agencies engaged in drug interdiction but also those conducting operations related to the War on Terror, homeland security, and emergency re-

Table 5.1. Subset of Weapons Acquired by Local Law Enforcement, 2006–June 2014.

Category	Description	Number of Items
Mine-Resistant Ambush Protected Armored Vehicles (MRAPs)	Armored vehicle specifically designed to sustain attacks against improvised explosive devices (IEDs)	432
Other Armored Vehicles	Other protected vehicles including cars and trucks	435
Night-Vision Pieces	Equipment designed to see in the dark, including sights, binoculars, goggles, lights, and other accessories	44,900
Aircraft	Planes and helicopters	533
Machine Guns	5.56 mm and 7.62 mm rifles (for example, M-16 assault rifle)	93,763
Magazines	Ammunition storage/feeding device that may be attached to a weapon (for example, a magazine for a 5.56 rifle can increase the number of rounds by 30)	180,718

Source: Table created by the authors with data from Department of Defense, via Apuzzo 2014. See also Bouie 2014 and Giblin 2017.

sponse.[85] Items available for purchase include pistols, rifles, ammunition, aviation parts, night-vision goggles, personnel carriers, boats, aircraft parts, and body armor.[86]

Other programs from the Department of Justice further contributed to the acquisition of military weaponry, technology, and training. For example, the Edward Byrne Memorial Justice Assistance Grants have awarded over $5 billion since 1988, with the bulk going to law enforcement.[87] Grants from the DHS allow even the smallest of local departments to obtain heavy military hardware—illustrating once again the erosion of the division between the federal and state governments and increased dependence of many smaller agencies on the political center.

In one often-cited example, the town of Keene, New Hampshire, obtained a DHS grant for $285,933 to purchase a BearCat, an eight-ton armored personnel carrier. Keene has a population of 23,000 and has seen only two murders since 1999.[88] Other examples abound.[89] In the past decade more than $35 billion in DHS grants have been awarded to local law enforcement in the name of combating terrorism.[90] All these programs facilitate and strengthen the integration of local government agencies with the fed-

Table 5.2. Top Ten U.S. Counties Receiving Guns
via the 1033 Program (Guns per 1,000 Residents),
2006–April 2013.

County, State	Guns per 1,000 People
Franklin, KY	28.4
Hughes, SD	18.2
Niobrara, WY	14.5
Petroleum, MT	14.1
Starr, TX	12.7
Hinsdale, CO	11.4
Chautauqua, KS	8.8
Wheeler, OR	8.5
Cheyenne, KS	8.1
Wahkiakum, WA	7.5

Source: Table created by the authors with data from Rezvani,
Pupovac, Eads, and Fisher 2014.

eral government. As Dan Klein, a retired sergeant with the Albuquerque, New Mexico, Police Department, noted, "[i]t seems like Homeland Security is taking more of a local law enforcement role. . . . I'm not a conspiracy theorist, but at least here [in Albuquerque], we are moving more toward a national police force. Homeland Security is involved with a lot of little things around town. Somebody in Washington needs to call a timeout."[91] In creating a national police force, the DHS has increasingly made local governments dependent on and subservient to the national government.

This entanglement is further illustrated by the rise in the FBI's Joint Terrorism Task Forces (JTTFs) following 9/11. JTTFs, coordinated by the federal government, allow for the sharing of intelligence, training, and other materials among a variety of agencies at the state, local, and federal levels. Though the original JTTF was created as a result of the War on Drugs, seventy-one task forces were added for the War on Terror. To illustrate the agglomeration of the different levels of government, consider that the JTTFs currently include more than forty-four hundred individuals from over six hundred local and fifty distinct federal agencies.[92]

The impact of these relationships is not trivial. Equipment and tactics once reserved exclusively for the military or federal agencies are now easily transferred to state and local law enforcement for use against civilians. Take, for example, the use of "Stingrays," or "cell site simulators." This technology allows the user to "trick" people's cell phones into transmitting information, such as location and other identifiers. Originally developed for use abroad as part of the War on Terror, these devices are now used by federal, state, and local law enforcement to combat terrorism domestically.[93] According to one investigation, at least thirty-nine of the country's fifty largest police departments have acquired military surveillance technologies over the 2013–2017 period.[94]

The use of these surveillance technologies by local police has extended far beyond counterterrorism efforts. Police are now using the devices to track common criminals, and these devices gather information on *all* cellular devices in a given area, meaning uninvolved civilians are having their data collected and viewed by law enforcement.[95] Such tactics are used with little or no oversight.[96] In fact, it's unknown how many federal and other agencies use Stingray technology. Moreover, the technology is often subject to a nondisclosure agreement, allowing many agencies to have these devices without providing details of when and how they are used.[97] Use of this technology illustrates not only how much federal power has expanded post-9/11, but also how equipment for surveillance and social control abroad has returned home and is being transferred to local police for use against average Americans who do not even realize it.

Unfortunately, the American people cannot rely on the courts to protect their liberties by checking abuses of police power. Legal scholar Barry Friedman notes that when it comes to policing, the courts have "failed to require warrants when they should, they've watered down the 'probable cause' standard in the Fourth Amendment to the point that it fails to serve as an appreciable restraint on who is a proper target of policing and who is not, and they've allowed the most blatant invasions of person and property. . . ."[98] The absence of adequate checks on state power, combined with technological advances in the tools of social control, is a recipe for losing liberty.

Events in Ferguson, Missouri; New York City; and Baltimore, Maryland, have brought police militarization to the forefront of national attention. In May 2015 President Obama announced that he intended to issue an executive order banning certain types of military weapons from being transferred to local police departments. The goal was to encourage police agencies to "embrace a guardian—rather than a warrior—mindset to build trust and legitimacy both within agencies and with the public."[99] While many were optimistic that President Obama's mandate would slow the militarization of police, those hopes were quickly dashed. In August 2017 Attorney General Jeff Sessions announced that the Trump administration planned to resume the transfer of military equipment to state and local law enforcement.[100]

Beyond the shift in policy by the Trump administration, there is a deeper issue to consider: the fundamental change in modern police departments that has resulted from the incorporation of military tactics and hardware. Just as Vollmer, Nelson, Gates, and others used their former military training to carve out careers in law enforcement, today's military veterans, particularly of the global War on Terror, have sought similar employment in police departments. According to a survey conducted by the IACP, 86 percent of police leaders stated they currently employ veterans who had been deployed in the last five years.[101]

This trend is also apparent from police-recruitment records. In discussing the latest crop of police recruits, Topeka, Kansas, police sergeant Ron Gish stated, "[m]any of [the applicants for the police academy] have combat experience."[102] After the first round of cuts for Gish's incoming class of officers, 60 percent of those still being considered for admission had had military training.[103] The appeal of policing for returning soldiers is easy to understand. The familiar equipment and military-friendly organizational dynamics are a serious draw for combat veterans looking to put their skills to use. According to Yeffry Disla, a former marine and member of the U.S. Army who was deployed three times to Iraq and Afghanistan, working as "a cop would be my fallback if I can't do something else, simply because I was an infantryman and those are my skills. Anything you want to see in a soldier, you want to see in a policeman."[104]

While veterans may find many aspects of policing appealing after their tenure in the military, their transition is not without problems. According to the IACP, veterans of the most recent conflicts in the War on Terror are particularly inclined to use the undesirable parts of their military training in their dealings with civilians.[105] Significant numbers of veterans-turned-police-officers report a variety of mental-health problems that undermine their work with the communities they are tasked with protecting and serving.[106] In discussing how combat experience affected veterans' police work, commanders said they "have exaggerated survival instincts" and "tend to come back ill-prepared for the civilian world."[107] The statement of one veteran who joined the police force nicely captures this assessment:

The hardest thing for me during my transition was control issues. . . . A student told me recently that I was so intimidating. . . . I didn't see myself as intimidating. I had two complaints lodged on me. Both of them dealt with people perceiving me to be very military in bearing and unbendable on the scene. . . . That is the hardest thing I had to deal with.[108]

This warrior, "us versus them" mentality is not tempered or discouraged. Rather it is often encouraged by law-enforcement agencies, even among officers with no military training. For example, Steve Claggett, a Dallas SWAT veteran speaking at the 25th Annual Conference of the Illinois Tactical Officers Association, outlined eight ways in which officers can "recharge [their] warrior mindset." While suggesting that they immediately be put into the position of warriors among civilians, Claggett continuously referred to an officer's patrol area not as a neighborhood or beat, but as a "battleground" or "battlefield" on which he must be prepared to fight. "As you approach a scene," he stated, "assess your . . . battlefield. . . . Keep your battlefield in front of you."[109]

In his research on the subject, Radley Balko, the same journalist to investigate no-knock raids, has noted the growth of this "battlefield mentality." This way of thinking has become so ingrained that officers literally wear it on their sleeves. Balko reports that clothing marketed to police departments and worn off duty include such text as the following:

"NARCOTICS: You huff and you puff and we'll blow your door down"

"Human Trash Collector" (above a picture of a pair of handcuffs)
"Save the Police Time, Beat Yourself Up"
"Happiness is a Confirmed Kill"
"Law Enforcement: Helping Perps Slip Down the Stairs Since 1776"
"Be Good or You Might Get a Visit From the Bullet Fairy"
"Math for Cops: 2 to the Chest + 1 to the Head = Problem Solved"[110]

Police militarization is unlikely to reverse course in the foreseeable future. The continued integration of new technology further expands the power of government agencies at all levels. Government programs continue to intertwine the missions of the federal government with state and local agencies. Perhaps most important, within the context of the status quo, there is no clear mechanism for reestablishing the demarcation between police and military. The massive drug-terror complex, which benefits from a permanent state of war domestically and internationally, has no incentive to constrain itself and will actively work to undermine any efforts by others to do so. This complex includes an array of government officials, bureaucracies, contractors, unions, and consultants whose very existence is predicated on the culture of fear and crisis that serves to expand the scope of government power over the lives of Americans.

CHAPTER 6

Drones

In June 2011 six cows wandered onto Rodney Brossart's thirty-six-hundred-acre farm located in North Dakota. After Brossart refused to return the animals to their owner and failed to appear in court, the SWAT team from Grand Forks, North Dakota, was sent to arrest him. Things did not go smoothly. Refusing to be taken into custody, Brossart and his three sons engaged the police in a sixteen-hour standoff.[1] Brossart was eventually captured, tried, and sentenced to three years in prison for "terrorizing police."[2]

Under normal circumstances Brossart's arrest and sentencing would have probably made only the local news, but his case made national headlines. The intrigue surrounding his case had nothing to do with the cows, the farm, or even the deployment of a SWAT team. What made the case so interesting was that local police used a drone to locate the Brossart family and to gather evidence.[3] A drone, or unmanned aerial vehicle (UAV), is an aircraft controlled remotely or autonomously by a computer without a human pilot.[4] Drones have seen extensive use in the global War on Terror and have been used for decades as tools of war abroad.[5] As this story illustrates, however, this technology has now come to be used domestically.

The use of the drone in the Brossart case, loaned to the police department from the U.S. Customs and Border Patrol (CBP), created controversy. Brossart and his attorney argued that the use of the drone was illegal and amounted to "guerrilla-like tactics" by police.[6] They further claimed that the drone was used "without judicial approval or a warrant," making the surveillance and arrest illegal.[7]

Though perhaps the most publicized, the Brossart case was not the first time a drone was used in the United States. In fact, the first domestic use of drones occurred in the early 2000s, along the southern border. The use of such technology domestically has not been limited to border areas, however. Brian Bennett, a journalist for the *Los Angeles Times*, reported that the CBP had been making its drones available to a variety of agencies throughout the United States, including local law enforcement, the Federal Bureau of Investigation (FBI), and the Drug Enforcement Agency (DEA).[8] Between 2010 and 2012 alone, CBP used drones in some 687 missions for *other agencies* in the United States.[9] The Federal Aviation Administration (FAA) says it has issued 1,428 permits to domestic drone operators between 2007 and early 2013, including police, universities, state transportation departments, and at least seven federal agencies.[10] More than thirty states have applied to use drones in their law enforcement and other operations.[11]

The prospect of local and domestic federal agencies using drones raises serious questions regarding privacy and civil liberties. While drones have many potentially beneficial uses, such as tracking wildfires, search and rescue operations, boosting agricultural production, and even delivering goods ranging from packages to human blood, the government can use them to undermine liberty.

Covert drone technology is directly linked to domestic surveillance and police militarization discussed in previous chapters. In principle these tools can be used to protect citizens and their property, but drones also lower the cost of controlling the lives of peaceful Americans, undermining the very rights government is tasked with protecting. Many UAVs are equipped with technologies such as high-power zoom lenses, night-vision cameras, and radar imaging that allows operators to see through ceilings, walls, and other barriers. Other UAVs are outfitted with additional video analytics, granting operators more surveillance power than ever before.[12] The technology further weakens the constraints on surveillance because drones are difficult, if not impossible, to detect by those being watched. The result is that citizens' rights may be violated without their knowledge.

Critics cite a variety of potential problems with widespread domestic drone use by the government, including enhanced opportunities for law enforcement and other government agents to track and target civilians and nonviolent criminals. Others express concerns regarding voyeurism and whether drones would be used to target particular racial, socioeconomic, or other groups.[13] The potential use of drones to spy on Americans has been identified as a threat to some of the fundamental rights protected by the U.S. Constitution, including the Fourth Amendment protection against unreasonable search and seizure.[14] In 2015 North Dakota became the first state to legalize the use of "weaponized" drones by police. Police drones in the state may now be equipped to shoot tear gas, rubber bullets, beanbags, pepper spray, and Tasers.[15]

Further complicating the issue is the lack of transparency regarding the use of UAVs by various government agencies. In 2013 FBI director Robert Mueller admitted in testimony before the Senate Judiciary Committee that the Bureau uses drones for domestic surveillance. He failed to elaborate, stating only that the FBI uses the technology in a "minimal way, and seldom."[16] His refusal to state how his agency uses the technology is typical. A variety of government agencies have refused to answer questions about their use of UAVs, if they admit to using them at all.

In 2011 the Electronic Frontier Foundation (EFF), a nonprofit organization dedicated to privacy, expression, and technology policy, requested that the FAA and the Department of Transportation (DOT) release a list of entities authorized to operate UAVs domestically. After nearly a year with no response, the group filed a lawsuit against the DOT.[17] While the DOT and FAA later produced a list, a subsequent congressional hearing revealed that it was woefully incomplete. The EFF renewed its request and ultimately filed a second lawsuit. The case was ongoing in early 2017.[18]

Meanwhile, others have begun to seriously question the current use of drones domestically. For example, in 2014 the White House stated it was preparing a directive to force federal agencies such as the Departments of Defense (DoD), Justice (DOJ), and Homeland Security (DHS), and the CBP to publically disclose when they use UAVs and what they do with the data they collect. At the time of this writing, however, these agencies do not have to disclose this information, and promises of increased transparency remain unfilled.[19]

On the basis of publicly available information, the domestic use of drones is a relatively new phenomenon. However, the U.S. military has used drones in foreign interventions for decades in a variety of contexts. The boomerang effect illuminates how their use abroad facilitated their use at home.

Prior to the subsequent discussion, it is important to note two things. First, our analysis purposefully excludes private commercial drone use.

While increased commercial use is undoubtedly important and is worthy of discussion, our focus is on the development of drones as a means of surveillance by the state. Thus commercial use falls outside the purview of our analysis. Commercial drone technology would have developed absent the influence of the U.S. government. However, the purpose and use of these technologies differs across private and government use. We limit our focus to the latter, which entails employing drones as a tool of control over domestic and foreign populations.

Second, our analysis is limited by the extent of the data available. As just discussed, drones have only come to be used domestically over the past decade, meaning the longer-term, detailed historical illustrations of the boomerang effect present in the cases of surveillance, police militarization, and torture will not be present here. Moreover, current laws do not require government agencies to disclose when and how drones are used, meaning that comprehensive data are simply unavailable. Despite these caveats, the ongoing relevance of the topic and the connection of domestic drone use to foreign intervention militate in favor of study rather than neglect. Without a doubt, as more information becomes available, this analysis is likely to expand as is the connection between foreign intervention and the use of drones at home.

A BRIEF HISTORY OF THE USE OF DRONES ABROAD

The use of drones by the U.S. government dates back nearly a century.[20] From the very first drone to the modern incarnations, UAV technology was developed expressly to enhance the government's ability to engage in war. The first UAVs were designed in the midst of World War I. Throughout prior conflicts the United States (and other military powers) relied on manpower, investing relatively little in military technology.[21] During World War I, however, this dynamic changed dramatically. Both the Allied and Central powers saw potential in using new technologies to gain an advantage over their enemies and mobilized substantial resources toward this end. These ambitions resulted in a new type of war, which emphasized technological differences. It wasn't simply a matter of the sheer size of a country's military in terms of number of soldiers, but instead an issue of relative technological strength. The first drones were part of this shift.

In 1915, nearly two full years before U.S. entry into the conflict, inventors Elmer Sperry and Peter Cooper Hewitt worked to produce a "pilotless aerial torpedo," the modern drone's ancestor.[22] These "proto-drones" were to be loaded with TNT and launched against enemy targets.[23] While these early UAVs were never used in the war, military leaders saw their potential for future interventions and continued to refine the technology to enhance military capabilities. Drones were further developed after the war to serve as targets in the training of traditional fighter pilots. By 1939 both the navy and the army used target drones to train anti-aircraft gunners. Over fifteen thousand of these early drones would be used throughout the first half of the twentieth century.[24] Beginning in the late 1940s, after World War II and at the beginning of the Cold War, the use of UAV technology changed. Technological advances allowed drones to be used not just for training those who would pursue social control, but as a direct means of state-produced surveillance.

The Cold War and fear of the "Soviet threat" provided opportunities for the U.S. government to invest in developing new ways of spying and collecting data. Looking to gather data on the perceived enemies of the United States and prevent the spread of communism around the globe, the U.S. government renewed its interest in drones. Their appeal was obvious. If a manned aircraft was shot down over the Soviet Union, for example, the death or capture of the pilot would undoubtedly make international news. At a minimum, such an event would further strain the relationship between the global superpowers. If a drone was shot down, in contrast, the U.S. government could more easily deny responsibility and more easily prevent a public outcry, since no human pilot would be killed or captured.[25]

With such incentives working in the background, drones were equipped to carry film cameras and used for reconnaissance missions throughout Soviet territory beginning in 1955. The technology was further refined and put into mass production in 1959. In all, more than fourteen hundred spy drones would be used in foreign missions to gather intelligence throughout the Cold War.[26] The space race between the Soviet Union and the United States further enhanced the capabilities of drones and engendered additional uses. Increases in defense spending, particularly during the Reagan administration, led to the development and integration of technologies such as "microelectromechanical" system sensors and miniature global positioning systems into drone design, advancements that would prove pivotal in modern UAVs.

Military missions in Grenada, Libya, Lebanon, and elsewhere led to the additional use of drones. It was the First Gulf War, however, that propelled the expanding use of drones in foreign intervention.[27] At least 522 drone missions took place during the brief conflict, logging more than sixteen hundred hours of flying time.[28] Humanitarian missions throughout the 1990s in Somalia, Bosnia and Herzegovina, Rwanda, Kosovo, and elsewhere would provide additional testing grounds for drones abroad.[29] Other examples of drone use during this period abound. For example, drones were used to confirm that the Serbian military had failed to uphold their agreement to withdraw weapons out of Sarajevo, thus prompting a change in military action. The technology provided a lower-cost method (fewer boots on the ground) of enhanced surveillance. Coalition forces could now gather valuable intelligence on enemies from a safe distance and use this information to achieve the goals of the intervention. By the end of 1996, UAVs had completed more than 1,575 surveillance missions in support of coalition forces in former Yugoslavia.[30]

The global War on Terror provided a substantial opening for the increased use of drones by the U.S. government abroad. The DoD's drone inventory increased forty-fold from the beginning of the war in 2001 to more than 7,400 UAVs in 2012.[31] It was also during this war that drones began to be used in a new capacity—to strike and kill targets. In addition to conducting surveillance in Iraq, Afghanistan, Pakistan, Somalia, and Yemen, the U.S. military has conducted well over one thousand known offensive strikes in at least five countries.[32] At least 2,464 people were killed in strikes between President Barack Obama's inauguration and 2015, although there likely were more.[33]

Proponents of drone use abroad offer a variety of arguments for the continued and expanded use of UAV technology. In essence, nearly *every* argument for the recent expansion of the military use of drones stems from the idea that they are a cheaper, more effective means of achieving foreign policy goals than the alternatives.[34] Obama explicitly stated that drones are better at targeting and killing foreign adversaries. Drones "are effective . . . ," he said. "Dozens of highly skilled al Qaeda commanders, trainers, bomb makers and operatives have been taken off the battlefield. . . . [T]he primary alternative to [drones] would be the use of conventional military options. . . . Conventional airpower or missiles are far less precise than drones."[35]

UAVs are also said to reduce the costs of engaging in conflict in other ways, such as by reducing civilian casualties, or "collateral damage." CIA director John Brennan, for example, stated that UAVs have "surgical precision—the ability with laser-like focus to eliminate the cancerous tumor called al Qa'ida, while limiting the damage to the tissue around it."[36] The idea is that the U.S. government can intervene in and control other societies with precision to achieve its ends. Proponents also argue that drones reduce the cost to military personnel. Fewer "boots on the ground," they posit, means it's easier to engage in foreign operations without putting the lives of pilots and other members of the military at risk.

Taken together, these qualities illustrate how drones have come to be used so extensively in foreign intervention. From target practice to surveillance to offensive attacks to reducing the risk to pilots, drones provide many potentially lower-cost ways of intervening abroad to shape outcomes in other societies according to the plan of interveners. It will come as no surprise that the technology has come to be used domestically.

DRONES RETURN HOME

To understand the applicability of the boomerang framework to drones, consider the career of Vice Admiral Arthur Cebrowski. A naval officer and former president of the Naval War College, Cebrowski headed the Office of Force Transformation (OFT) in the DoD from 2001 to 2005[37] and is credited with being "directly responsible for the rise in the number of robots and drones within the U.S."[38] While the U.S. military had used drones abroad before Cebrowski came along, his integration of them into standard military operations would ultimately set the stage for their use domestically. Indeed, the use of drones and other automated technologies by law enforcement and other domestic government agencies is a direct outcome of Cebrowski's work. His story illustrates how technology, once integrated into foreign operations, may quickly come to be used at home.

Cebrowski's naval career lasted nearly forty years, beginning with two tours of duty in Vietnam. Just as that war would prove vital to the development and importation of SWAT teams (Chapter 5) and torture (Chapter 7) to the United States, it is also important in explaining the rise of domestic drones. It was in Vietnam that Cebrowski first began to develop his ideas regarding the need to integrate advanced technologies into military operations. He would explain later in life (as discussed further on) that his dangerous missions directly informed his ideas about military technology. During his tours Cebrowski flew some 154 combat missions, mostly over enemy territory in North Vietnam.[39]

His experiences in Vietnam led him to believe that substantial changes were needed in the military: that the armed forces had to be bold and adaptive, and that they should seek new and innovative ways to carry out their missions and better achieve their objectives of foreign intervention. These changes, which he would later implement, would ultimately pave the way for drones to be used domestically. Throughout the 1970s and 1980s Cebrowski made his way up the chain of command in naval aviation. With his new positions of increasing authority, Cebrowski focused on large-scale integrated systems—complex computer and information-sharing systems. He believed such technologies would be vital in future combat scenarios by increasing efficiency and technical reliability while reducing the risk to pilots. He noted that these ideas came directly from his combat tours:

My experience had come from flying combat aircraft. . . . It was a complex situation, and success depended on manipulating that complexity. . . . Transistors and the large-scale integrated circuits [complex computer systems] . . . promised to shift some of that complexity [from the pilot] to the aircraft and the weapons it carried. [If the] military could do that on a large scale . . . [it] would have an edge. It could lead to a strategic advantage, an ability to shift the terrible burden of warfare complexity and the risks it carried away from you onto your opponent.[40]

In 1980 the navy established the Strategic Studies Group at the Naval War College to propose improvements. In this effort, the navy sought the opinions of "war fighters," as opposed to individuals with little to no combat experience. It is here that Cebrowski found the opportunity to push his ideas forward. His appointment to the group allowed him to further develop his idea that the military needed to incorporate more advanced technologies into its aviation operations.[41]

After his year-long appointment to the Strategic Studies Group, Cebrowski returned once again to participating in foreign intervention. In 1990 he engaged in combat in the First Gulf War as the commander of the USS *Midway* during Operation Imminent Thunder. Operation Imminent Thunder and the larger Operation Desert Storm influenced Cebrowski's views and his later work. During Imminent Thunder, the U.S. military conducted drills in an effort to deceive and intimidate Iraqi forces into moving their military activities to the coast of Kuwait. While Cebrowski was on the *Midway*, the Navy launched 228 sorties and more than one hundred Tomahawk missiles.

It was during Desert Storm that the U.S. military realized the potential of drone technology not only for surveillance but also to intimidate the enemy. During Desert Storm the crew of the USS *Missouri*, one of the ships that worked with the *Midway* during Imminent Thunder, launched surveillance drones over Iraq. These missions provided further evidence that drones were effective as a means of combat. The crew of the *Missouri* reported that groups of Iraqis intimidated by drones attempted to surrender to the unmanned aircraft on at least two occasions.[42]

For the next ten years Cebrowski attempted to advance his ideas about transforming the military through automated warfare, which he had developed during his combat experience. He initially met strong resistance. As discussed by his biographer, James Blaker, Cebrowski was keenly aware that his plan would be extremely difficult to accomplish due to the military's bureaucratic structure.[43] According to Blaker, Cebrowski understood the opportunity that a crisis could provide: "[M]ilitaries institute change with extreme caution. When they are not at war. In war, change is easier and often faster, for in the clash of armed conflict it becomes clear, very quickly, what of the tried, traditional, doctrinal—the way 'things are to be done'—is no longer true. Conflicts, coupled with advances in military technology, are sharp goods for change."[44]

The necessary crisis materialized on 9/11. Just as the resulting War on Terror was integral to the stories of domestic surveillance and militarized police, so too was it important to the return of drones. The attacks on the Pentagon and World Trade Center on September 11, 2001, in addition to opening the door for a variety of new agencies, bureaus, and measures aimed at "combatting terror," blew the door wide open for Cebrowski, enabling him to push for the adoption of advanced automated systems. In October 2001 Defense Secretary Donald Rumsfeld appointed him to run the OFT, which was tasked with developing new military tactics and technologies to keep the United States the dominant military power on the globe.

With the War on Terror the U.S. government was eager to develop new capabilities and technologies to help defeat terrorism both abroad and at home. As head of the OFT, Cebrowski was in a prime position to put his combat-inspired ideas into action. He worked as the agency's "conceptual engine," looking for ways to implement and assess "transformational" initiatives.[45] In addition to providing the opportunity to put his ideas into practice, the War on Terror also provided the necessary funds. Flush with resources dedicated to fighting terrorism, backed by expanded and newly created agencies, and supported by Rumsfeld, the OFT had the means to transform the military in ways that would likely not have otherwise occurred. Cebrowski had significant discretion in establishing the size, budget, and operations of his office and exhibited substantial influence within the Bush administration. Discussing the impact of Cebrowski and his ideas, the political scientist P. W. Singer noted,

After Bush's inauguration, his new leadership team at the Pentagon led by Donald Rumsfeld as secretary of defense, moved quickly to make the vision of network-centric warfare a reality. The cantankerous Rumsfeld saw this as his opportunity to put his own stamp on the U.S. military. . . . Perhaps the greatest sign that the new team at the Pentagon was drinking the network-centric Kool-Aid was what happened next for Admiral Cebrowski. As an article in the U.S. Navy official journal put it, "If 'Rummy' was the president's high priest of Defense Transformation, Cebrowski was his major prophet, or better yet messiah announcing the New World Order just on the horizon."[46]

Although he focused on expanding UAV technology for foreign intervention, the unique nature of the War on Terror and continuing War on Drugs was conducive to the domestic use of drones. As discussed in previous chapters, these two wars are fundamentally different from other U.S. conflicts in that they feature both external and internal enemies who are not easily identified. Therefore, the distinction between "us" (innocent U.S. persons) and "them" (enemies), or the "in group" and the "out group," is much less clear. Moreover, the general fear surrounding drugs and terrorism prevented, and continues to prevent, a backlash from many Americans. Tactics such as warrantless wiretapping, the collection of electronic communications, and drone surveillance, once considered unthinkable, became reasonable and normalized to many people. The supposed threat of homegrown terrorists not only continued the centralization of government power but also allowed for the "network-centric warfare" championed by Cebrowski to be used—within the United States.[47] "Network-centric warfare" or "network-centric operations" is the formal incarnation of Cebrowski's ideas of using complex computer systems in conflict. Specifically, network-centric warfare involves using the U.S. government's advanced information technology to create a competitive advantage through the tight coordination of geographically dispersed forces and weapons.[48]

The adaptation of drones for domestic purposes was swift. In 2002 the Customs and Border Patrol began using drones along the U.S. border as a way to stop illegal immigration and prevent those with possible terrorist ties from entering the country.[49] Lawmakers used the War on Terror to start and expand domestic drone programs. State and federal officials declared that the use of stealth drone technology was "invaluable" to counterterrorism operations along the border.[50] Former Texas governor Rick Perry, for example, championed the use of drones in his state, claiming that Predator drones would be a valuable asset in the state's efforts to combat terrorism.[51] He stated, "[t]here may already be ISIS cells—ISIS individuals—in America. . . . They may have used our southern border, because it's porous."[52]

The use of drones domestically by authorities gained further appeal when combined with the War on Drugs. It's been suggested that Mexican drug cartels, for example, have helped ISIS militants cross the border to "explore targets."[53] The alleged connections between terrorist organizations and illegal drugs have prompted the use of drones in operations supposedly targeting both problems. Former Arizona governor Jan Brewer illustrated this dynamic when she stated that Predator drones are "ideal for border security and counter-drug missions."[54] Some have suggested that drones may be beneficial in fighting drugs independent of their possible connection to terror groups. Lawmakers and others claim that drones may provide a more cost-effective means of counterdrug operations in a time when many are questioning the billions spent on the drug war. Senator Thad Cochran (R-MS), for example, stated that drones have "operational readiness and potential to provide more persistent and cost-effective intelligence, surveillance and reconnaissance [for illegal drugs]."[55]

Intermingling the War on Drugs and the War on Terror offers the perfect justification for expanding surveillance of Americans and other U.S. residents who are viewed as potential enemies. In lowering the cost of monitoring and intervention, drones serve as an ideal tool for government to control people in a clandestine and efficient manner.

THE CURRENT STATE OF AFFAIRS

To many individuals the supposed threats posed by the government's domestic use of drones are mere fantasy. In 2012, for example, journalist David Horsey referred to reports of spy drones as "paranoid lunacy" and a tale that "will show up in the future dark musing of radio preachers, in the ravings of right wing conspiracy mongers and in casual coffee shop discussions in small towns."[56] We now know that Horsey's condescending dismissal of such concerns was wrong, since drones have in fact been used to spy on Americans on U.S. soil and elsewhere.

As noted, drone technology has greatly reduced the cost of surveillance. By design, the technology is covert and difficult, if not impossible, for the average civilian to detect. And officials have been less than forthcoming about how and when drones are used on U.S. soil. All of this makes an accurate accounting of drone use in the United States practically impossible. However, we can still make several important observations regarding the use of drones domestically and abroad, and the impact on U.S. citizens in each case.

We know, for example, that drones such as the Sky Warrior and the Reaper (Predator B) continue to see extended use in the global War on Terror in a variety of countries including Afghanistan, Iraq, Pakistan, Yemen, Somalia, and Libya, and that these attacks have resulted in civilian casualties. Although the air force recently announced the "retirement" of the famed MQ-1 Predator drone, they plan to use the drones at least through 2018.[57] While the exact number of casualties is unknown, the strikes have been particularly hazardous for civilians. Recent estimates are that nearly 90 percent of people killed by U.S. drone strikes were not intended targets. Parents in Pakistan have reported keeping their children home from school lest the buildings be mistaken for al-Qaeda compounds and targeted.[58] A related concern is that the use of drones by the U.S. government to combat terrorism results in widespread terror for those foreign populations who must live with drones overhead.[59] Among other things, this has generated anger, resentment, and hatred toward the United States government and the citizens it represents.

More important, for our analysis, we also know these controversial drone strikes have not targeted only foreign nationals. Lack of oversight of U.S. activities overseas has eroded critical constraints on government power, and as a result, U.S. citizens have been killed. Some of these deaths have been accidental, but at least one was intentional. In 2013 the Justice Department confirmed that four U.S. citizens had been killed by CIA drone strikes abroad since 2009, either intentionally or unintentionally. One of these Americans, Abdulrahman al-Awlaki, was only sixteen years old.[60] When asked how the U.S. government justified killing a U.S. citizen—a minor child yet—White House press secretary Robert Gibbs replied, "I would suggest that [al-Awlaki] should have a far more responsible father." He was referring to Anwar al-Awlaki, a suspected terrorist who had been killed in a drone strike two weeks earlier. Gibbs's statement suggested that being related to a "known terrorist" was grounds for killing the teenager.[61] The young al-Awlaki, however, had not been linked to any terror-related activity nor charged with any crime at the time of his death. He was eating dinner at an outside café when the strike occurred.

The killing of U.S. citizens without due process has rightfully stirred significant controversy. The American criminal justice system is designed to permit conviction (and execution) only when guilt has been proven beyond a reasonable doubt. Indeed, the Fourth and Fourteenth Amendments to the U.S. Constitution each contain a due process clause intended to shield citizens from the possibility of arbitrary actions by the U.S. government. The use of drones, however, has undermined this critical constraint on government power, allowing the almost unthinkable—the execution of U.S. citizens without formal charges or due process.[62] Moreover, these strikes are conducted under the sole authority of the executive branch; that is, there is practically no oversight, no checks, and no accountability. The "kill list" created by government agents, including the president, is secret.[63] They serve as the judge, jury, and executioner under secret guidelines.

In 2011, after numerous protests and attempts by the Obama administration to keep it private, an appeals court released a government memo outlining the supposed justification for killing U.S. citizens in drone strikes. The memo concluded by stating, "we do not believe that U.S. citizenship imposes constitutional limitations that would preclude the contemplated lethal action under the facts represented to us by the DoD, CIA and the intelligence community."[64] President Obama echoed these sentiments. In discussing the order to kill a U.S. citizen abroad, Obama stated bluntly that "as president, I would have been derelict in my duty had I not authorized the strike that took him out."[65]

The abuse of drones is not only a problem for U.S. citizens abroad in countries with supposed links to terrorism. Per the logic of the boomerang effect, drone technology and its abuses have found their way onto U.S. soil. Individuals such as Arthur Cebrowski used human and physical capital developed through decades of foreign intervention to push drones into the U.S. arsenal. The War on Terror provided the necessary crisis and centralization of government to expand the use of drones domestically.

Nowhere is this more apparent than in the use of UAVs along the U.S. border. As discussed earlier, CBP has used drones extensively in border operations and conducted myriad operations for other agencies. The justification for many CBP activities, drone use included, centers largely on the idea of preventing those with terrorist and drug ties from coming into the United States through the border. According to the agency's website, the CBP maintains a "priority mission" of "preventing terrorists and terrorists [sic] weapons, including weapons of mass destruction, from entering the United States."[66] As its mission is now inextricably linked to the War on Terror, the agency operates without much oversight or transparency. In fact, a report commissioned by the CBP found a "lack of due diligence" in investigating inappropriate behavior by CBP officers and officials.[67] Despite these problems and clear reports of abuse throughout the agency, federal and state lawmakers insist the use of stealth drone technology is "invaluable" to U.S. counterdrug and counterterrorism operations along the border.[68]

The expanded use of drones in these operations, and the documented lack of oversight and constraints, is particularly jarring when one considers that the "border" extends a full hundred miles inland, meaning that in some cases, entire states fall under the purview of the CBP. These include Maine, Massachusetts, Connecticut, New Jersey, Maryland, Hawaii, Florida, and Rhode Island. Nine out of ten of the largest U.S. metropolitan areas also fall within this zone: New York City, Los Angeles, Chicago, Houston, Philadelphia, Phoenix, San Antonio, San Diego, and San Jose.[69]

The response to the supposed threat of illegal immigrants with terrorist or drug-trafficking ties has already led to abuses of Americans. To give but one example, consider a fifty-four-year old woman from New Mexico who filed a lawsuit after CBP agents subjected her to a manual inspection of her genitals and anus, an x-ray and CT scan, a rectal exam, and a bimanual search of her vagina—while she was handcuffed to an exam table. After refusing to sign a consent form, she was billed $5,272.25 for "services provided." She was never charged with any crime.[70]

While this case did not involve the use of drones, it raises serious, related questions. If current operations involve the gross mistreatment and abuse of U.S. citizens, what does the introduction of deliberately stealthy technology mean for individual rights? If individuals may be so brazenly abused, what does this imply about covert technology for which the oversight and rules of use are much less clearly defined?

Other state and local agencies have likewise used or applied to use drones or other new technology. According to the EFF, local law enforcement agencies in Idaho, Oregon, North Dakota, Ohio, and Florida have all asked to use UAV technology, though in many cases it is unclear why.[71] In other cases, limited information is known. Police in Ogden, Utah, for example, requested to use a "lighter than air" drone platform (a blimp-like drone) to conduct surveillance over "high crime" areas at night.[72] Law enforcement officials in Arlington, Texas, have requested to use drones for a variety of operations, including surveillance and counternarcotic operations.[73] Police in Gadsden, Alabama, asked to use drones as part of a multi-agency narcotics operation. According to the EFF, the police intend to use the drones for "covert surveillance of drug transactions and [to] develop video evidence of such activities."[74]

In perhaps the best illustration of the intermingling of state, local, and federal agencies with regard to drones and the War on Drugs, the Queen Anne's County, Maryland, sheriff's department, in conjunction with the DOJ and the DHS, was granted permission for a program in which local law enforcement agents trained at Eglin Air Force Base would use drones to engage in drug-enforcement and surveillance operations.[75] More broadly, it has been reported that the DHS has distributed some $4 million in grants to help police purchase and maintain their own drones.[76]

In addition to these local agencies, the Pentagon has admitted to conducting spy and surveillance missions over U.S. soil in operations not necessarily linked to terrorism or narcotics. In 2016 *The Atlantic* reported that the DoD "has deployed drones to spy over U.S. territory for non-military missions over the past decade."[77] While government officials say the use of drones is rare and lawful, the specifics are unclear due to a lack of transparency. In perhaps the most startling statement regarding the use of drones on U.S. soil, Attorney General Eric Holder sent a letter to Senator Rand Paul (R-KY) responding to questions about the president's authority to kill U.S. citizens on U.S. soil. He said, "[i]t is possible, I suppose, to imagine an extraordinary circumstance in which it would be necessary and appropriate . . . for the President to authorize the military to use lethal [drone] force within the territory of the United States."[78]

Another ongoing issue is the weaponization of domestic drones. As noted at the beginning of this chapter, North Dakota became the first U.S. state to legalize the weaponization of police drones. This authorization is restricted to what are considered less lethal weapons such as rubber bullets, stun guns, and tear gas. However other states, such as Connecticut, are considering laws that would allow police to arm drones with deadly weapons.[79] Irrespective of what happens in Connecticut, the very fact that outfitting drones with lethal weapons is being seriously debated as policy shows how far the domestic use of drones has come and the potential they possess for expanding the scope of state power over the lives of American people.

There is every reason to believe that drones will continue to be used and that the scale and scope of their operations will expand. Private defense firms are investing significant sums of money to design the next generation of drones with the goal of replacing domestic police helicopters starting within the next decade.[80] Moreover, the Department of Defense's Third Offset Strategy, which was announced in November 2014, explicitly emphasized the use of drone technology.

An offset strategy is a long-term plan that aims to generate and sustain a military advantage. The two prior offset strategies sought to maintain U.S. military dominance through the creation of advanced technologies. The First Offset began in the 1950s and sought to maintain nuclear superiority over the Soviet Union. When the USSR acquired nuclear capabilities similar to those of the United States, the DoD launched the Second Offset with a focus on such things as precision-guided missiles, microprocessors, and other information technologies. As other nations have come to acquire and use similar technologies, the U.S. government once again looks to technology to keep the U.S. military ahead of the rest of the world. At the core of the new offset strategy is the use and integration of a variety of new technological advances, including drones and other unmanned systems.[81] With additional labor, research, and funds pouring into these technologies, the continued use of drones abroad and domestically is inevitable.

As noted at the outset, drones have some potentially valuable uses. The technology has been used to increase agricultural production, to fight fires, and to assist in search and rescue missions.[82] Drones have the potential to protect persons and property. As we've shown, however, the lack of oversight and constraints on the use of drones domestically and abroad has created conditions in which civil liberties can and have been abused.

The full extent of domestic drone use is still unfolding. But despite the lack of detailed information, it is apparent that the technology poses a real threat to U.S. citizens. The concern is not necessarily that that the U.S. government will launch a violent drone war against its own citizens tomorrow, but rather that drones will allow for the scope of government to slowly expand in ways that are not readily observable by Americans. By lowering the cost of surveillance, violence, and other activities, drones allow government agents to undertake activities that undermine liberty. The covert nature of drones combined with the lack of transparency and oversight means that the constraints on domestic drones are lax at best. While the full extent of how drones ultimately will affect Americans remains to be seen, the technology has the potential for grave abuse. Once again, the boomerang effect is at work.

CHAPTER 7

Torture

In 2004 CBS News and the *New Yorker* issued disturbing reports regarding the treatment of prisoners at Abu Ghraib prison in Iraq. Ghastly photos of inmates accompanied the reports. In one photo a naked Iraqi man cowers before two German shepherds restrained by smiling American soldiers. In another, taken but a few minutes later, the same man is lying on the ground, a soldier pressing his knee into his back. Other photos depicted prisoners naked on the ground with dog collars attached to leashes around their necks. Yet others showed U.S. soldiers smiling next to an inmate's dead body, a variety of images of sexual assault, and other forms of humiliation.[1] In response to the photographs and the public outcry that ensued, the Bush administration blamed a few "bad apples," that is, low-ranking rogue military personnel who failed to follow orders. The American government, the administration claimed, does not torture prisoners and does not condone their mistreatment.[2]

This was far from the end of the story. In late 2014 the Senate Committee on Intelligence released 525 pages of its report on the use of torture in the War on Terror.[3] The document revealed that the treatment of detainees was far more brutal than what had been previously disclosed. Among other things, prisoners were subjected to "rectal rehydration" and "rectal feeding," in which nutrition is delivered rectally.[4] Although it was claimed such methods were used when detainees refused to eat, the medical community states that rectal feedings "have zero medical application and are nothing more than full-bore torture."[5] Detainees were also subjected to sleep deprivation for up to 180 hours, typically while being forced into stress positions, in which their hands were shackled above their heads or behind their backs.[6] Other captives were waterboarded—an interrogation technique in which a person is strapped down and water is poured over the face to simulate drowning. Such episodes resulted in convulsions, vomiting, and in at least one case, a "series of near drownings."[7] In other cases,

U.S. military personnel threatened to physically harm detainees' children and to rape and murder their mothers.[8]

In anticipation of the report's release, President Barack Obama held a press conference at which he acknowledged the misconduct of government agents, stating, "I was very clear that in the immediate aftermath of 9/11 we did some things that were wrong. We did a whole lot of things that were right, but we tortured some folks. We did some things that were contrary to our values."[9]

Americans have mixed views on torture (also referred to by the U.S. government as "enhanced interrogation"). According to polls, roughly half of Americans believe at least some torture was justified following the 9/11 attacks, while the other half claim such actions are rarely or never defensible.[10] However, the torture documented at Abu Ghraib and elsewhere is largely objectionable to most Americans. In the wake of the Abu Ghraib scandal a 2005 Gallup poll found that nearly 80 percent of American adults believed the use of stress positions and nudity in U.S. operations abroad was unacceptable. Approximately 70 percent opposed threatening detainees with dogs.[11] Nearly half agreed it was wrong to subject prisoners to sleep deprivation, and 82 percent were against waterboarding.[12] A similar poll, conducted after the release of the Senate torture report, found a deep political divide between Democrats and Republicans, with the latter being considerably more supportive of torture. Even still, many surveyed disapproved of the U.S. tactics in Iraq. More than half of all respondents stated that it was "unacceptable" to threaten to harm a detainee's family members. Seventy-three percent said it was wrong to "feed a detainee by pumping food into his anus."[13]

In the United States, discussions of torture, to the extent they exist, focus on abuse abroad against foreigners. Indeed, the idea that the U.S. government could engage in torture domestically is unfathomable to most Americans. Yet despite the view that torture by the U.S. government is rare and only happens abroad, evidence indicates that members of the government have engaged in widespread and systematic torture against Americans, mainly within the U.S. prison system, though other cases exist as well. The boomerang effect offers one explanation for the establishment and use of various torture techniques in the United States. Foreign intervention, or preparation for it, has enabled the government to experiment with torture as a technique of social control over distant populations. Once developed, these methods found their way back to the United States, only to be used against Americans.

Although torture has a variety of definitions, we use the definition adopted by the United Nations in the "Convention Against Torture and Other Cruel, Inhuman, or Degrading Treatment or Punishment":

"[T]orture" means any act by which severe pain or suffering, whether physical or mental, is intentionally inflicted on a person for such purposes as obtaining from him or a third person information or a confession, punishing him for an act he or a third person has committed or is suspected of having committed, or intimidating or coercing him or a third person, or for any reason based on discrimination of any kind, when such pain or suffering is inflicted by or at the instigation of or with the consent or acquiescence of a public official or other person acting in an official capacity.[14]

We adopt this definition for three reasons. First, it is widely accepted: more than 140 countries have ratified the U.N. "Convention Against Torture."[15] Second, the definition allows us to examine cases using the same commonly accepted metric as most other analyses. Third, this definition allows us to discuss a broad spectrum of torture techniques. While many individuals think of torture as purely physical and requiring pain, the U.N. definition makes two important inclusions. First, it allows for the discussion of psychological torture. These methods, though they do not leave physical scars, are just as detrimental to victims as physical abuse.[16] In fact, many experts argue that psychological torture is worse than physical torture. Second, and related, this definition also highlights that torture does not necessarily require pain. Other types of suffering can likewise qualify as torture. The common thread is that acts of torture are used in order to obtain information or actions from an unwilling subject. Using this definition allows us to offer a more complete picture of the torture used by the U.S. government abroad and domestically.

Before we continue, a caveat is in order. Given that torture is widely considered an unacceptable means of interrogation, it comes as no surprise that detailed data regarding torture practices are severely limited. Individuals engaged in torture face strong incentives to keep their activities a secret and therefore tend not to document their actions. This issue is further compounded when considering historical cases due to elapsed time and poor historical records. It follows that comprehensive, time-series data regarding torture simply do not exist. So although it may be widely accepted that specific forms of torture were used during certain periods, exact instances and individuals may be impossible to identify due to the intentional obfuscation of events by parties involved and a general lack of documentation. Therefore our analysis is limited by the extent of the data available. In spite of these difficulties, the fact that torture continues to be used and debated indicates that its study, however imperfect, is one of immense import.

TORTURE AND THE AMERICAN FOUNDING

Torture is certainly not an American invention. Depictions of torture can be seen throughout human history. The Old Testament documents several instances of torture, including one in which seven brothers were tortured to death by King Antiochus IV Epiphanes in the second century B.C. after they refused to eat pork.[17] In ancient Greece torture victims were roasted to death inside a brass container known as the "Brazen Bull."[18] Later, devices such as the "heretic's fork" were developed—an object with sharp metal prongs that was placed under a victim's chin and rested on the sternum. If the person fell asleep or dropped his head, the metal spikes would pierce his throat and chest. Other forms of torture, such as crucifixion; thumbscrews; the iron maiden; and devices to rip or cut tongues, fingers, and other body parts, were developed well before the advent of modern war or government.

Although the American founders did not witness the use of the Brazen Bull, heretic's fork, or crucifixion in their time, they recognized that torture is a favorite tool of governments to control people. From the time the first colonies were established in the New World, the governing bodies in America attempted to limit the government's use of torture in order to protect the rights of the citizenry. For example, in 1631 the Massachusetts

Body of Liberties limited the instances in which torture could be used, and prohibited outright torture that was considered "barbarous or cruel."[19]

Following the Revolutionary War, the founders sought to curtail the use of torture by the newly formed government. During the war colonists accused the British of war crimes, including torturing and killing colonial troops outside of what was considered acceptable behavior in warfare.[20] Such incidents induced a variety of key figures from the period, including George Washington, Benjamin Franklin, and John Adams, to denounce torture.[21]

When the leaders of the new United States of America began to put together the rules under which the government would operate, torture was again addressed—and expressly forbidden. In April 1781 the Continental Congress forbade the kind of torture it deemed "cruel and inhuman." The Bill of Rights, which amended the Constitution in 1791, contains a prohibition directly pertaining to torture. The Eighth Amendment expressly forbids the government from inflicting "cruel and unusual punishments."[22]

Despite these early and strict bans on torture, the U.S. government historically has engaged in it—including on U.S. soil against Americans. The logic of the boomerang effect offers insight into how the constitutional constraint on government torture fails to protect Americans from abuses by their government.

TORTURE IN THE PHILIPPINES AND U.S. POLICING

As discussed previously, the U.S. occupation of the Philippines in the late 1800s served as the origin of the modern domestic surveillance state (Chapter 4) and played a critical role in the militarization of domestic police departments (Chapter 5). Likewise, the Philippine-American War is important in understanding torture in the United States. The occupation allowed for a wide range of experimentation in social-control techniques, since U.S. forces faced limited or no constraints on their activities.

The Philippine Constabulary engaged not only in wiretapping, intimidation, and other activities related to surveillance and militarized policing, but in torture as well. Such actions were not only permitted but also encouraged by those at the highest levels of the U.S. government and military. For example, in 1901 General J. M. Bell wrote that he planned on using his twenty-five hundred men "to destroy everything [we] find outside of towns. All able bodied men will be killed or captured. . . . These people [the Filipinos] need a thrashing to teach them some good common sense."[23]

Not a month later, General Bell issued Circular Order No. 3 to all American field commanders in the occupied territory, giving the "green light" to engage in whatever actions they deemed appropriate, up to and including torture.

Commanding officers are *urged and enjoined to use their discretion freely in adopting any or all measures of warfare* authorized by this order which will contribute, in their judgment, toward enforcing the policy or accomplishing the purpose above announced . . . Neutrality should not be tolerated. Every inhabitant . . . should either be an active friend or be classified as an enemy. . . . [A]rrest anyone believed to be guilty of giving aid or assistance to the insurrection in any way or of giving food or comfort to the enemies of the [U.S.] government, it is not necessary to wait for sufficient evidence to lead to conviction by a court. . . . *It will frequently be impossible to obtain any evidence against persons of influence as long as they are at liberty; but, once confined, evidence is easily obtainable.*[24]

Another American commander, General Jacob H. Smith, expressly ordered his men to murder Filipinos, including children, via particularly cruel methods if necessary. As he indicated in his orders to those under his command, "I want no prisoners. I wish you to kill and burn, the more you kill and burn the better it will please me. I want all the persons killed who are capable of bearing arms in actual hostilities against the United States."[25] When asked for a "limit of age" with regard to the order, Smith replied, "ten years of age." [26] When questioned regarding such a low age limit, he repeated his command.[27]

Subordinates quickly adopted the callous attitudes displayed by their superiors. Widespread abuse and torture ensued. One illustration of this torture is evident in a letter to Senator George Frisbie Hoar (R-MA) from Private Clarence Clowe. Clowe wrote that during his time in the Philippines he was

[L]iable to be called upon to go out and bind and gag helpless prisoners, to strike them in the face, to knock them down when so bound, to bear them away from wife and children, at their very door, who are shrieking pitifully the while, or kneeling and kissing the hands of our officers, imploring mercy from those who seem not to know what it is, and then, with a crowd of soldiers, hold our helpless victim head downward in a tub of water in his own yard, or bind him hand and foot, attaching ropes to head and feet, and then lowering him into the depths of a well of water until life is well-nigh choked out, and the bitterness of death is tasted, and our poor, gasping victims ask us for the poor boon of being finished off, in mercy to themselves. All these things have been done at one time or another by our men . . . generally in cases of trying to obtain information. . . . *Nor can it be said that there is any general repulsion on the part of the enlisted men to taking part in these doings. I regret to have to say that, on the contrary, the majority of soldiers take a keen delight in them, and rush with joy to the making of this latest development.*[28]

He asked to be discharged from the army, a "service that [was] outraging his conscience."[29]

Torture and other atrocities appeared to be not merely intermittent occurrences, but rather standard operating procedure.[30] The resulting public outcry over the torture scandal in the Philippines led to a formal Senate investigation. The Senate Committee on the Philippines, known informally as the Lodge Committee, released its report in 1902, discussing its findings regarding torture throughout the Philippines and in the concentration camps set up for Filipinos.

While it is known that torture occurred, the true extent of U.S. government activities is not. Those who testified before the Lodge Committee largely denied any wrongdoing, and investigations were either lacking in critical inquiry or never completed. According to historian Stuart Creighton Miller, calls for a committee to travel to the islands to speak to Filipino leaders were ignored. Further, he indicated that those compiling the committee report "[gleaned] from the record anything that remotely supported [the] conclusion that the war was one of the most humane ones in history and then [published] this deceitful cut-and-paste job as a separate senate document."[31] People soon forgot the Lodge Committee had even been formed, and any outcry against torture in the Philippines quickly faded from memory.[32]

One explanation for the dismissal of torture in the Philippines was the widespread view that there was a distinction between torture "over there" and torture at home, and a supposed difference between Americans and foreigners.[33] National newspapers sought to downplay or outright deny the torture that was identified by the Lodge Committee and others or presented the actions of the U.S. military as justifiable or "mild." In some cases, the Filipinos were blamed for the torture they endured at the hands of their American occupiers! One paper from the period captures these sentiments well. It states, "the natives [Filipinos] have, in some cases, moved our soldiers to transgress the line of gentleness desirable for ordinary warfare. . . . [T]he transgressions were very slight. And at the worst, they have been few."[34] Another stated that the army "has obeyed orders. It was sent to subdue the Filipinos. Having the devil to fight, [they] sometimes used fire." President Theodore Roosevelt echoed these attitudes, stating, "nobody was seriously damaged. . . . The Filipinos had inflicted incredible torture upon our own people."[35]

It would not be long before some of the most nefarious torture methods employed by U.S. soldiers in the Philippines would be seen again. Only this time the victims would not be the men, women, and children of the Philippines, but Americans.

THE "WATER CURE"

The end of the Philippine-American War brought a cadre of veterans back to the United States along with the skills they had acquired abroad. As discussed in Chapter 5, these veterans significantly influenced the evolution of America's police forces. August Vollmer, for example, incorporated military structure, technology, and techniques into the police departments of Berkeley and Los Angeles, California; worked as the head of national police organizations; and served as a consultant to a number of other police groups.[36] Others like Jesse Garwood, known for their brutal tactics in the Philippines, returned to the United States and established constabularies modeled after the one created in the islands.[37] Lieutenant Colonel Harry Bandholtz employed the psychological techniques he learned in the war against miners in West Virginia.[38] Major General Smedley Butler used his wartime training in the battle against alcohol during national Prohibition, leading his team on an estimated five thousand raids.[39]

It is within this context that one observes the connection between the use of torture in the Philippines and in the United States. We do not know which person, or group of people, was responsible for first introducing these techniques to the United States. However, we observe the appearance and use of torture techniques in the United States following the war. In fact, in the years after the U.S. conflict in the Philippines, people became increasingly concerned about the pervasive use of torture by domestic police forces.

In one case from 1930, an eighteen-year-old Ohio man was detained for twenty-six hours; threatened, screamed, and cursed at; deprived of food and water; beaten with fists and a rubber hose on his bare back and feet; and stripped naked. Legal expert Richard A. Leo stated, "[b]y the standards of the time, there was nothing unusual about the manner in which Cleveland detectives obtained a confession [from the suspect]. His interrogation was in many ways representative of the methods police generally used. . . . In fact, detectives frequently employed far more violent ways . . . and over even longer periods of time."[40]

Just as the use of torture in the Philippines caused a public outcry, so too did the mistreatment of suspects and prisoners in the United States. Media exposés, as well as court cases like *State v. Nagle*, in which confessions were thrown out and convictions overturned due to police torture, caused such a public disturbance that the federal government launched an investigation.[41] Unbeknownst to those outraged by torture at home, however, was the intimate connection between these law-enforcement tactics and the earlier conflict in the Pacific.

In 1931 President Herbert Hoover authorized the National Commission on Law Observance and Enforcement, which would come to be known as the Wickersham Commission after its chair, George Wickersham. The Report on Lawlessness of Law Enforcement, released by the Commission later that year, provided insight into the scope of torture and other questionable and criminal practices in U.S. police departments. It documented that many of the tactics used in the Philippine War were widely used in the United States, including stress positions, battery, psychological torture, and the water cure (described further on). The torture methods it discussed had become so common that police had given them a name—the "third degree." The report defined "third degree" as "the employment of methods which inflict suffering, physical or mental, upon a person in order to obtain information about a crime,"[42] a definition consistent with the modern notion of torture. By all accounts the use of the "third degree" became systematic and widespread throughout the United States by the 1920s. The Commission reported on its use in New York, Buffalo, Boston, Newark, Philadelphia, Cincinnati, Cleveland, Detroit, Chicago, Dallas, El Paso, Denver, Los Angeles, San Francisco, and Seattle.[43]

Techniques included "sweat box treatments," in which suspects were placed in a small cell next to a stove into which officers would throw materials to produce extreme heat and foul smells, prompting suspects to confess.[44] Other techniques included making suspects walk barefoot on an electrified carpet or sending electricity directly into detainees' spines.[45] The Wickersham report revealed not only that these tactics were widespread, but also that the police were essentially unconstrained in their treatment of suspects.[46]

Exactly how many of the individuals perpetrating these acts were veterans of the Philippine-American War is unknown. And while the link between veterans and the use of all of the torture methods identified in the report is unclear, some techniques appear to be direct imports from the conflict. Perhaps the clearest illustration of how the human capital forged by the war in the Philippines, and the torture it engendered abroad, came to be used in the United States is the aforementioned "water cure." The water cure was one of the most widely used and most feared methods of torture in the Philippines during the U.S. occupation. According to legal and international relations expert Richard J. Prevost, "[a] variety of punishments were employed by Americans on Filipinos. . . . Yet this particular technique [the water cure], garnered great interest in the press and in the Congress."[47]

The "cure," as described by Darius Rejali, a political scientist and expert on torture, falls under the broader torture category of "pumping," or forcibly filling the stomach and intestines with water.[48] In 1902 the New York Evening Post printed a description by a witness in the Philippines.

If the tortures I've mentioned are hellish, the water cure is plain hell. The native is thrown upon the ground, and, while his legs and arms are pinioned, his head is raised partially so as to make pouring in the water an easier matter. An attempt to keep the mouth closed is of no avail: a bamboo stick or a pinching of the nose will produce the desired effect. And now the water is poured in, and swallow the poor wretch must or strangle. A gallon of water is much, but it is followed by a second and a third. By this time the victim is certain his body is about to burst. But he is mistaken, for a fourth and even fifth gallon are poured in. By this time the body becomes an object frightful to contemplate; and the pain, agony. While in this condition, speech is impossible; and so the water must be squeezed out of him. This is sometimes allowed to occur naturally, but is sometimes hastened by pressure and "sometimes we jump on them to get it out quick." . . . How often is it [the cure] given? . . . [A] sergeant told me he has seen it taken by two and three hundred, by as many as twenty sometimes in a day. . . . The unconcerned way in which the soldiers . . . speak of the water cure, the exulting way in most cases, is the saddest phase of all.[49]

The use of the water cure was widespread in the Philippines. In testimony before the Lodge Committee, for example, it was alleged that General Frederick Funston had said he had "helped to administer the cure to one hundred sixty natives, all but twenty-six of whom died."[50] And this is just a single testimony regarding the use of the technique.

After the war, domestic police forces in America began to use the water cure with some frequency in the interrogation of suspects. The Wickersham Commission included the cure in its 1931 report, in addition to electrocution, beatings, and other torture techniques, the use of which began in the early 1900s.[51] The Wickersham Commission was not the only written documentation acknowledging the use of the water cure domestically. In the case of *Fisher v. State*, the Supreme Court of Mississippi found that law enforcement officials had obtained a confession via use of the water cure, which it stated was "a species of torture well known to the bench and bar of the country."[52] Writing in 1918, more than a decade before the Wickersham Commission received its charge, political activist and pacifist Norman Thomas discussed the use of the water cure on U.S. citizens who identified as conscientious objectors during World War I.

[M]en were bayoneted, clubbed with guns, beaten and robbed . . . and, above all, tortured by various forms of water cure. . . . Mr. K—was forced to remain seated while cold water was poured on to his head. This process was continued until he fainted. Mr. H—was bound with his arms above his head in a manner so painful that he felt his arms were being broken, and the pain caused him to scream repeatedly. While in this position the hose was played first on one side and then on the other.[53]

Further, by the time the National Commission on Law Observance and Enforcement's report on "third degree" methods, including the water cure, was published in 1931, there is evidence that the use of such tactics was well established in major urban areas. For example, the report bluntly stated that "[t]he third degree is widely employed in New York City."[54] Moreover, in a letter published in 1929, former district attorney R. H. Elder indicated that the third degree had become standard operating procedure throughout New York City. He wrote, "[t]he third degree has now become established and recognized practice in the police department of the city of New York. Every police station in the city is equipped with the instruments to administer the torture incident to that process."[55]

As this suggests, established torture techniques and the "us versus them" mentality that rationalized torture abroad was also present in the U.S. criminal justice system. Reflecting on his treatment of suspects between 1900 and 1925, New York City police officer and detective Cornelius Willemse stated, "I never hesitated." He continued, "I've forced confessions—with fist, black-jack, and hose. . . . The hardened criminal knows only one language and laughs at the detective who tries any other. . . . Remember that this is war after all!"[56] Just like intervention abroad, the "war" at home required methods of social control, and the Philippines provided an excellent laboratory for honing such methods.

A RENEWED VOW AGAINST TORTURE

The problems revealed in the Wickersham report, issued in the early years of the Great Depression, were lost to concerns over unemployment and the economy. Torture would not receive much public attention for the next decade.

The conclusion of World War II, however, brought renewed international attention to torture with the collapse of the Nazi regime and the liberation of the concentration camps. A variety of domestic and international laws sought to ban torture in future conflicts. The U.S. government quickly adopted the Nuremberg Code, an international code that bans human experimentation and requires informed consent for all studies involving human beings, as a complement to its existing restrictions on torture (the Eighth Amendment) and human experimentation (policies adopted by the military, the Atomic Energy Commission, and so on). In 1948 the UN adopted the Universal Declaration of Human Rights, which included, among other things, a provision banning the use of torture or inhumane treatment. The declaration was a product of a drafting committee famously chaired by former first lady Eleanor Roosevelt. Forty-eight of fifty-eight member states, including the United States, voted for the Declaration; none voted against it (eight members abstained and two cast no vote).[57] In addition to this international effort, state laws were also passed. For example, in 1946 the Georgia legislature outlawed the use of corporal punishment in prisons, including the use of "all shackles, manacles, picks, leg-irons, and chains."[58] Whipping was also forbidden.[59]

But the "Soviet threat" and the Cold War that came with it provided a new opportunity and justification for the development and use of torture by the government. Fearful of bad publicity and public outrage like that seen after the use of the water cure in the early 1900s and the use of torture by the Nazis in concentration camps, U.S. officials focused on developing "clean" torture techniques. In other words, they sought to create and refine torture methods that leave few or no physical marks but nonetheless inflict immense physical, psychological, or emotional pain.[60] The Cold War and the war in Vietnam would offer ample chances for the U.S. government to develop these techniques abroad. Just as important for our purposes, however, the Cold War, the War on Drugs, and the War on Terror would provide the opportunity for such techniques to be used domestically.

THE CIA, TORTURE, AND MIND CONTROL

When Allied Forces landed on the beaches of Normandy in France on June 6, 1944, they sought to finally put an end to the fighting in the European and Pacific theaters. Having observed the capabilities and technologies used by the Nazis, the U.S. government sought to shorten the war by learning what knowledge the Nazis possessed. In an effort to uncover this information, the U.S. government sent some ten thousand intelligence personnel into Europe directly behind the D-Day troops as part of Operation Overcast. While Overcast was initially implemented for the sole purpose of interviewing Nazi scientists to understand the technological capabilities of the Third Reich, the mission quickly morphed into one of recruiting German scientists to work for the U.S. government. The reason behind such recruiting was simple—fear of the Soviet Union. These scientists, and those who worked with them, facilitated the importation of torture techniques developed abroad into the United States.

The possibility of war with the Soviet Union empowered the federal government to expand its portfolio of operations. Throughout the Cold War government programs expanded, resources flowed to those bureaus engaged in counter-Soviet operations, and officials expanded their control over the lives of everyday U.S. citizens. Schoolteacher John Driscoll, recalling this period, stated, "It seems surreal now. Every summer when I heard heat lightning over the city and the sky would light up, I was convinced it was all over. My whole childhood was built on the notion the Soviets were the real threat."[61] For decades, the U.S. government implemented programs to teach school children to "duck and cover" to supposedly protect themselves from Soviet air raids. School systems across the country issued identification bracelets or dog tags to students—with the idea that they would help identify lost or dead children if the Russians were to attack. New York City spent $2.5 million in 2003 dollars on such a project.[62] Thousands of Americans, with prompting from the Federal Civil Defense Administration, installed bomb shelters in their backyards.[63]

The possibility of communists and communist sympathizers living in the United States further cultivated anxiety among the populace and opened the door for the government to expand its activities domestically. Moreover, Americans actively encouraged and accepted government encroachments on their freedoms in the name of combating communism. In fact, these sentiments were present even before the Cold War started. A Gallup poll from June 1938, for example, found that 97 percent of Americans agreed with the freedom of speech promised by the First Amendment. However, only 38 percent believed in this right "to the extent of allowing communists to hold meetings and express their views."[64] A poll from April 1941 found that 64 percent of Americans believed that "repressive measures" should be used against communists living in the United States. Only 8 percent favored doing nothing. At the start of the Cold War, in June 1946, 16 percent of those surveyed stated they wished to "curb or make [communists in the U.S.] inactive."[65] More than a third of respondents, however, took a much stronger stance. Thirty-six percent said communists in the United States should be immediately killed or imprisoned.[66]

There was also a great deal of fear regarding the spread of communism outside of the USSR. A 1943 survey conducted by the Roper Organization found that 41 percent of Americans believed that Russia would try to spread communism throughout Europe after the war's end.[67] In a 1950 survey, the National Opinion Research Center found that a plurality of Americans thought the U.S. government should curtail such efforts. When asked, "how important do you think it is for the United States to try to stop the spread of communism in the world," 83 percent stated such efforts were "very important."[68] Only 4 percent thought such activities were "not important."[69]

This "Soviet threat" not only engendered fear and created room for the expansion of government activity, it also provided an opportunity for the development and importation of "battle tested" human capital in the United States. Specifically, President Truman looked to bring in those with skills that could be helpful in defeating the Soviets in a possible war. As a result, Truman approved Project Paperclip (also called Operation Paperclip) in September 1946. A revamping of the earlier Operation Overcast, Project Paperclip would bring over a thousand German scientists to the United States.[70] These scientists had expertise in a variety of areas, including aeronautics, electronics, medicine, rocketry, and torture.

As noted in Chapter 2, human capital associated with state-produced social control can be imported from outside the country. By importing German specialists through Project Paperclip, the U.S. government sought to further develop and refine methods and techniques of social control under the claim that such human capital was essential in combating the Soviets and preventing the USSR from gaining access to similar information. In fact, denying the scientists to the Soviets became the primary justification for the program. According to historian John Gimbel, denying the scientists to the Soviets "was apparently the only argument for bringing Germans to the United States that made an impression in the State Department."[71]

With this justification, through programs like Project Paperclip and others (such as Project National Interest), the U.S. government integrated scientists, many of whom had been ardent Nazis, into the American military, intelligence, and academic communities. Taken together, the fear of communism within the United States and the importation of individuals who had, among other things, specialized in creating torture techniques created an atmosphere conducive to a variety of abuses against Americans.

It is well known that the Nazi scientists brought into the United States would prove integral to the American government's research in rocketry and chemical and biological warfare. What is less known, however, is that so too would their skills be important to the development of torture techniques, particularly "clean torture," or techniques that leave little to no physical marks. The Nazis had experimented with their own methods of psychological torture throughout the war. While the Dachau concentration camp would become infamous for its experiments with altitude and salt water, another group of Nazis at the camp engaged in an altogether different form of human experimentation—psychological torture.

Nazis connected to both the Gestapo and the SS, for example, dosed unknowing prisoners with mescaline, a psychedelic alkaloid created from the extract of the peyote cactus, which is known for producing hallucinations and other effects similar to those of LSD. The purpose of these experiments was to see if unwilling subjects could be brought under the control of their captors—that is, "to eliminate the will of the person examined."[72] Doctors dosed at least thirty prisoners with the drug, but determined it was "impossible to impose one's will on another person . . . even when the strongest doses of mescaline had been given."[73]

As the Dachau scientists were conducting their experiments, the U.S. government, through the Office of Strategic Services (OSS), was assembling a group of scientists in the United States to undertake similar research. They sought to develop a "truth drug" and other psychological techniques for the purposes of extracting information, confessions, and other information from U.S. enemies. According to American authors Martin Lee and Bruce Shlain, "[t]he OSS chief pressed his associates to come up with a substance that could break down the psychological defenses of enemy spies and POWs, thereby causing uninhibited disclosure of classified information. Such a drug would also be useful for screening OSS personnel in order to identify German sympathizers, double agents, and potential misfits."[74] The OSS examined a variety of drugs, including alcohol, barbiturates, and marijuana.

Following World War II the CIA took over the project and continued the search for a truth drug. Under Project Paperclip and its affiliated projects, the government would employ not only numerous American scientists but also German scientists who had conducted the mescaline and other experiments at Dachau. To give but one example, under Project Paperclip the government recruited Dr. Kurt Plötner, who had overseen the Dachau mescaline experiments, for the sole purpose of continuing his research in the United States to combat the Soviet threat.[75]

The CIA initiated Project CHATTER in 1947 to conduct a variety of psychological experiments aimed at mind control and information extraction. Although these efforts were unsuccessful, the CIA was undeterred in its quest for mind control as a means of social control. Its efforts only intensified in the early 1950s, following the show trial of Cardinal József Mindszenty, a staunch critic of communism and supporter of religious freedom in Hungary.[76] In 1948 the cardinal had been arrested and accused of treason and conspiracy by the communist government. Mindszenty would confess to the false charges, leading many in the CIA, including the chief of the agency's medical staff, to believe he had been subjected to some new form of torture, which agents called the "Mindszenty Effect."[77] On this basis, the medical chief suggested the agency should further examine mind control and other forms of psychological torture as means of acquiring information. "There is ample evidence," he wrote, "that the communists were using drugs, physical duress, electric shock, and possibly hypnosis against their enemies. . . . *We are forced by this mounting evidence to assume a more aggressive role in the development of these techniques.*"[78] With the Mindszenty trial fresh on the minds of CIA officials, Project

CHATTER gave way to Project BLUEBIRD in 1950 and then to Project ARTICHOKE in 1951. Both projects continued the search for a truth drug and expanded to include studies of hypnosis and addiction and the use of natural and synthetic substances to produce amnesia.

By 1953, U.S. government agencies were more interested than ever in finding their elusive mind-control drug and uncovering new ways to gain some sort of advantage over their Soviet rivals. In its quest for mind control the CIA began testing a variety of chemicals on unwilling and unknowing U.S. citizens. Under Project MKUltra the CIA funded and conducted a wide array of studies and experiments with the goal of controlling minds and enhancing social-control capabilities. More than 140 projects were set up, including experiments with hypnosis, LSD, marijuana, alcohol, sleep and sensory deprivation, carbon dioxide, and hallucinogenic mushrooms.[79] Projects also sought to understand the effects of stress on the brain, ways to control animal brains remotely, and extrasensory perception (ESP).[80]

These projects involved myriad private and public institutions, including a variety of hospitals and schools. Princeton, Stanford, the University of Denver, the University of Minnesota, Emory University, the University of Illinois, Montana State College, the University of Richmond, the University of Oklahoma, Cornell, and the University of Delaware were all sites of MKUltra projects. George Washington University, the University of Maryland, Indiana University, Rutgers, the University of Wisconsin, Harvard, Johns Hopkins, MIT, Ohio State, Penn State, the University of Houston, Columbia, Texas Christian University, the University of Florida, and the University of Texas at Austin were also home to various tests.[81] Researchers at each of these institutions received significant sums of money from the government to conduct their research projects. The exact nature of many of these projects remains unknown, however, because most were and remain classified "Top Secret."

In some of the first experiments with mind control, CIA agents slipped drugs to one another. For example, CIA personnel were known to put doses of LSD into their officemate's morning coffee. While subjects were unaware of the exact time of the dosing, they generally understood that being drugged was part of the job description. Many of the first to be dosed were members of the Manhattan Project, which developed the government's nuclear capabilities.

The repercussions from these experiments were quickly evident. While on a joint CIA/Army Special Ops retreat at Fort Detrick, for example, CIA personnel slipped LSD into the drinks of the attendees. Twenty minutes later those responsible asked if anyone felt any change, explaining they had been dosed. While most attendees felt no long-lasting effects (accounts state that the men were boisterous and chatty the rest of the evening), one recipient, Dr. Frank Olson, experienced a "bad trip."[82] Unfortunately for Olson, the LSD triggered a long-lasting psychosis. Realizing he was apparently having an adverse reaction, CIA personnel took him to a doctor in New York City. The doctor had no training in psychology, but was an allergist with an interest in LSD and had been receiving money from the CIA to study its effects. Returning to the retreat, Olson, convinced he had gone insane and had been made a laughingstock, jumped out of a hotel window, killing himself.[83]

In another instance a CIA employee experienced a frightening episode after being dosed with LSD. According to one of his colleagues, "he couldn't pull himself together."[84] The agent ran away from his work building and out into the streets of Washington, D.C., where, according to his colleague, "every automobile that came by was a terrible monster with fantastic eyes, out to get him personally. Each time a car passed he would huddle down against a parapet, terribly frightened."[85]

These events eventually led the CIA to question its experimentation with LSD and other hallucinogenic drugs on one another. When a plan was discovered to lace the punch with LSD at the 1954 CIA Christmas party, a security memo was issued, stating that the drug could "produce serious insanity for periods of 8 to 18 hours and possibly longer. . . . [We do] not recommend testing [LSD] in the Christmas punch bowls usually present at the Christmas office parties."[86]

The CIA soon ceased testing drugs on their own personnel and instead began to experiment on the American public. In addition to enlisting a small army of university scientists, as noted, the government continued its own experiments. In one such case, the CIA set up test sites in New York and San Francisco to extract information on the effects of LSD on human behavior from unknowing and unwilling subjects. In Operation Midnight Climax, the agency recruited area prostitutes to pick up clients in area bars and slip them doses of LSD. The women would bring the men back to one of the test sites, a converted hotel room, where CIA personnel would record the drugged men. The men would then leave without receiving follow-up care or even knowing they had been drugged. If one of the men ever figured out what had happened, he would likely be too embarrassed to do anything about it. Even if he told someone, such a fantastic tale would hardly be believed. Either way, the CIA could conduct its experiments in secrecy with little fear of repercussion.[87]

The CIA viewed these experiments as having a broader application, namely, covert warfare. According to Martin Lee and Bruce Shlain,

[T]op-level military brass waxed enthusiastic over the prospect of a new kind of chemical weapon that would revolutionize combat. They imagined aircraft swooping over enemy territory releasing clouds of "madness gas" that would disorient people and dissolve their will to resist. . . . Suppose [the government] found a way to spike the city's water supply or to release a hallucinogen in aerosol form. For twelve to twenty-four hours all the people in the vicinity would be hopelessly giddy, vertiginous, spaced out. Those under the spell of the madness gas would be incapable of raising a whimper of protest while American troops established themselves. . . . Victory would be a foregone conclusion.[88]

Other examples of mind-control experiments are plentiful. Prisoners in Lexington, Kentucky, for example, were also used to test the effects of LSD. Primarily using drug addicts, Dr. Harris Isbell would offer convicts their drug of choice in exchange for their willingness to be used as human guinea pigs. Instead of reforming prisoners and assisting them in getting off drugs, the tests effectively reinforced their addictions and repeatedly exposed them to highly addictive hallucinogens. Over eight hundred compounds were sent to the prison for testing.[89] One inmate was given LSD for seventy-seven straight days.[90] In other cases unsuspecting civilians were dosed with LSD and other mind-altering drugs while relaxing at beaches or enjoying cocktails at city bars.[91]

The total number of experiments conducted is unknown, but clearly enough were done to understand the effects of LSD and other substances.

According to a memo from former CIA executive director Lyman B. Kirk-patrick, "[t]he effectiveness of the substances on individuals at all social levels, high and low, native Americans and foreign is of great significance, and testing has been performed on a variety of individuals within these categories."[92]

Psychological torture was not exclusive to drugs, however. Other CIA projects undertaken with the goal of enhancing social control in the Cold War period explored techniques such as sensory deprivation to force subjects to confess and divulge information. For example, U.S. officials approached scientist John Lilly about his neurophysiology research, in-cluding a sensory deprivation tank in which subjects were deprived of all stimulation. Government agents wanted to know, "[C]ould involuntary subjects be placed in the tank [of water] and broken down to the point where their belief systems or personalities could be altered?"[93] Lilly tested his creation on himself and his collaborators, placing themselves in a tank of body-temperature water, wearing masks that allowed for oxygen flow but eliminated all light and sound. Once he realized his research was going to be used to manipulate potentially innocent people, Lilly promptly re-signed, refusing to compromise his personal ethics.[94] While Lilly refused to participate, others who did not share his convictions undertook similar research programs.

At the National Institutes of Health in Bethesda, Maryland, for example, the CIA's ARTICHOKE program funded Maitland Baldwin's research on sensory deprivation. Unlike Lilly, however, Baldwin would experiment on unknowing individuals. Placing subjects in a box, Baldwin would cover their eyes, muffle noise or expose them to white noise, prevent movement and touch, and preclude exposure to any external smells.[95] During one ex-periment Baldwin put an army volunteer into what would become known as "Baldwin's Box" and refused to release him for more than forty hours, a direct violation of the Nuremberg Code and other mandates. According to Baldwin, "after an hour of crying loudly and sobbing in a heartbreak-ing fashion," the man kicked his way out of the box. This led Baldwin to declare that his box "could break any man, no matter how intelligent or strong-willed."[96] He agreed to continue his tests if the CIA "could provide the cover," since he felt the box would "almost certainly cause irreparable [psychological] damage" to those subjected to it.[97] In discussing the effects of such methods of sensory deprivation created by Lilly, Baldwin, and others, one 1966 study found that "only one subject lasted ten hours."[98] On the basis of this research, another researcher concluded that the tanks were "the most severe situation used" in sensory-deprivation studies.[99]

The extent of the search for a "truth drug" and other means to acquire information from unwilling individuals will likely never be known. Following the Watergate scandal, CIA director Richard Helms ordered that the files related to MKUltra be destroyed. The lack of information regarding the magnitude of human experimentation on private persons by the U.S. government has long been a source of frustration for those interested in understanding the programs and preventing similar events from occurring in the future. In joint hearings on MKUltra before the Select Committee on Intelligence and Subcommittee on Health and Scientific Research of the Committee on Human Resources in 1977, no comprehensive data were offered. However, hearing transcripts do definitively declare that experiments on citizens took place over a span of at least twenty years.

Specifically, the transcripts state that the "CIA engaged in a program of human experimentation from the 1950s into the 1970s."[100] At another point the report indicates that "[b]eginning in 1967, the CIA's Office of Research and Development and the Edgewood Arsenal undertook a Joint program for research in influencing human behavior with drugs, which included human experimentation (including on prison inmates)."[101] The late Senator Ted Kennedy expressed his frustration at the lack of transparency from officials involved in the experiments, declaring,

[T]he Senate Health Subcommittee heard chilling testimony about the human experimentation activities of the Central Intelligence Agency. The Deputy Director of the CIA revealed that over 30 universities and institutions were involved in an "extensive testing and experimentation program" which included covert drug tests on unwitting citizens "at all social levels" . . . Several of these tests involved the administration of LSD to "unwitting subjects in social situations."[102]

He continued,

Other experiments were equally offensive. For example, heroin addicts were enticed into participating in LSD experiments in order to get a reward—heroin. . . . Perhaps most disturbing of all was the fact that the extent of experimentation on human subjects was unknown. . . . In spite of persistent inquiries by both the Health Subcommittee and the Intelligence Committee, no additional records or information were forthcoming. And no one—no single individual—could be found who remembered the details, not the Director of the CIA, who ordered the documents destroyed, not the official responsible for the program, nor any of his associates.[103]

While detailed information is, unfortunately, limited, what is clear is that the U.S. government, in preparing for a possible conflict with the Soviet Union, imported individuals who had developed the techniques and mind-sets necessary to engage in torture. Moreover, these traits were fostered in others domestically, as experiments were authorized and conducted throughout the country. As a result, the government subjected private persons, including U.S. citizens, to what undeniably amounts to torture in the name of protecting those very people from the potential threat posed by the Soviets.

VIETNAM AND PROJECT PHOENIX

While preparations for a war with the Soviet Union and the importation of Nazi scientists provided an avenue for the creation and expansion of torture techniques in the United States, the war in Vietnam also provided a unique testing ground for U.S. forces to hone both traditional and clean torture techniques that would eventually boomerang to the United States. Like the war in the Philippines some eighty years earlier, the constraints on U.S. forces in Vietnam were lax at best. In fact, until March 1966 commanders in Vietnam were not obligated to report war crimes, including torture, perpetrated by U.S. forces and their allies.[104] Even then the rules on reporting torture and other crimes were grossly deficient. Not until 1970 were the rules amended when the military realized that the commanders obligated to submit reports on torture and other abuses might be personally involved. Still, there was no process for independent investigation of torture allegations and there were no significant penalties for failing to report abuse.[105]

The torture techniques of the U.S. government's South Vietnamese ally were the traditional brutal methods of torment. South Vietnamese torturers "beat and whipped prisoners to death. . . . Guards crushed fingers and toes, removed teeth with pincers, stuck pins under nails and into knees, and burned flesh with lamps and cigarettes. They forced chopsticks, Coke bottles, and eels up orifices, and they exposed prisoners to ants. They suspended prisoners by the toes, testicles, or the hands."[106] U.S. forces employed similar techniques along with clean torture, such as electrocution, against the North Vietnamese.

In his report on events leading to the My Lai Massacre, in which U.S. soldiers murdered more than five hundred Vietnamese civilians, gang-raped women, and carved "C Company" into their victims' corpses, Lieutenant General W. R. Peers detailed the use of torture by U.S. forces.[107] Specifically, he noted the use of electric shock to obtain information, beatings, and the infliction of knife wounds on the backs of the hands, after which detainees were "taken to the beach where salt was rubbed in the fresh wounds."[108]

Though poorly documented, at least 141 cases of torture perpetrated by U.S. forces against Vietnamese civilians or detainees with fists, sticks, water, or electric shock have been corroborated.[109] One favorite interrogation technique used by U.S. forces involved electrocution with modified field telephones. It left no long-term physical marks but inflicted excruciating pain.

In his testimony before the Bertrand Russell Vietnam War Crimes Tribunal, the POW interrogator Peter Martinsen described the use of the field telephone and other torture methods during interrogations, and how his time in Vietnam allowed him to experiment with new forms of torture, although this violated international law.

The lieutenant had an Army field telephone, which runs on batteries and generator. You crank it and it gives a nasty shock, a very nasty shock, quite painful. The interrogation commenced with the prisoner being tortured by field telephone. The telephones were first placed on his hands and then . . . on his sexual organs.

My interpreter was beating this man. . . . He beat the man on the kneecaps and the shoulder blades. . . . This didn't yield much information. . . . I decided to try out a new idea. I had the man dig his own grave with a gun at his head, and he dug his grave until I counted off the minutes he had to live. I counted them off in Vietnamese so that he knew I wasn't kidding. He broke down and cried. This is the absolute power the interrogator has. . . . I described what kind of death he was going to have. . . . After he was "broken," to keep him broken I just kept reminding him, in Vietnamese, that he was not yet dead.

I have read the 1949 Geneva Convention on the treatment of prisoners of war. Coercion is quite illegal. It [my conduct] was a war crime.

Electric torture was very common. . . . Beatings were extremely common. An interrogator came to me and said, "My hands are getting tired from hitting this man in the mouth." It [torture] was something that occurred in almost every interrogation and it was clearly condoned by the officers. The commanding officer of the unit stated for the record that there must be no torturing. . . . However, he allowed it to continue and watched it. He knew of it.[110]

Perhaps the most egregious torture in Vietnam took place under the covert CIA-initiated Phoenix Program (also known as Project Phoenix or the Phoenix Project), which was designed to find, capture, interrogate, and kill Vietnamese citizens sympathetic to the Viet Cong (VC).[111] The program launched in 1965, the same year the United States agreed to abide by the Geneva Convention in Vietnam, including the provision protecting captured civilians from threats, violence, coercion, murder, torture, and other mutilations.

Under Phoenix Program operations, Provincial Reconnaissance Units would capture civilians believed to be affiliated with the Viet Cong Civilian Infrastructure and move them to interrogation centers, where CIA personnel and their Vietnamese counterparts would torture them to obtain information. Tactics used in the Phoenix Program were notoriously brutal, intending to inflict both physical and psychological damage. According to Elton Manzione, a former Navy SEAL who worked in the Phoenix Program, murder was often used to torture other detainees.

We wrapped det [detonator] cord around necks and wired them to the detonator box. And basically what it did was blow their heads off. . . . The general idea was to waste [murder] the first two [prisoners]. They planned the snatches that way. Pick up this guy because we're pretty sure he's VC cadre—the other two guys just run errands for him. Or maybe they're nobody. . . . But bring in two. Put them in a row. By the time you get to your man, he's talking so fast you got to pop the weasel just to shut him up. I guess you could say we wrote the book on torture.[112]

By 1966, forty-four interrogation centers, one in every province in South Vietnam, were operating under Project Phoenix.[113] A variety of torture techniques were used, many of them clean, including electro-torture, sexual abuse, sensory deprivation, and sustained stress positions. John Patrick Muldoon, the first director of the Phoenix Program's Province Intelligence Coordinating Committees, noted that the cleaner techniques had to be taught to the soldiers working in the centers: "[The interrogators were using] the old French methods [of physical torture]. . . . All this had to be stopped. . . . [T]hey had to be retaught with more sophisticated techniques."[114]

The techniques developed and used during the Vietnam War under the Phoenix Program would not remain in Southeast Asia. Instead, per the boomerang effect, they would be used against Americans by their own government.

CHICAGO, JON BURGE, AND THE "VIETNAM SPECIAL"

Just as the end of the war in the Philippines brought soldiers home to local police forces, so too did the end of the Vietnam War bring an influx of military personnel into state and local law enforcement. Census data indicates that while some 38 percent of the total U.S. population in 1968 were classified as veterans, 66 percent of law enforcement officers held veteran status.[115] These veterans brought the techniques and methods of social control they learned abroad back home, with some actively putting it to use. Perhaps the most well-known and disturbing example is Jon Burge. Burge, a Chicago native, had enlisted in the Army Reserves in 1966 and later volunteered for two tours of duty in Vietnam with the ultimate goal of returning to Chicago and working for the Chicago Police Department (CPD).[116] He was assigned to the Ninth Military Police Company, which was responsible for a variety of duties, including processing, transporting, and guarding prisoners in Dong Tam, one of the many POW holding centers operated under the Phoenix Program.[117] Members of Burge's company would later confirm that they were present during interrogations and sometimes stood guard as "interviews" were conducted.[118]

According to John Conroy, a Chicago journalist and author, Burge claimed he never guarded prisoners and did not know where they were interrogated. However, according to Burge's company commander, Edwin Freeman, the interrogation rooms of the Dong Tam compound were a mere twenty steps from Burge's command post. Members of the unit stated they knew of and participated in the torture of prisoners. Sergeant D. J. Lewis, for example, stated that interrogations using electro-torture, often via field telephones, were "not uncommon."[119] Dennis Carstens, also with the Ninth MPs, said that it was standard for MPs to attend interrogations. "We could pretty much do anything as long as we didn't leave scars on people," he said.[120]

Burge returned from Vietnam and became a police officer with the CPD in 1970. Just a little more than a year after joining the force, he was assigned to a particular part of the city, "Area 2," and promoted to detective. It was not long after his promotion that torture became common practice in Area 2. Suspects taken into custody were frequently beaten and subjected to other abuses that constituted torture. In discussing Burge and his unit, G. Flint Taylor, a lawyer who has represented survivors of police torture in Chicago, stated, "Burge and his midnight crew escalated their brutality, employing torture tactics Burge had most likely learned from his fellow soldiers in Vietnam."[121] One of the most widely cited methods was the use of electric shock via a cattle prod, field telephone, or what came to be known as the "third device," an instrument plugged into an electrical outlet.[122]

Burge and his colleagues subjected at least 110 African American men to torture, leading to false confessions and wrongful convictions. Suspects would often have an electronic device, which their torturers called the "nigger box," attached to their genitals, hands, and other body parts. Some were beaten with ashtrays, flashlights, phone books, and rubber hoses. Others were sexually assaulted, having their genitals kicked, stepped on, and electrocuted. Some suspects were deprived of food and water, stripped naked, held in stress positions, and denied sleep. Victims were "bagged," in which a bag is placed over the head to disorient and create feelings of suffocation. Some were also subjected to mock executions; this included simulated Russian roulette, having nooses placed around their necks, guns being put in their mouths, and being dangled out of open windows by their captors.[123]

The connections between the torture in Chicago throughout the Burge era and in Vietnam are clear. The use of the field telephone and other methods of electric torture were hallmarks of Vietnam atrocities. As if the association among Vietnam, Burge, and the Chicago cases was not readily apparent, one of Burge's colleagues leaves little room for doubt. In a sworn statement Walter Young, a thirty-five-year veteran of the CPD, testified that torture had indeed occurred. More important, he stated he heard Burge and other officers refer to torture as the "Vietnam Special" or "Vietnamese Treatment."[124]

In 1989 one of Burge's victims filed a civil suit claiming Burge and his men had tortured him. Burge won the case, but the verdict led to increased scrutiny of the CPD. An investigation conducted by the Office of Professional Standards produced the Goldston Report, which found that under Burge's command "abuse did occur and that it was systematic. The time span . . . covers more than ten years. The type of abuse described was not limited to the usual beating, but went into such esoteric areas as psychological techniques and planned torture."[125]

In subsequent court proceedings Burge invoked his Fifth Amendment right against self-incrimination, but was ultimately charged with two counts of obstruction of justice and one count of perjury. He was convicted in 2010, but sentenced to only four-and-a-half years in prison out of a possible forty. He was released in 2015.[126] The city of Chicago subsequently set aside $5.5 million in reparations for Burge's victims.[127] He was never convicted of crimes against the men he allegedly tortured, since the statute of limitations prevented prosecutors from filing charges.

While the total number of people tortured by Jon Burge and the CPD is unknown, abuse clearly occurred and not in one-off, isolated incidents. Further, there is good reason to believe that this torture on U.S. soil was connected to Burge's experiences in Vietnam. Burge developed the attitudes and human capital necessary to engage in "clean" torture while abroad. When he returned home, he brought these skills with him and implemented them while in his new position in the CPD, allowing the torture that took place in Vietnam to boomerang to the United States.

TORTURE TODAY AND TOMORROW

The interest in torture and state-produced social control developed under Project Paperclip and affiliate programs unfortunately remains relevant, particularly the connection between unethical (possibly illegal) government operations and private organizations. A recent 542-page report, for example, revealed that the largest professional organization of psychologists, the American Psychological Association (APA), has worked closely with the CIA on its torture program in the War on Terror.[128] The report found that some of the APA's senior officials, including its ethics director, Stephen Behnke, tried to "curry favor with Pentagon officials by seeking to keep the association's ethics policies in line with the Defense Department's interrogation policies, while several prominent outside psychologists took actions that aided the CIA's interrogation program and helped protect it from growing dissent."[129] Two former APA presidents served on the CIA advisory committee. One held an ownership stake in a consulting firm founded by the individuals who oversaw the CIA interrogation program.[130]

There are other recent examples of torture in the United States. In early 2015, reports emerged of an off-the-books location, or "black site," in Chicago known as Homan Square, in which police were accused of holding and possibly torturing people. People claim they were held in stress positions, sexually assaulted, and held incommunicado without access to legal representation. In discussing the Homan Square allegations, Chicago lawyer G. Flint Taylor stated that these allegations of torture are only the latest. He said, "[o]ver the last 25 years, we have repeatedly brought the justice department and the US attorney powerful evidence of systemic police torture . . . and a myriad of other patterns of outrageous police conduct."[131] Chicago isn't the only city where police have been accused of torture. In August 2015 the *New York Times* reported that sixty inmates at the Clinton Correctional Facility in New York had lodged complaints of abuse against their prison guards. Following the prison break of two inmates, it's alleged that guards tortured other prisoners with the goal of extracting information about the escapees. At least one prisoner said officers placed a bag over his head and threatened him with waterboarding.[132]

Although these cases are still unfolding, we may note certain similarities between the Burge case and current allegations of torture in the U.S. prison system. Just as Burge utilized the clean torture techniques observed and practiced in Vietnam, it is possible that veterans of recent conflicts in the transnational War on Terror may likewise import techniques developed and honed abroad. In the reports on the Chicago black site, for example, there were clear similarities between the methods used in the facility and those discussed in the Senate report on torture conducted by the U.S. military abroad.[133]

The similarity between techniques makes sense when one considers the influx of former military personnel into the criminal justice system. As noted in Chapter 5, many veterans of the wars in Iraq and Afghanistan have found their way into state and local police departments, contributing to the militarization of U.S. domestic police. In a similar way, veterans are finding a variety of employment opportunities working within prisons as guards and in other capacities. In some cases, hiring veterans is a stated priority.

For instance, the Florida Department of Corrections hired more than 270 veterans between July 1 and November 10, 2015.[134] The Pennsylvania Department of Corrections gives preference to former military applicants who have been on active duty.[135] In 2015 the Virginia Department of Corrections (VDOC) hired more than 100 veterans as part of the Virginia Values Veterans Program, and hoped to hire 100 more within six months. As of November 2015 approximately 13 percent of the VDOC's 11,500 employees were veterans.[136] This is representative of overall trends in law enforcement. The percentage of veterans in law enforcement has declined, along with the overall number of veterans in the United States. (In 1968, approximately 38 percent of the population were veterans. By 2016, this number had fallen to 7 percent.) However, veterans still constitute a significant portion of law enforcement officers. As of 2016, some 20 percent of all law enforcement officers had prior military service.[137]

The connection between the government's use of torture abroad and its subsequent use at home is only beginning to be fully recognized and appreciated. In discussing the recent claims at the Clinton facility, for example, Reverend Ron Stief, executive director of the National Religious Campaign Against Torture, stated, "[f]aith and human rights leaders who worked to stop the CIA's torture program have long feared its corroding influence on our civilian authorities. These events [at the Clinton Correctional Facility in New York] prove that we must fight the torture of Americans here at home just as we have fought the use of torture abroad."[138] Perhaps unbeknownst to Stief and his colleagues, however, is that their fear is not only well founded but also a long-standing reality.

It is important to note that, unlike surveillance (Chapter 4) and police militarization (Chapter 5), the use of torture within the United States does not appear to have affected the general American population en masse. While the anti-Soviet programs associated with MKUltra inflicted real physical and psychological damage on a range of private U.S. persons, tortures such as the water cure, the "Vietnam special," and current torture techniques have been limited to detainees in the U.S. prison system. To understand why this may be the case, we return to our framework and caveats presented in Chapter 2 to identify two explanatory factors.

First, it is not clear how, under current circumstances, mass torture would be implemented against the general domestic population of the United States. Given that the purpose of torture is typically to elicit information, a confession, or desired action from the victim, it is unclear how mass torture would serve a useful purpose from the perspective of those in the government. Second, the ideology of the American public, along with still functioning constitutional constraints, has likely limited the magnitude of the expansion of torture on U.S. soil. Unlike domestic surveillance or prisoner abuse, which the vast majority of the American public may never observe, wide-scale torture against the general public would be directly evident and likely met with resistance. While we cannot rule out this possibility in the future, to date these factors have limited the reach of government torture. There is still reason, however, for concern.

Although this chapter has focused on the torture of U.S. persons at home, it is not just domestic torture that should concern Americans. According to the recent decision in *Meshal v. Higgenbotham*, American citizens cannot sue federal agents who illegally detain or torture them in other countries.[139] This case revolved around Amir Mohamed Meshal, a natural-born American citizen captured while fleeing from Somalia to Kenya. Meshal, who was never charged with a crime, claims that the FBI agents who detained him violated his Fourth and Fifth Amendment rights and the Torture Victim Protection Act of 1991. In 2015 the U.S. Court of Appeals for the District of Columbia Circuit upheld a lower court's 2014 decision to dismiss Meshal's case. The appeals court stated that "[m]atters touching on national security and foreign policy fall within an area of executive action where courts hesitate to intrude absent congressional authorization."[140]

In other words, the court held that in matters of national security, constitutional constraints are limited, if not completely ineffective, in protecting the rights of citizens against abuses by the U.S. government. This is a stark example of how coercive foreign intervention creates not only the opportunity for the U.S. government to develop tools of torture but also the possibility of using those innovations of control with near impunity against Americans. So while current constitutional constraints limit, at least to some degree, what government is able to do domestically, it is important to remember that constraints are far from perfectly binding. This slack grants significant scope to the government, which potentially can be used to reduce the freedom of domestic persons. As the aforementioned quote from the court in the Meshal case indicates, courts have been reluctant to actively limit the menu of actions available to government in matters of national security.

This realization has important consequences for limiting the power of the state. In the face of constitutional slack and reluctant courts, the ideology of citizens regarding the appropriate role of the state is of central importance as a constraint on government. In the concluding chapter we discuss the role of ideology in greater detail, as well as the other implications of our analysis of the boomerang effect.

Conclusion: Reclaiming the Great Republic

Domestic life is not immune to the foreign policies undertaken by a country's government. Preparing for and engaging in coercive foreign intervention leads to refinements and innovations in state-produced social control that often return home to destroy liberties, as per the logic of the boomerang effect. While some of the domestic effects of foreign intervention are direct and immediate, others seep into domestic life in a slow and unpredictable way, eroding individual freedom over time. Foreign intervention can create institutional possibilities that lay dormant for years, if not decades, until they are revived and exploited in new and previously unforeseen ways by the political elite. Because the specifics of this process are unpredictable and take time to unfold, the full consequences of foreign intervention on domestic life are not immediate or readily observable by citizens.

An understanding of the boomerang effect and its costs is especially important given the U.S. government's foreign policy. In the introductory chapter we provided some insight into the significant global reach of the U.S. military. Since the world wars a militaristic foreign policy has become institutionalized in the United States government.[1] This includes not only continuous interventions of differing sizes and contexts, but also constant preparation for future intervention. For this reason General David Shoup recognized that in the wake of the world wars "America has become an aggressive and militaristic nation."[2] These characteristics are evident in the government's grand strategy, which has been described as "liberal hegemony."[3] According to this strategy, the U.S. government uses the country's military and economic power to promote Western liberal values in other societies.[4] But as history shows, these foundational values are often pushed by the wayside, if not outright discarded, in order to control distant populations.

The mentality of militarism fueling the U.S. government's foreign policy, in turn, serves to reinforce the spirit underpinning that mind-set. Colonel

James Donovan noted that militarism "is defined as the tendency to regard military efficiency as the supreme ideal of the state, and *it subordinates all other interests to those of the military.*"[5] The historian Alfred Vagts defines militarism as an environment in which people "rank military institutions and ways above the ways of civilian life, carrying military mentality and modes of acting and decision into the civilian sphere."[6] Militarism, President Woodrow Wilson said, "is a spirit. It is a point of view. It is a purpose. The purpose of militarism is to use armies for aggression."[7] He believed, however, that America was immune to militarism, arguing that "as long as America is America, that spirit and point of view is impossible with us."[8] He was wrong.

The spirit of militarism has come to dominate many aspects of American political and civilian life.[9] Shoup noted that "[t]he American people have become more and more accustomed to militarism, to uniforms, to the cult of the gun, and to the violence of combat."[10] Historian Garry Wills argues that the world wars and introduction of the atomic bomb "fostered an anxiety of continuing crises, so that [American] society was pervasively militarized."[11] Historian Andrew Bacevich suggests that "mainstream politicians today take as given that American military supremacy is an unqualified good, evidence of a larger American superiority." He goes on to say that "[o]ne result of that consensus over the past quarter century has been to militarize U.S. policy and to encourage tendencies suggesting that American society itself is increasingly enamored with its self-image as the military power nonpareil."[12] Bacevich also observes that the spirit of militarism has become ingrained in the lives of many young Americans, meaning that "for the rising generation of citizens, war has become the new normal, a fact they readily accept. . . ."[13]

As Mark Twain cautioned, when a society adopts the values of an aggressive empire, it runs the real risk of adopting imperial characteristics at home. Americans would do well to heed Twain's warning, as it suggests that if they do not give up their empire, they will come to live under it in their own daily lives. With this in mind, our analysis has four main implications:

1. The costs of coercive foreign intervention tend to be understated.

2. Existing formal constraints are limited in protecting freedom from abuses of power associated with intervention.

3. Ideology can constrain foreign policy and is crucial to protecting against abuses of power.

4. An antimilitarist ideology is necessary to curtail intervention and its assaults on liberty.

UNDERSTATING THE COSTS OF COERCIVE FOREIGN INTERVENTION

When considering intervention, focus tends to be on the immediately observable benefits and costs. The boomerang effect, however, is long and variable. This means that the full extent of the expansions of state power, and the concomitant loss of domestic freedom, are not known or seen at the time of the intervention. Thus the costs of preparing for and engaging in intervention will tend to be understated; that is, intervention will appear more attractive than it actually is.

Consider the history of the national surveillance state discussed in Chapter 4. When the U.S. government intervened in the Philippines in the late nineteenth century, there was no way for anyone to know that the occupation would serve as the origins of the modern-day domestic surveillance state. Likewise, the current War on Terror will produce unforeseen costs that will be borne by Americans for years and decades to come. Many legal scholars have noted, for example, that post-9/11 the U.S. government has expanded its powers and undermined domestic liberty.[14] Some of these expansions are directly evident to those who care to observe them. But our analysis suggests that the full consequences of current interventions will be even greater and will only become evident in the future. Current policy has created an array of institutional possibilities for future expansions of government power.

This implication counters one common criticism of concerns over government overreach, which are often dismissed as the exaggerations of myopic civil libertarians.[15] Critics of noninterventionism often note that the garrison state and authoritarian leader that civil libertarians warn of never seem to appear despite numerous instances of intervention. But this mischaracterizes the concern. The central concern is not that a single event will result in the immediate rise of an authoritarian despot. Rather the worry is that a series of seemingly minor encroachments over time will result in a significant loss of liberty that cannot be recovered.

As Supreme Court Justice William O. Douglas observed, "[a]s nightfall does not come all at once, neither does oppression. In both instances there is a twilight when everything remains seemingly unchanged. And it is in such twilight that we all must be most aware of change in the air—however slight—lest we become unwitting victims of the dark."[16] The logic of the boomerang effect helps to explain how intervention can contribute to advances in this darkness of oppression by creating new possibilities for state-produced social control at home.

LIMITATIONS OF EXISTING FORMAL CONSTRAINTS

Ideally, formal political constraints would limit the government's threat to Americans' freedom. Recall that the paradox of government is that a government empowered to protect liberty has the power to undermine it. If constitutional rules could be designed correctly, then government would protect its citizens' freedom without violating their rights. But as discussed in Chapter 3, when it comes to intervention, existing constitutional constraints are, at best, speed bumps: they might slow, or even temporarily reverse, expansion of government power, but they are by no means hard constraints against abuse.

Existing constitutional constraints tend to grant significant discretion in matters of national security, with the traditional checks and balances—courts and the legislators—typically deferring to the executive branch and the extended security state.[17] This is especially true during times of crisis. Political scientist Clinton Rossiter notes that during a crisis "the government will have more power and the people fewer rights."[18] He illustrates this with the example of World War II: "[A]t the very moment when the people of the United States were shouting about the differences between democracy and dictatorship, they were admitting in practice the necessity of conforming their own government more closely to the dictatorial pattern!"[19]

Economist Robert Higgs is also keenly aware of the adverse effects of discretion granted to government leaders during crises.[20] "Besides the Normal Constitution, protective of individual rights," he notes, "we [the United States] now have a Crisis Constitution, hostile to individual rights and friendly to the unchecked power of government officials."[21] Crises, however, often do not have a clean start and finish, and it is common for one national emergency to overlap with or bleed into the next. The result is that in the face of permanent crisis, as has existed for decades, "the Crisis Constitution will simply swallow up the Normal Constitution."[22] There is good reason to believe that it already has. Historian Garry Wills argues,

[S]ince the inception of World War II we [the United States] have had a continuous state of impending or partial war, with retained constitutional restrictions. World War II faded into the Cold War, and the Cold War into the war on terror, giving us two-thirds of a century of war in peace, with growing security measures, increased government secrecy, broad classification of information, procedural clearances of those citizens able to know what rulers were doing in secret. The requirements became more stringent, not less, after World War II and then again after the Cold War. Normality never returned, and the executive power increased decade by decade, reaching a new high in the twenty-first century—a continuous story of unidirectional increase in the executive power.[23]

By carrying out national security activities in the shadows, the security state can avoid both oversight by citizens and the checks and balances established by the Constitution, which are intended to limit abuses of power.[24]

It is not just domestic constraints that are weak. The constraints provided by formal international law are also severely limited. As has been glaringly evident over the past fifteen years, the U.S. government can simply ignore or redefine international law when it so chooses. This allows its members to use foreign intervention to develop, test, and hone new methods of social control over distant populations, methods that often return home, as per the boomerang effect.

This significant slack in existing formal constraints allows the government to adopt new means of expanding its powers over private persons domestically. The implication, as noted by legal scholar Norman Dorsen, is that "[f]oreign affairs, and its close relation national security, has [sic] been a graveyard for civil liberties for much of our [America's] recent history."[25] As we have emphasized, these reductions in liberty can occur during preparation for intervention, during an intervention, and in the future due to new institutional possibilities produced by the intervention.

Many commentators and scholars have attempted to identify additional formal mechanisms that supposedly limit the government during and after emergencies—such as sunset clauses, increased transparency, and new checks and balances.[26] Likewise, significant resources have been spent on numerous government committees and commissions, typically after a scandal, that propose a variety of reforms to prevent further abuses of power. Yet these proposals have not been implemented in any meaningful way precisely because those in power have little incentive to constrain themselves. As journalist Glenn Greenwald notes, "the last place one should look to impose limits on the powers of the U.S. government is . . . the U.S. government. Governments don't walk around trying to figure out how to limit their own power, and that's particularly true of empires."[27] On the contrary, they—government bureaucrats, elected officials, and a wide array of private interests—have a strong incentive to preserve the national security state and its militaristic foreign policy precisely because of the benefits generated by its expansive powers.

IDEOLOGY IS CRUCIAL

Recognizing the limitations of existing formal constraints is not to suggest that all is lost. The underlying spirit animating America's foreign policy is not fixed. It is in the control of citizens and can be changed over time. In general, the exercise of power by the government requires the voluntary consent of those living under that government.[28] This means that the U.S. government's ability to act in a militaristic manner requires Americans to go along either directly—by actively supporting such a foreign policy—or indirectly—through indifference.[29]

While militarism may prevail in present-day America, it need not continue to prevail. The historian Arthur Ekirch documents the deep antimilitarist tradition in America.[30] Although the government has frequently gone to war, Ekirch writes, Americans historically have been skeptical of such a foreign policy. This skepticism weakened during World War II and further eroded with the onset of the Cold War and

the entrenchment of a permanent war economy focused on preparations for future conflicts.[31]

The transition from skepticism to acceptance makes clear that the beliefs
of citizens regarding the appropriate role of government, both in foreign
and domestic policy, are important. That is, ideology can constrain the
state. "If the dominant ideology gives strong support to the Normal Constitution," Higgs notes, "it will survive, no matter what else happens."[32]
However, "[i]f the dominant ideology does not give strong support to the
Normal Constitution," he warns, "that constitution will eventually be
overwhelmed by the Crisis Constitution," which grants significant discretionary power to those in control.[33]

Ideology is the "somewhat coherent, rather comprehensive belief system
about social relations."[34] A person's ideology frames his or her perception of the world, provides moral content ("good" or "bad") to actions,
and serves as a catalyst for participation in political groups.[35] Thus ideology expresses the relationship between citizens and their government
over a range of issues, including foreign intervention. Psychologist Gordon Allport emphasizes that "[t]he indispensable condition for conflict
is that people must expect war and must prepare for war, before under
war minded leadership they make war."[36] A central driver of America's
militaristic culture, according to General Shoup, is "millions of proud,
patriotic, and frequently bellicose and militaristic citizens" who enable
their government to engage in foreign wars.[37] Along similar lines, Colonel Donovan suggests that "[t]he ultimate source of war and militarism,
then, lies in the ideologies of men."[38] What these authors are highlighting
is that militarism begins in the beliefs of the people and what they see as
appropriate behavior by their government.

Ultimately, the ability of formal rules to protect freedom is only as
good as the ideology of the people living under the government. As Judge
Learned Hand wrote, "[l]iberty lies in the hearts of men and women;
when it dies there, no constitution, no law, no court can save it; no constitution, no law, no court can even do much to help it. While it lies there
it needs no constitution, no law, no court to save it."[39] In other words,
citizens have the power to influence how politicians behave with respect
to foreign policy and the maintenance of domestic freedom. Along similar

lines, political scientist Gene Sharp notes that "[t]he degree of liberty or tyranny in any government is . . . a reflection of the relative determination of the subjects to be free and their willingness and ability to resist efforts to enslave them."[40] His point is that people possess the power to be free and must choose to exercise that power accordingly.

Legal scholar David Cole also recognizes the central role of private individuals in maintaining freedom when he argues that civil society is a central mechanism for limiting government during crises, when formal checks are typically curbed.[41] He documents numerous instances when civil-liberties and human-rights groups, that is, organizations of private citizens, have played a central role in constraining expansions of government power that threaten freedom during national emergencies. Underlying those efforts was the ideology of the members of civil society combined with a willingness to exert their power over the state.

In general citizens are not helpless pawns, but instead possess significant power over the state in the form of required consent. Each person can choose to remove their support, whether active or based in indifference, for a proactive, militaristic foreign policy. Recognizing the power of ideology leads to the final implication.

THE NEED FOR AN ANTIMILITARIST IDEOLOGY

Ideology influences the extent to which people embrace militarism. Acceptance of militarism in turn enables a proactive, aggressive foreign policy that consists of preparing for and engaging in intervention. The techniques of social control invented and honed throughout this process often boomerang to the homeland, affecting domestic life and undermining freedom. Curtailing the boomerang effect thus requires rolling back the American empire. Given the slack in existing formal constraints, this requires that enough citizens possess an antimilitarist ideology with certain characteristics.

Placing significant weight on individual freedom. Nothing threatens liberty like indifference from those who are fortunate enough to possess freedom. Indifference can mean taking freedom for granted or trading it off for promises of increased safety. Indifference includes failing to protect liberty against the corrosive effects of an interventionist foreign policy.

In contrast, the antimilitarist mind-set requires that citizens value liberty more than the potential benefits of intervention.

Citizens must maintain a commitment to individual freedom even in the face of concrete benefits promised by politicians in return for expansions of government power. "The preservation of a free system," F. A. Hayek wrote, "is so difficult precisely because it requires a constant rejection of measures which appear to be required to secure particular results, on no stronger grounds than that they conflict with a general rule [a steadfast commitment to individual liberty], and frequently without our knowing what will be the costs of not observing the rule in the particular instance."[42] With each proposed intervention, the government promises tangible benefits to citizens. However, per the boomerang effect, aspects of the intervention will likely come home in unforeseen ways to threaten individual liberty. A commitment to liberty requires rejecting the potential benefits of intervention precisely because it can erode liberty. This is why, Hayek concludes, "[f]reedom will prevail only if it is accepted as a general principle whose application to particular instances requires no justification."[43] This requires citizens to value their freedom more than the potential benefits of foreign intervention.

Understanding the paradox of government. The state poses a threat to the domestic freedom it purports to protect. This is not a new idea. As legal scholars Frederick Schwarz and Aziz Huq note, the "framers of the Constitution and those that ratified it were acutely aware of threats both from overseas and from chief executives who wished to set aside the law."[44] The framers' solution was to attempt to design formal checks and balances to limit the powers of all branches of government. As discussed, however, these formal constraints have failed to limit expansion of government power and prevent the loss of freedom associated with an interventionist foreign policy.

The antimilitarist recognizes the limitations of formal rules in national security and foreign intervention and therefore does not rely on such rules to constrain government. Antimilitarism understands that intervention diverts citizens' focus away from the basic conflict between domestic government and liberty by shifting their attention to purported foreign enemies. A pro-militarist compares external threats to protection by a benevolent government that uses military power to further the "national interest." The antimilitarist, in contrast, compares the risk to liberty from external enemies with the same risk from his own government.

Recognizing that foreign intervention has real, lasting effects on domestic institutions. Domestic life and foreign policy cannot be separated; they are intimately related. Intervention shapes the human and physical capital of those who carry it out, as well as the dynamics of the institutions of domestic life. Further, expansions in the scope of domestic state power cannot be turned on and off as desired. As sociologist William Graham Sumner warned, "it is not possible to experiment with a society and just drop the experiment whenever we choose. The experiment enters into the life of society and never can be got out again."[45] This suggests that the growth of government tends to be sticky and difficult to reverse.

Acknowledging that the security-liberty trade-off is simplistic, if not altogether incorrect. With national security and foreign policy, the relevant trade-off facing citizens is often presented as security versus liberty.[46] According to this logic, citizens can have more security or more liberty, but not both. In exchange for giving up some liberty, political leaders promise more protection. Public-spirited politicians and courts, the people are told, will find the right balance between freedom and security. But in principle, this trade-off is only one of three possible scenarios.

Another possibility is that after giving up their liberty, citizens become less safe due to ineffective or even counterproductive government policies, that is, policies which themselves threaten freedom.[47] In this scenario the trade-off would be less liberty for less safety. Second, even if trading off liberty did increase security against some potential external threats, a new potential coercive threat, from the newly expanded government, would remain. A final possibility is that more, not less, liberty would increase security.

Regarding this last possibility, a recent study by two political scientists, Nilay Saiya and Anthony Scime, explores the relationship between religious liberty and religious-based terrorism.[48] They find that a lack of religious liberty is a key factor motivating religious-based violence and conclude that "the best way to combat religious terrorism is not by restricting religious practices but rather by safeguarding their legitimate manifestations."[49] In this case, increasing liberty may increase security by reducing the likelihood of violence. This alternative should cast doubt on promises that reducing freedom and expanding state power will guarantee greater security.

Recognizing that patriotism requires a critical attitude toward one's government. Those who are critical of the U.S. government in military and foreign affairs are commonly described as "unpatriotic," "un-American," or even "hating America."[50] From this perspective patriotism and love of one's country are defined by an unquestioning attitude toward government's handling of foreign affairs. The antimilitarist recognizes that governments foster this attitude to rally support for and neutralize dissent against their foreign policies. As Hermann Göring, a leader of the Nazi party, noted during an interview in his Nuremberg prison cell,

> Why of course people don't want war. But after all it is the leaders of the country who determine the policy and it is always a simple matter to drag the people along whether it is a democracy or a fascist dictatorship or a Parliament or a Communist dictatorship. . . . [V]oice or no voice the people can always be brought to the bidding of the leaders. That is easy. All you have to do is tell them they are being attacked and denounce the pacifists for a lack of patriotism and exposing the country to danger. It works the same in any country.[51]

There is an alternative perspective, however, offered by the essayist Randolph Bourne, who distinguished among "Country," "State," and "Government." For Bourne, *Country* referred to "the non-political aspects of people" and included the "loose population spreading over a certain geographic portion of the earth's surface, speaking a common language, and living in a homogenous civilization."[52] *State*, in contrast, is "the country acting as a political unit, it is the group acting as a repository of force. . . ."[53] This has implications for international relations, which is "'power politics' because it is a relation of States and that is what States infallibly and calamitously are, huge aggregations of human and industrial force that may be hurled against each other in war."[54] The concept of *Government* is closely related to *State* and refers to the "machinery by which the nation, organized as a State, carries out its State functions."[55]

These distinctions suggest that one can be deeply committed to America the country while simultaneously being critical and distrusting of the American state and government. In fact, to the extent one prefers peaceful cooperation to relations based on force, one can love one's country and concurrently abhor the state, which is the embodiment of force. As Bourne makes clear, "Country is a concept of peace, tolerance, of living and letting live. But State is essentially a concept of power, of competition; it signifies a group in its aggressive aspects."[56] Far from being unpatriotic, then, a critical attitude toward state and government is necessary to protect against the potential threats they pose to the country. As this book has shown, this is especially important in foreign affairs.

Understanding the often perverse incentives facing politicians and bureaucrats. Those in political office face an array of incentives to perpetuate and expand their power by increasing their control of resources (scale) and the range of their activities (scope). Expansion can occur in a variety of ways, including through new powers to the executive branch or to existing agencies, through new agencies and budgets, and through the reorganization and expansion of existing agencies and their budgets. These incentives have been evident since 9/11, when significant additional resources and powers were granted to the executive branch to combat terrorism.

According to terrorism researchers John Mueller and Mark Stewart, "[a]t least 263 government agencies devoted to counterterrorism were created or reorganized after 9/11."[57] They document sixty-two cases of terrorism since then, in which a hundred terrorists were apprehended for apparently targeting the United States. This means that "the United States has created or reorganized *more than two entire counterterrorism organizations* for every terrorist arrest or apprehension it made of people plotting to do damage within the country."[58]

Consider also the substantial growth in the Department of Homeland Security (DHS) since its inception in 2001. In 2003 the agency employed 180,000 full-time workers, with an annual budget of $29 billion. By 2014 the number of full-time employees had increased to 240,000 and the department's budget had increased to $61 billion.[59] Observable results were required to support the department's expansion and demand for additional resources. This led to mission creep such that "[t]oday, in addition to protecting America's borders and airports, the department is interrogating people suspected of pirating movies at Ohio theaters, seizing counterfeit NBA merchandise in San Antonio and working pickpocket cases alongside police in Albuquerque. Homeland Security agents are visiting elementary schools and senior centers to warn of dangers lurking on the Internet."[60]

This expansion into everyday life has little to do with national security, even under the broadest possible conception. As a report from Senator Tom Coburn concluded, "a review of DHS's programs, including those related to counterterrorism, raise [sic] questions about whether counterterrorism is actually DHS's primary mission, and also whether these programs are succeeding in making the United Sates safe from the threat of a terrorist attack on American soil."[61]

Because of how political institutions operate, the antimilitarist recognizes that foreign intervention is among the greatest threats to domestic liberty. Interventionists defend their foreign policy on the grounds of "protecting the homeland" from foreign threats, but a closer review of the evidence suggests that many supposed national security activities have little to do with external threats in practice. Instead, these activities serve the purpose of justifying past expansions in the scale and scope of government while serving as a foundation for calls for further growth.

Seeking a realistic understanding of risks and threats by potential enemies. Fear is a fundamental tool used by those in the national security state to convince citizens to acquiesce in expansions of government power. This was evident following the 9/11 attacks, when, as former National Security Advisor Zbigniew Brzezinski recognized, a "[c]onstant reference to a 'war on terror' stimulated the emergence of a culture of fear."[62] This fear, he continued, "obscures reason, intensifies emotions and makes it easier for demagogic politicians to mobilize the public on behalf of the policies they want to pursue."[63] As the poet and novelist Margaret Atwood recognizes, "[g]overnments know our desire for safety all too well, and like to play on our fears. How often have we been told that this or that new rule or law or snooping activity on the part of officialdom is to keep us 'safe'?"[64] This culture of fear exaggerates potential external threats while understating the potential risks the government poses to Americans.

In reality, violent external threats are less of a risk for Americans than other dangers. Using data from 1970–2007, Mueller and Stewart estimate that the odds that a U.S. resident will be killed by terrorism is 1 in 3.5 million.[65] Their estimate includes the 9/11 attacks, an outlier over that period. Another estimate, based on 2005–2010 data, places the chance of an American being killed in a terrorist attack, either domestically or abroad, at 1 in 20 million.[66] To provide some comparison, consider that the annual risk of death from a car accident is 1 in 19,000, while the risk of death by drowning in a bathtub is 1 in 800,000.[67]

Beyond terrorism, America is largely insulated from external threats. Political scientist Barry Posen argues that America is in a favorable strategic position due to its economic dominance and location between oceans and neighbors—Canada and Mexico—which have no reason or desire to attack. In addition, Posen notes that America's substantial nuclear arsenal serves as a deterrent against direct attacks by other governments.[68] Journalist Stephen Kinzer similarly recognizes that "[t]he United States has no potent enemies. We are not only safe, but safer than any big power has been in all of modern history."[69]

In seeking to assess the true risk from enemies, the antimilitarist understands the tendency of those associated with the national security state to overstate the dangers to gain more power and resources. This dynamic is evident in the politicians' rhetoric. On the one hand, American politicians boast about the awesome power of the U.S. military; at the same time, however, they constantly stoke fears of new and more dangerous threats requiring greater resources, power, and control over Americans and foreigners.[70] Anyone who blindly listened to the politicians would have no sense whatsoever of just how safe Americans are from external threats.

Understanding the price of living in free society. Living in a free society carries the risk that people will occasionally do bad things to others, even terrorism and mass murder. If people wish to live in a truly free society, however, they must realize that this risk cannot be removed and so must be accepted as a part of life. Of course those in government can and often do pretend they can neutralize all potential threats, both domestic and foreign, if given enough resources and control. But there are two related issues to consider.

First, even the most benevolent and resource-rich government cannot possibly remove all risks. As discussed, the government could potentially reduce some risks, but only by increasing others—for example, by creating new enemies or by expanding domestic government powers. An entirely riskless world, however, is not possible.

Second, the cost of relying on government to reduce risk is significant. This point is captured by Stephen Kinzer, who writes that "[t]he safest and most terror-free country I ever visited was Iraq under the secular dictatorship of Saddam Hussein. If a fellow in a café casually asked a friend whether he thought Iraq should become more religious, he was likely to be quickly arrested. Disturbing public order was a capital crime. Al Qaeda never had a chance in Saddam's Iraq."[71] This illustrates that *potential* reductions in the risk of *potential* harms require granting more power to the state. We purposefully emphasize the dual potentiality because government may fail to reduce the risks to citizens despite increases in power. Likewise, harms may never come to fruition irrespective of government action.

The price of potentially reducing potential harms—namely, increased state control over people—is real. It includes killing American citizens without due process, surveillance, secret watch lists and dragnets, military-style police raids, and property confiscation without warrant for unproven crimes. And this list does not even include the significant, wide-ranging costs imposed on foreigners by the U.S. government.

Today many Americans are comfortable in granting government expanded powers over their lives in the name of safety. A common refrain is that "if you have done nothing wrong you have nothing to fear." The implicit assumption is that increased government powers will be used in the public interest only to target criminals and potential threats. But this ignores the reality that expanded powers create opportunities for future abuse.

The late Senator Frank Church, who headed the Church Committee discussed in Chapter 4, recognized this point in the context of surveillance. He warned that this "capability at any time could be turned around on the American people, and no American would have any privacy left, such is the capability to monitor everything—telephone conversations, telegrams, it doesn't matter. There would be no place to hide."[72] He went on to caution that "[i]f this government ever became a tyranny, if a dictator ever took charge in this country, the technological capacity that the intelligence community has given the government could enable it to impose total tyranny, and there would be no way to fight back because the most careful effort to combine together in resistance to the government, no matter how privately it was done, is within the reach of the government to know."[73] What Church was highlighting is that once granted, expansions in government power create an array of institutional precedents and possibilities for social control for those who assume power in the future.

The conflict between government and liberty requires constant vigilance. It pertains not only to those currently in power, but also to those who might come to power in the future under different circumstances. Thus it is important to consider whether the potential benefits of intervention, and its associated social control, will exist in the future. This principle is an extension and application of the insight of the eighteenth-century philosopher David Hume, who wrote,

> Political writers have established it as a maxim, that, in contriving any system of government, and fixing the several checks and controls of the constitution, every man ought to be supposed a *knave*, and to have no other end, in all his actions, than private interest. By this interest we must govern him, and, by means of it, make him, notwithstanding his insatiable avarice and ambition, co-operate to public good. Without this, say they, we shall in vain boast of the advantages of any constitution, and shall find, in the end, that we have no security for our liberties or possessions, except the good-will of our rulers; that is, we shall have no security at all.[74]

This maxim has important implications for foreign policy.[75] Policies that seem desirable in the abstract may very well appear undesirable, if not outright repugnant, when one envisions Hume's knave implementing them. This is due not only to narrow self-interest, but also to the fundamental nature of the interventionist mind-set discussed in Chapter 2. As the Guantánamo Bay detention camp and Abu Ghraib prison make clear, the interventionist mind-set can lead to the adoption of atrocious techniques of coercion and control. And as we have emphasized, foreign intervention provides new tools and methods for future knaves to control and repress private persons, both abroad and at home. Hume's principle by no means offers all the answers regarding foreign policy, but it does provide a guide for thinking through the potential consequences of alternative courses of action and what they would mean for freedom.

Members of the U.S. government often use the rhetoric of freedom and virtue to legitimize intervention. This supposed commitment to higher ideals is indicated by the names assigned to the government's actions, such as "Operation Just Cause," "Operation Enduring Freedom," "Operation Iraqi Freedom," "Operation Valiant Guardian," and "Operation Falcon Freedom." Despite this rhetoric, the boomerang effect operates: preparing for and carrying out intervention abroad undermines freedom at home. As Mark Twain cautioned over a century ago, when citizens and their government become comfortable with the "crushing of other people's liberties," they will eventually "suffer for their mistake in their own persons."[76] Twain's warning must be sounded regularly until we all realize that domestic liberty is not immune to the tyranny of foreign intervention and the militarism at its foundation.

Notes

Chapter 1

1. See Twain 1972a, 1972b, and 1992; Kinzer 2017.

2. Twain 1972a, 1972b.

3. Twain 1972b, 395.

4. The term *boomerang effect* has been used before; in psychology literature, see Hovland, Janis, and Kelley 1953, and in political science, see Keck and Sikkink 1998. The use of the term in these literatures is different, both from each other and from the manner in which we employ the term.

5. See McCoy 2009 and Barder 2015.

6. See Greenwald 2014a and Granick 2017, 41–52 for a detailed discussion of these revelations.

7. Bilmes and Intriligator 2013, 9.

8. Ibid.

9. See Bacevich 2016.

10. Bilmes and Intriligator 2013, 10.

11. Turse 2015.

12. U.S. Department of Defense 2014, 6.

13. Ibid., 2.

14. Vine 2015, 3.

15. Theohary 2016, 2.

16. Ibid.

17. Ibid.

18. See Johnson 2000, 2004; Bacevich 2002, 2010; Dudziak 2012; Posen 2014.

19. See U.S. Department of State 1967, Goldwater 1973, Collins 1991, Torreon 2016.

20. Lal 2004, 63. See also Aron 1974, Ikenberry 2012, Posen 2014, McCoy 2017.

21. Bacevich 2005, 1.

22. Posen 2014, xii.

23. Ibid. On the significant costs of America's military dominance, see Preble 2009.

24. Boot 2002; Ferguson 2003, 2004; Ferguson and Schularick 2006; Lal 2004; McCarthy 2014; Kane 2014; Cohen 2016. See also Mitchener and Weidenmier 2005.

25. Johnson 2004, 13. Also see Garrett (1953, 117), who argued, "We [the United States] have crossed the boundary that lies between Republic and Empire. If you ask when, the answer is that you cannot make a single stroke between day

and night; the precise moment does not matter. There was no painted sign to say: 'You now are entering Imperium.' Yet it was a very old road and the voice of history was saying: 'Whether you know it or not, the act of crossing may be irreversible.'" Similarly, see Ekirch (1956), who argued that United States involvement in World War II and the Cold War led to an expanded role of the military in domestic society threatening the liberties of U.S. citizens.

26. See Coyne and Mathers 2010.

27. For more on the CIA-backed coup, see Cullather 2006.

28. See Kinzer 2003.

29. Hazlitt 1946, 17.

30. Madison 1865, 491.

31. Washington 1796.

32. Quoted in Edel 2014, 163 (emphasis original).

33. Tocqueville 1840, 285.

34. Bourne 1964, 71.

35. See Buchanan 1975; Brennan and Buchanan 1985; Weingast 1995; Hardin 1999; Gordon 2002.

36. See Peacock and Wiseman 1961; Porter 1994; Denson 1999; Bilmes and Stiglitz 2008; Eland 2013; and Duncan and Coyne 2013a.

37. See Garrett and Rhine 2006 for a review of some the evidence regarding each set of theories.

38. Higgs 1987 and 2008a.

39. See Porter 1994.

40. See Peacock and Wiseman 1961 and Eland 2013.

41. See Cowen 2009.

42. Higgs 1987.

43. Ibid., 62.

44. See Higgs 1987, 1991.

45. Higgs 2008b.

46. Buchanan 1975, 163.

47. For example, the Organization for Economic Cooperation and Development has an index of labor and product regulation. Dudley and Warren (2014) use the budgets and staffing of federal regulatory agencies as a proxy of the overall regulatory burden. See also Dawson and Seater 2013.

48. See Office of the Federal Register, https://www.federalregister.gov/uploads/2014/04/OFR-STATISTICS-CHARTS-ALL1-1-1-2013.pdf, for the annual number of pages in the *Federal Register*: 1937–2013.

49. Peltzman 1980, 209.

50. Ibid.

51. Buchanan 1975, 163.

52. See Coyne 2015 and Coyne and Lucas 2016 for a discussion and critique of the way economists discuss and model defense.

53. Dunne 1995, 409.

54. Newport 2015.

Chapter 2

1. For more details on the 1953 Iranian coup, see Roosevelt 1979; Risen 2000; Kinzer 2003, 2006; and National Security Archives 2000.

2. Kinzer 2006, 1.

3. See Fuller 1964; Brennan and Buchanan 1985, ix; Ellickson 1991; and Leeson and Coyne 2012.

4. Ellickson 1987.

5. Weber 1958, 78. See also Oppenheimer (1972) on the economic means and the political means.

6. Weber 1958, 83.

7. Robin 2004, 2.

8. Posner and Vermeule (2007) argue that fear of (real or perceived) crises do not produce bad policies and overreaching on the part of the government. Cole (2008) provides a response and critique of their arguments.

9. Smith 1776, 873.

10. Hayek 1981, 124. See also Bloom 2004, 79.

11. Ibid.

12. Higgs: 2007a, 2. See also Robin 2004; Svendsen 2008; Cole 2008, 1343–1347; and Thrall and Cramer 2009.

13. Russell 1943, 25. See also Fettweiss 2013, 26–28.

14. Robin 2004, 25.

15. Dye 1975, 199. See also Higgs 1987.

16. Cole 2008, 1343.

17. MacArthur 1965, 333. See also Svendsen 2008, 111.

18. See Mueller 2009; Thrall and Cramer 2009; and Priest and Arkin 2011.

19. Bennett 2006, 6.

20. See Bennett 2006 and Mueller and Stewart 2011, 2016.

21. See Sauer 2005.

22. Pierson 2004, 10.

23. See Coleman 2014a, 2014b.

24. See Coleman 2014a. On the ill-defined notion of "homeland security," see Reese 2013.

25. See Olson 1965.

26. Higgs 1987, 73.

27. Porter 1994, xv.

28. Ibid., 13. See also Jacoby 1973; Higgs 1987, 2004, 2007a, 2012; and Gottfried 1999.

29. See Hedges 2002.

30. Shakespeare 1823, 295.

31. Bodin 1955, 168.

32. Polsby 1964, 25. See also Mueller 1970; Lian and O'Neal 1993; and Chapman and Reiter 2004.

33. See Vagts 1937.

34. See Ekirch 1956; Shoup 1969; Donovan 1970; Sherry 1997; Bacevich 2005; Turse 2008; Glain 2011; and Goodman 2013.

35. Donovan 1970, 23.

36. Bacevich 2005, 19.

37. Wagner 2014, 5.

38. Ibid., 4. See also Greve 2012.

39. U.S. Senate Permanent Subcommittee on Investigations 2012, 35.

40. Jefferson 1854a, 543.

41. Jefferson 1854b, 216. See also Jacoby 1973, 213.

42. See Coyne 2008, 2013 and Duncan and Coyne 2015b.

43. See Higgs 2007b; Duncan and Coyne 2013a; McCartney 2015.

44. See Coyne, Michaluk, and Reese 2016.

45. See Tullock 1965; Niskanen 1971, 1975, 2001; Coyne, Michaluk, and Reese 2016.

46. See Brenner 2014.

47. See McCoy 2006; Slahi 2015; and Physicians for Social Responsibility et al. 2015.

48. See Root 2008 and Carpenter and Innocent 2015.

49. Quoted in Tirman 2015.

50. See Tirman 2011.

51. See Tirman 2011, 2015.

52. Quoted in Beschloss 2003, 137.

53. See Ostrom 1991, 242.

54. For a first-hand-account illustration of these dynamics, see Fair 2016.

55. Donovan 1970, 39.

56. Willers 1977, 45.

57. Shoup 1969, 54.

58. Donovan 1970, 80.

59. See Rejali (2007, 454–458) for a discussion of this dynamic of "professionalism" in the context of torture.

60. See Coyne and Coyne 2013.

61. See Rejali 2007, 457–458.

62. See Lasby 1971 and Jacobsen 2014 for comprehensive histories of Operation Paperclip.

63. See McCoy 2006 for a history of the development of torture techniques by the U.S. government.

64. See Price 1945, 3.

65. Citizens for Responsibility and Ethics in Washington 2013.

66. See Donovan 1970, 54–55; Duncan and Coyne 2015a.

67. On the unique nature of the military-industrial complex, see Donovan

1970, 44–63; Higgs 2007b; Duncan and Coyne 2013a, 2015a; McCartney 2015; Coyne, Michaluk, and Reese 2016.

68. See http://www.l-3com.com/careers/transitioning-military.html.

69. Simon 1997, 18.

70. Donovan 1970, 33.

71. Hodgson 1990, 384–5.

72. Shoup 1969, 52.

73. Donovan 1970, 32.

74. Ibid, 37.

75. Cowen 2009.

76. U.S. Department of Defense 2017, 9.

77. See Reel 2016.

78. See Berkowitz and LePage 1967; Turner, Layton, and Simons 1975; Carlson, Marcus-Newhall, and Miller 1990; Anderson, Benjamin, and Bartholow 1999; Hemenway, Vriniotis, and Miller 2006; and Subra, Muller, Bègue, Bushman, and Delmas 2010.

79. See Zimbardo 2007 on the role of context in shaping the behaviors of those embedded in the situation.

80. See Higgs 1987 and Porter 1994.

81. Buchanan 2005.

82. Johnson 2000.

83. See Porter 1994, 17–19.

84. The ideology of the judiciary will be influenced by a variety of factors, including the process of selecting judges, whether they have lifetime tenure, and the source of compensation (see Mitchell and Simmons 1990, 740–744). These factors will influence how judicial candidates are initially filtered while also delineating their ability to pursue and further their ideological worldview once in power.

85. Glennon 2015, 39–49.

86. Ibid., 40.

87. See Friedberg 1992.

88. See Hochschild 1999.

89. Ibid., 226.

90. We would like to thank Mike Munger for bringing this point to our attention.

91. Cole 2008, 1349–1350.

92. Ibid., 1353.

93. See Friedberg 1992.

94. Quoted in Grigsby 1890, 130.

95. Sweeney 2001, 18.

96. See Radack 2014.

97. Murphy 1943.

Chapter 3

1. Yardley 1931.

2. Hersh 1974.

3. Greenwald 2014a and Granick 2017, 41–52.

4. See Buchanan 1975; Brennan and Buchanan 1985; Weingast 1995; Hardin 1999; Gordon 2002; and Whittington 2009.

5. Quoted in Vile 2005, 916.

6. Weingast 1995, 1.

7. Glennon 2015. The idea of a "double government" can be traced back to William Bagehot (1963), who argued that a dual set of institutions emerged in Britain.

8. Quoted in Vile 2005, 916.

9. For more on the "deep state" and associated "elite theory," see Mills 1956; Dye 2001, 2014; and Lofgren 2016.

10. Hogan 1998, 24–25.

11. Ibid., 14.

12. Page and Shapiro 1992, 332.

13. Ekirch 1956. See also Dunlap 1994, 344–350.

14. See Glennon 2015, 11–25. Also see Hogan (1998) on the origins of the U.S. security state. Corwin (1947) argues that the "peacetime Constitution" ended with World War II when the scope of government powers was permanently expanded.

15. Hogan 1998, 3. See also Neu 1987.

16. Hogan 1998, 4. See also May 1990.

17. Complementing these reforms and the erosion of checks and balances was the increased emphasis on secrecy that allowed those in the security community to avoid accountability. The 1950 National Security Council directly stated that "any publicity, factual or fictional, concerning intelligence is potentially detrimental to the effectiveness of an intelligence activity and to the national security." It went on to order that "[a]ll departments and agencies represented by membership on the Intelligence Advisory Committee shall take steps to prevent the unauthorized disclosure for written or oral publication of any information concerning intelligence or intelligence activities. The head of each department or agency will determine his channel for granting such authorization as may be necessary" (National Security Council Intelligence Directive No. 12 1950). This led to the default position of classifying any and all information that insulated the members of the security state from public scrutiny regarding their activities and potential abuses.

18. For analysis and discussion of the evolution, global reach, and magnitude of various aspects of the U.S. national security complex, see Bamford 1983, 2008; Hogan 1998; Powers 2004; Weiner 2007; Mueller 2009; Priest and Arkin 2011; Esman 2013; Mazzetti 2013; Scahill 2013; and Risen 2014.

19. Glennon 2015, 6–7.

20. Ibid., 58–65.

21. Ibid., 58.

22. See Mazzetti 2013, 228.

23. Quoted in Mazzetti 2013, 228.

24. Quoted in Bamford 2017.

25. See Axelrod and Rand 2016; Cooper 2016; U.S. House of Representatives Joint Task Force on U.S. Central Command Intelligence Analysis 2016.

26. See Axelrod and Rand 2016.

27. Bamford 2013.

28. Fettweis 2013, 19. See also pp. 24–93 for the presence and nature of American fear regarding external threats.

29. Glennon 2015, 46.

30. Corwin 1947, 177.

31. See Krasner 1972.

32. The territories were governed by the U.S. War Department's Bureau of Insular Affairs, hence the name the *Insular Cases*.

33. U.S. Constitution: http://www.archives.gov/exhibits/charters/constitution_transcript.html.

34. Quoted in Vignarajah 2010, 790.

35. Vignarajah 2010, 791.

36. Quoted in Sparrow 2006, 102.

37. See Raustiala 2009, 83–86 and Kinzer 2017, 200–202.

38. Ibid., 83.

39. Quoted in Vignarajah 2010, 791.

40. Sparrow 2006, 236.

41. On the establishment of relationships with client states, see Kinzer 2006 and Carpenter and Innocent 2015. On the history of the U.S. government's global network of bases, see Vine 2015.

42. Cogan 2006, 190.

43. Mearsheimer 1994-1995, 7.

44. Posner 2009.

45. Krisch 2003, 42.

46. McCoy 2015.

47. This is by no means the only instance of this type of reasoning. For example, a 1954 executive panel commissioned by President Eisenhower concluded the following regarding U.S. foreign policy in the face of the threat of communism: "It is now clear that we are facing an implacable enemy whose avowed objective is world domination by whatever means and at whatever costs. There are no rules in such a game. Hitherto acceptable norms of human conduct do not apply. If the US is to survive, longstanding American concepts of 'fair play' must be reconsidered. . . . It may become necessary that the American people be made acquainted with, understand and support this fundamentally repugnant philosophy" (quotes in Leary 1984, 144).

48. Yoo and Delahunty 2002, 2.

49. Gonzales 2002, 2.

50. For a discussion of why governments follow international law despite the

lack of enforcement mechanisms, see Koh 1997 and Sykes 2013. For a discussion of the relationship between international law and U.S. domestic law, see Paulsen 2009.

51. *The Economist* 2014.

52. Paulsen 2009, 1842.

53. Weber 1958, 121.

54. United Nations Human Rights Council 2015, 6.

55. Ibid.

56. Ibid.

57. Ibid., 7.

58. Ibid., 9.

59. Ibid.

60. Ibid., 11.

61. Ibid.

62. Ibid., 12.

63. See Taguba 2004; Cole and Dempsey 2006; Rejali 2007; McCoy 2006; Cole 2008; Cole and Lobel 2009; Mazzetti 2013; Scahill 2013; Bacevich 2014; Greenwald 2014a; U.S. Senate Select Committee on Intelligence 2014; and Slahi 2015.

64. United Nations Human Rights Council 2015, 14.

Chapter 4

1. For a detailed, first-hand account of the Snowden revelations, see Greenwald 2014a.

2. See Greenwald 2013a.

3. See Greenwald and MacAskill 2013; Miller 2013; and Greenwald 2014a, 108–119.

4. See Gellman and Soltani 2013.

5. See Ball and Ackerman 2013.

6. Savage and Poitras 2014.

7. See Gellman, Tate, and Soltani 2014.

8. See Greenwald 2013b; Marquis-Boire, Greenwald, and Lee 2015; and Lee, Greenwald, and Marquis-Boire 2015.

9. See Poitras, Rosenbach, and Stark 2014.

10. See Perlroth, Larson, and Shane 2013.

11. See Gellman and Soltani 2013.

12. See Gellman 2013.

13. For a more detailed treatment of intelligence and surveillance during the American Revolutionary War, see Rose 2007;, Nagy 2011; Sulick 2012; and Misencik 2013.

14. See Central Intelligence Agency 2007a.

15. Ibid.

16. Ibid.

17. For a more detailed treatment of intelligence and surveillance during the Civil War, see Sulick 2012 and Towne 2015.

18. For a detailed history of the Signal Corps, see Brown 1974.

19. See Central Intelligence Agency 2007b, 17

20. Ibid., 23.

21. *Treaty of Peace Between the United States and Spain* 1898, Article III. Available online at http://avalon.law.yale.edu/19th_century/sp1898.asp.

22. Guevara 2005, 104–120.

23. U.S. Department of State Office of the Historian 2015.

24. See Constantino 1975.

25. McCoy 2009, 2017, 113-115.

26. Millett 2010, 7.

27. McCoy 2009, 21–29.

28. Ibid., 21.

29. Ibid., 74.

30. See Millett 2010, 8–12.

31. McCoy 2009, 105.

32. Ibid., 127.

33. Ibid., 77.

34. Ibid., 96.

35. Ibid., 17.

36. Ibid., 76–82.

37. U.S. Army n.d., 3.

38. Quoted in U.S. Army n.d., 4.

39. Finnegan 1998, 24.

40. Lynn 1989, 155.

41. Finnegan 1998, 24.

42. Ibid., 28.

43. Ibid., 31.

44. Ibid., 31.

45. Yardley (1931) provides a first-hand account of the operations of MI-8. For more on the American Expeditionary Force in France, see Finnegan 1998, 32–38.

46. See Bamford 1983, 28; 2008, 163–164 and Kahn 1996, 352–360.

47. Bamford 1983, 29; 2008, 164.

48. Bamford 1983, 29.

49. U.S. War Department 1914, 106 and Bamford 1983, 27–28.

50. Finnegan 1998, 29.

51. Quoted in Cherny 2008, 23. See also McCoy 2009, 301.

52. Quoted in McCoy 2009, 300.

53. See Hagedorn 2007, 58-9.

54. Quoted in Stimson and Bundy 1971, 83.

55. See USAICoE History Office 2013. The United State Army Signal Corps had existed since 1860 with the purpose of managing network operations in support of the U.S. armed forces. The Code and Compilation section of the Signal Corps was established in 1918 to author a code book for use during battle (see

U.S. Army Signal Corps 1919, 536–538) and was the precursor to the SIS, which was focused on code-breaking activities.

56. Finnegan 1998, 78–79.

57. Ibid., 102.

58. Burns 1990, 59.

59. Finnegan 1998, 111.

60. See Burns 1990, 81–96.

61. See Brownell Committee 1952; Burns 1990, 97–111.

62. See Brownell Committee 1952.

63. U.S. Senate Select Committee to Study Governmental Operations with Respect to Intelligence Activities 1976, 104.

64. McCoy 2009, 523.

65. Ibid., 339–340.

66. Gentry 1991, 110.

67. Ibid., 707.

68. McCoy 2009, 342.

69. See Lyon 1990.

70. See Holzman 2008, 241–242.

71. Epstein 2007.

72. Helms 2003, 275.

73. U.S. Senate Select Committee to Study Governmental Operations with Respect to Intelligence Activities 1976, 170.

74. See Halperin, Berman, Borosage, and Marwick 1976, 145, Lyon 1990.

75. U.S. Senate Select Committee to Study Governmental Operations with Respect to Intelligence Activities 1976, 175.

76. Quoted in U.S. Senate Select Committee to Study Governmental Operations with Respect to Intelligence Activities 1976, 104–5.

77. Aid and Burr 2013.

78. U.S. Senate Select Committee to Study Governmental Operations with Respect to Intelligence Activities 1976, 147.

79. Hersh 1974.

80. Ibid., 1.

81. U.S. Senate Select Committee to Study Governmental Operations with Respect to Intelligence Activities 1976, 169.

82. Ibid..

83. Ibid., 3.

84. The original Foreign Intelligence Surveillance Act structured the court so that it included seven judges. This was amended, and increased, to eleven judges as part of the USA PATRIOT Act in 2001 to handle the increased workload expected as part of the War on Terror.

85. Quoted in Wallsten, Leonnig, and Crites 2013.

86. Glennon 2015, 45.

87. Source of data: Electronic Privacy Information Center, n.d. See, however,

the letter from Reggie Walton (2013, 3), the FISC president, to Senator Patrick Leahy, in which he suggests that the high acceptance of warrant requests is due to more careful *ex ante* scrutiny on the part of the government regarding which warrant applications are filed or withheld. See also Granick 2017, 248–250.

88. See Mueller 2009.

89. Priest and Arkin 2010. See also Priest and Arkin 2011.

90. Priest and Arkin 2010.

91. See Granick 2017, 196–199.

92. Risen and Lichtblau 2005.

93. Savage and Poitras 2014.

94. Quoted in Clarke et al. 2014, 46.

95. See U.S. Department of Justice, Office of the Inspector General 2007. Prior to the PATRIOT Act there were stronger constraints on the use of NSLs. However, the PATRIOT Act eased these constraints, making it easier for federal agencies to issue NSLs to access information. See Clarke et al. 2014, 44–49.

96. U.S. Senate Select Committee to Study Governmental Operations with Respect to Intelligence Activities 1976, v.

97. Bamford 2016. See also McCoy 2017, 122–130.

98. Savage 2016, 2017.

99. Savage 2016.

100. American Civil Liberties Union of Massachusetts 2016.

101. Froomkin 2015.

102. See Heath 2015.

103. See Pen America 2013, Marthews and Tucker 2015, Penney 2016.

Chapter 5

1. See McLaughlin, Savidge, and Sayers 2014.

2. See Sack 2017 for details and for an image of the playpen.

3. See Lynn and Gutman 2014.

4. Quoted in *Inquisitr* 2014.

5. See Sullum 2014 and Hastings 2014.

6. See Grigg 2015, 35 (emphasis added).

7. Sack 2017.

8. Ibid.

9. See Balko 2006, 2014 for numerous examples of no-knock raids gone wrong. See also Friedman 2017 for additional examples.

10. See Kraska 2001, 7.

11. See Kraska 2007, 506.

12. Keisling and Galik 2014.

13. Barnett and Alongi 2011.

14. See Burton 2014.

15. See Holpuch 2014.

16. Obama 2014.

17. Paul 2014.

18. Coakley 2011, 14.

19. Militia Act of May 2, 1792. See Vladeck 2004 for a history of the Militia Acts.

20. See Vladeck 2004, 159–163.

21. See Hall and Coyne 2013, 491–493 for a fuller discussion of the Posse Comitatus Act.

22. See *United States Army Field Manual 7–10* 1962, 1.

23. See Constantino 1975.

24. McCoy 2009, 127.

25. *Official Gazette* 1938, Section III.

26. Roth 2000.

27. Wilson 1953, 100.

28. Carte et al. 1983, vii, see also, Carte 1980, 57.

29. Carte 1980, 63.

30. Bennett 2010.

31. Wilson 1953, 97–98.

32. Ibid., 97.

33. Ibid.

34. Ibid.,95.

35. Ibid., 98.

36. Ibid., 94–95.

37. Carte 1980, 106.

38. Kuzmarov 2011.

39. Reppetto 2010, 1909–1910.

40. Reppetto 2010, 1910.

41. Kuzmarov 2012, 39.

42. McCoy 2009, 316.

43. Ibid., 193.

44. See Baldwin 1960, 357.

45. See Ramirez 2003.

46. See Zimmerman 2010.

47. Ibid..

48. See Clinton 2010.

49. See Katz 2012.

50. See the National Association of Destroyer Veterans 1998.

51. Domanick 2010.

52. See Woo and Malnic 2010.

53. See Gates 1992, 114.

54. See Los Angeles Police Department 2014.

55. See Gates 1992, 109–110.

56. See Los Angeles Police Department 2014.

57. The term *homegrown* refers to "terrorist activity or plots perpetrated within

the United States or abroad by American citizens, legal permanent residents, or visitors radicalized largely within the United States" (Bjelopera 2013, 1).

58. See Glenn 2006. Also see Baum 1996; Fe Caces and Zobeck 2001; and Hall and Coyne 2013.

59. See Robison 2002.

60. See U.S. Bureau of Justice Statistics 1994.

61. Ibid.. Also see U.S. Bureau of Justice Statistics 2003.

62. On the economics of probation and the war on drugs, see Timberlake 1963; Moore 1977; Thornton 1991; Miron and Zwiebel 1995; Resignato 2000; Miron 2003; Becker and Murphy 2013; Boettke, Coyne, and Hall 2013; and Redford and Powell 2016.

63. See Greenwald 2009.

64. United States Code, Title 10, sec. 371–378.

65. Defense Logistics Agency 2015.

66. U.S. General Services Administration 2015.

67. See the National Defense Authorization Act of 1994, 10 U.S.C. § 381, available online at https://www.law.cornell.edu/uscode/text/10/381.

68. U.S. General Services Administration 2012, 1.

69. See Mueller 2009 and Mueller and Stewart 2011, 2016.

70. U.S. General Services Administration 2012, 1.

71. Ibid.

72. See Saad 2002.

73. See U.S. Bureau of Justice Statistics 2003, 127, Table 2.27.

74. See Schann and Phillips 2011, 7–10.

75. See Epstein 2010 (emphasis added).

76. See U.S. Department of Homeland Security 2012.

77. Andreas 2003, 92.

78. See Whitehead 2013, 2015.

79. See Missouri Department of Public Safety 2012.

80. See Ruppert 2011.

81. Vibes 2014.

82. Rahall 2015, 7.

83. See Bove and Gavrilova 2017 and Harris, Park, Bruce, and Murray 2017.

84. See Delehanty, Mewhirter, Welch, and Wilks 2017.

85. See the Duncan Hunter National Defense Authorization Act of 2009, section 885.

86. U.S. General Services Administration 2014.

87. Rahall 2015, 11–16.

88. Balko 2012.

89. See Balko 2013a.

90. See Halperin 2013.

91. Quoted in Coleman 2014b.

92. U.S. Federal Bureau of Investigation 2012.

93. See Bates 2017.
94. See Joseph 2017.
95. See Wessler 2014.
96. See American Civil Liberties Union 2015.
97. Waddell 2015.
98. Friedman 2017, 21.
99. T. Lee 2015.
100. See Jackman 2017.
101. See the International Association of Chiefs of Police 2009, 25.
102. See Anderson 2011.
103. Ibid..
104. Quoted in Peterson 2013.
105. See International Association of Chiefs of Police 2009, 14 (emphasis added).
106. Ibid., 27.
107. Ibid., 29.
108. Ibid., 39.
109. Quoted in Remsberg 2013.
110. Balko 2013b.

Chapter 6

1. Fox News 2014.
2. Ibid..
3. Koebler 2014.
4. This definition is consistent with definitions used by the DoD. A UAV is defined as a single air vehicle, while a UAS (unmanned aerial system) consists of three to six vehicles, ground control, and support equipment. The term *drone* has become popular, referring to both UAVs and UASs, though it is not used by the DoD or private industry.
5. For background on the history and use of drones, see Whittle 2014; Plaw, Fricker, and Colon 2015; Kreps 2016; Scahill 2016; and Gusterson 2016.
6. Koebler 2014.
7. Ibid..
8. Bennett 2011.
9. Fulton 2014.
10. Bennett and Rubin 2013.
11. Electronic Frontier Foundation 2015.
12. American Civil Liberties Union 2011, 5.
13. Ibid., 11–12.
14. The Supreme Court has not ruled in any way on the use of drones domestically, though the court has allowed for warrantless searches in some cases by manned aircraft. See *California v. Ciraolo* 1986, *Dow Chemical Co. v. United States* 1986, and *Florida v. Riley* 1989.
15. Wagner 2015.

16. See Kopstein 2013 and Ingram 2013.
17. Electronic Frontier Foundation 2012.
18. Electronic Frontier Foundation 2014.
19. Whitlock 2014.
20. For a more complete history of the evolution of UAVs, see Hall and Coyne 2013.
21. Gibson 2011.
22. Newcome 2004, 16.
23. Cradle of Aviation 2016.
24. Newcome 2004, 58.
25. Ibid., 71.
26. Ibid., 59.
27. *Frontline* 2013.
28. Shelsby 1991.
29. Seybolt 2008.
30. Michel 2013.
31. See Gertler 2012, i, 8.
32. See Gregory 2011; Mazzetti 2013; Scahill 2013, 2016; and Hall 2015.
33. Serle 2015.
34. See Hall 2015.
35. Obama 2013.
36. Brennan 2012.
37. See Singer 2009 and Springer 2013.
38. Springer 2013, 145.
39. Blaker 2007, 130.
40. Quoted in Blaker 2007, 132.
41. Blaker 2007, 133–34.
42. Shelsby 1991.
43. Blaker 2007, 11.
44. Ibid., 3.
45. Ibid., 138.
46. Singer 2009, 187.
47. Shane 2015.
48. See Cebrowski and Garstka 1998.
49. Customs and Border Protections Today 2004; see also Perry 2008 and Operation Border Star 2014.
50. Booth 2011.
51. Ibid.
52. Quoted in Loeb 2014.
53. Judicial Watch 2016.
54. Quoted in Booth 2011.
55. Quoted in Padgett 2009.
56. Quoted in Horsey 2012.

57. Mizokami 2017.

58. Fang 2015.

59. See Coyne and Hall 2017.

60. A. Taylor 2015.

61. Friedersdorf 2012.

62. There is significant controversy regarding whether or not suspected terrorists, regardless of their citizenship, should be granted due process and other Constitutional rights. Although undoubtedly important to the larger discussion, this issue is beyond the scope of our analysis.

63. See Scahill 2016.

64. Office of the Assistant Attorney General 2010.

65. A. Taylor 2015.

66. Fernández 2014.

67. Bennett 2014.

68. Booth 2011.

69. American Civil Liberties Union of Massachusetts 2016.

70. Halpern and Martinez 2013.

71. Electronic Frontier Foundation 2015.

72. Electronic Frontier Foundation 2016d.

73. Electronic Frontier Foundation 2016a.

74. Electronic Frontier Foundation 2016c.

75. Electronic Frontier Foundation 2016b.

76. Dvorak 2012.

77. Friedersdorf 2016.

78. Glaser 2013.

79. See Collins 2017.

80. See Tucker 2017.

81. Work 2015.

82. McFarland 2015; see also van Vark 2015.

Chapter 7

1. See AntiWar.com 2006 for a gallery of these images.

2. Hersh 2007.

3. U.S. Senate Select Committee on Intelligence 2014. For a first-hand account of torture at Abu Ghraib by a former interrogator, see Fair 2016.

4. U.S. Senate Select Committee on Intelligence 2014, 11.

5. Sheets 2014.

6. U.S. Senate Select Committee on Intelligence 2014, 3.

7. Ibid., 3.

8. Ibid., 4.

9. White House Office of the Press Secretary 2014.

10. Dugan 2014.

11. In addition to generating fear, the dogs may have also been meant to in-

flict a different sort of pain. To some Muslims, dogs are viewed as unclean and impure. Exposure to a dog—touching it, or letting a dog come into contact with your belongings—requires *wudu*, an ablution or ritual washing. This is particularly important before engaging in *Salah*, or daily prayer. If not properly cleansed, a Muslim's *Salah* is not considered acceptable, thus impeding their ability to effectively engage in religious practice.

12. Ibid.
13. Edwards-Levy 2014.
14. United Nations General Assembly 1984.
15. Dignity Institute 2015.
16. See Landau 2009.
17. 2 Maccabees 7, New International Edition. See also Mannix 2014, 10–13.
18. See Donnelly and Diehl 2011, 37.
19. Pallitto 2011, 19.
20. Ibid., 24–27.
21. Ibid. It should also be noted that each stated the British should expect the same fates to befall their soldiers if such activities persisted.
22. The Constitution of the United States, Amendment Eight, 1789.
23. Storey and Lichauco 1977, 12.
24. Adams, Schurz, Smith, and Welsh 1902 (emphasis added).
25. Miller 1982, 220.
26. Ibid.
27. Ibid., 220.
28. Quoted in Adams, Schurz, Smith, and Welsh 1902 (emphasis added).
29. Teller 1902, 58.
30. The Anti-Imperialist League 1899.
31. Miller 1982, 245.
32. Ibid., 245–246.
33. Ibid.
34. Ibid., 247.
35. Kramer 2008.
36. See Chapter 5.
37. Kuzmarov 2012, 39.
38. McCoy 2009, 316.
39. Ibid., 316.
40. Leo 2008, 43.
41. *State v. Nagle* 1986.
42. National Commission on Law Observance and Enforcement 1931, 19.
43. National Commission on Law Observance and Enforcement 1931.
44. Leo 2008, 50.
45. Ibid.
46. Ibid., 45.
47. Prevost 2010, 8.

48. Rejali 2007, 279.
49. Adams, Schurz, Smith, and Welsh 1902, 65.
50. Ibid., 44. He denied the allegation.
51. Leo 2004, 47. See also the National Commission on Law Observance and Enforcement 1931.
52. See *Fisher v. State* 1926 at 127.
53. Thomas 1918, 547–548.
54. National Commission on Law Observance and Enforcement 1931, 90.
55. Ibid., 90–91.
56. Leo 2008, 31.
57. See Pallitto 2011, 126–128. See also Morsink 2000.
58. Quoted in Pallitto 2011, 126.
59. Pallitto 2011, 126.
60. See McCoy 2006, 2017, 135–144 and Rejali 2007, chapters 12 and 16.
61. Quoted in Brinkley 1992.
62. Greenberg 2003.
63. Ibid..
64. See White 1998.
65. Ibid.
66. Ibid.
67. See Roper Center Public Opinion Archives 1991, 29.
68. Ibid., 30.
69. Ibid., 30.
70. Callahan 2014. See Jacobsen 2014 for a detailed history of Operation Paperclip.
71. Gimbel 1990, 38.
72. Karlstrom 2012.
73. Lee and Shlain 1985, 16.
74. Ibid., 13.
75. McCoy 2006, 18; Otterman 2007, 19.
76. History 2008.
77. See McCoy 2006, 22.
78. Otterman 2007, 21 (emphasis added).
79. McCoy 2006, 28–30.
80. Ross 2006, 286–296.
81. Ibid.
82. Cockburn and St. Clair 1999, 217; McCoy 2006, 30.
83. Some claim that Olsen was murdered by his fellow CIA agents, though his death was officially ruled a suicide.
84. Lee and Shlain 1985, 32.
85. Ibid.
86. Ibid., 31.
87. Hooper 2012.

88. Lee and Shlain 1985, 36.
89. Cockburn and St. Clair 1999, 227–229.
90. Ibid.
91. Hooper 2012.
92. Quoted in Hooper 2012.
93. Rejali 2007, 370.
94. McCoy 2006: 39.
95. Rejali 2007., 368–369.
96. Ibid., 369.
97. Ibid.
98. Ibid., 370.
99. Quoted in Rejali 2007, 370.
100. Quoted in Senate Select Committee on Intelligence, Subcommittee on Health and Scientific Research of the Committee on Human Resources 1977, 239.
101. Ibid., 243.
102. Ibid., 7.
103. Ibid., 7–8.
104. Rejali 2007, 173.
105. Ibid., 173; see also Lewy 1980, 345–346.
106. Rejali 2007, 170–171.
107. BBC News 1998.
108. U.S.Department of the Army 1970, 7–15.
109. See Turse and Nelson 2006. See also Rejali 2007, 174.
110. Quoted in Coates 1971, 253–254.
111. McCoy 2006, 64–68; Otterman 2007, 61.
112. Quoted in Otterman 2007, 63–64.
113. Otterman 2007, 66.
114. Valentine 2004.
115. Data compiled from Flood, King, Ruggles, and Warren 2015. We thank Bryan Cutsinger for his assistance in collecting this data.
116. Conroy 2005.
117. Valentine 1990, 209.
118. Conroy 2005.
119. Ibid.
120. Ibid.
121. G. F. Taylor 2015, 330.
122. Conroy 2005.
123. People's Law Office 2014.
124. Conroy 2005.
125. Goldston 1990, 3.
126. Gorner 2015.
127. Ibid.
128. Hoffman et al. 2015.

129. Risen 2015.
130. Ibid.
131. Quoted in Ackerman 2015a. See also Ackerman 2015b.
132. Schwirtz and Winerip 2015.
133. Ackerman 2015a; see also Ackerman 2015b.
134. Florida Department of Corrections 2015.
135. Pennsylvania Department of Corrections 2016.
136. Associated Press 2015.
137. Data compiled from Flood, King, Ruggles, and Warren 2015.
138. McLaughlin 2015.
139. See Eddington 2015 and Hananel 2015.
140. Quoted in Hananel 2015.

Conclusion

1. See Sherry 1997.
2. Shoup 1969, 51.
3. See Ikenberry 2012 and Posen 2014.
4. See Posen 2014, 5–6.
5. Donovan 1970, 25–26 (emphasis original).
6. Vagts 1937, 15.
7. Wilson 1918, 128.
8. Ibid.
9. See Turse 2008. For discussions of the history and evolution of American militarism, see Ekirch 1956; Shoup 1969; Donovan 1970; Dunlap 1994; Sherry 1997; Bacevich 2005; Glain 2011; and Goodman 2013.
10. Shoup 1969, 53
11. Wills 2010, 1.
12. Bacevich 2005, 15.
13. Bacevich 2013, 14.
14. See Cole and Dempsey 2006; Cole 2008; Cole and Lobel 2009; Schwarz and Huq 2008; Herman 2011; and Glennon 2015.
15. See, for instance, Posner and Vermeule 2007.
16. Douglas 1987, 162.
17. See Cole and Dempsey 2006; Cole 2008; Cole and Lobel 2009; Schwarz and Huq 2008; Herman 2011; and Glennon 2015.
18. Rossiter 2009, 5.
19. Ibid.
20. See Higgs 1987, 2004, 2006, 2007a, and 2012.
21. Higgs 2004, 201.
22. Ibid.
23. Wills 2010, 2.
24. See, for example, Schwarz and Huq 2008, 19–20, and Glennon 2015.
25. Dorsen 1989, 840.

26. For a discussion of some of these mechanisms, see Rossiter 2009 and Schwarz and Huq 2008.

27. Greenwald 2014b.

28. See Sharp 2012, 25–32.

29. See Devins 2003 on the role of the public in constraining the executive branch during times of war.

30. Ekirch 1956. See also Dunlap 1994, 344–350.

31. On the origins of the permanent war economy, see Duncan and Coyne 2013b.

32. Higgs 2004, 214.

33. Ibid.

34. Higgs 1987, 37, 2008c, 548. Although they can relate and interact, "culture" and "ideology" are distinct concepts. Culture can be understood as a pattern of meanings through which individuals interpret their worldly experiences. Ideology, in contrast, is a systematic set of beliefs about how the world, including relations between people, works or should work. For a comprehensive treatment of culture and its importance for understanding social interactions and economic outcomes, see Storr 2013.

35. Higgs 1987, 39–45, 2008c, 548.

36. Allport 1950, 48.

37. Shoup 1969, 51.

38. Donovan 1970, 23.

39. Hand 1960, 189–190. See also Hayek 1973, 91–923; Buchanan 2005; and Schwarz and Huq 2008, 201.

40. Sharp 2012, 29.

41. Cole 2016. See also Devins 2003.

42. Hayek 1973, 61. See also Hayek 1960, 68.

43. Hayek 1973, 61.

44. Schwarz and Huq 2008, 2.

45. Sumner 1934, 473.

46. See, for example, Posner and Vermuele 2007 and Solove 2013.

47. See, for example, Johnson 2000.

48. Saiya and Scime 2015.

49. Ibid., 505.

50. See Bacevich 2005.

51. Quoted in Gilbert 1995, 278–279.

52. Bourne 1964, 67.

53. Ibid., 68.

54. Ibid.

55. Ibid., 69.

56. Ibid., 68.

57. Mueller and Stewart 2016, 2.

58. Ibid. (emphasis original).

59. Coleman 2014a.

60. Ibid.
61. Coburn 2015, 18.
62. Brzezinski 2007.
63. Ibid..
64. Atwood 2015.
65. Mueller and Stewart 2011, 43.
66. Bailey 2011.
67. Ibid.
68. Posen 2014, 16–20.
69. Kinzer 2015a.
70. See Mueller 2006 and Greenwald 2015.
71. Kinzer 2015b.
72. Quoted in Fenn 2015.
73. Ibid.
74. Hume 1963, 40 (emphasis original).
75. See Richman 2014.
76. Twain 1972b, 395.

References

Ackerman, Spencer. 2015a. "'I Sat In That Place for Three Days, Man': Chicagoans Detail Abusive Confinement Inside Police 'Black Site.'" *The Guardian*, February 27. Available online at https://www.theguardian.com/us-news/2015/feb/27/chicago-abusive-confinment-homan-square.

———. 2015b. "The Disappeared: Chicago Police Detain Americans at Abuse-Laden 'Black Site.'" *The Guardian*, February 24. Available online at http://www.theguardian.com/us-news/2015/feb/24/chicago-police-detain-americans-black-site?CMP=share_btn_tw.

Adams, Charles Francis, Carl Schurz, Edwin Burritt Smith, and Herbert Welsh. 1902. *Secretary Root's Record, Marked Severities in Philippine Warfare: Analysis of the Law and Facts Bearing on the Action and Utterances of President Roosevelt and Secretary Root*. Boston: Geo. H. Ellis.

Aid, Matthew M., and William Burr. 2013. "Secret Cold War Documents Reveal NSA Spied on Senators." *Foreign Policy*, September 25. Available online at http://foreignpolicy.com/2013/09/25/secret-cold-war-documents-reveal-nsa-spied-on-senators.

Allport, Gordon. 1950. "The Role of Expectancy." In *Tensions That Cause Wars*, ed. Hadley Cantril, 43–77. Urbana: University of Illinois Press.

American Civil Liberties Union. 2011. "Protecting Privacy from Aerial Surveillance: Recommendations for Government Use of Drone Aircraft." Available online at https://www.aclu.org/files/assets/protectingprivacyfromaerialsurveillance.pdf.

———. 2015. "Stingray Tracking Devices: Who's Got Them?" Available online at https://www.aclu.org/map/stingray-tracking-devices-whos-got-them.

American Civil Liberties Union of Massachusetts. 2016. "How New FBI Powers to Look Through NSA Intercepts Will Exacerbate Mass Incarceration." Privacy SOS blog, March 8. Available online at https://privacysos.org/blog/fbi-will-now-be-able-to-search-through-nsa-intercept-data.

Anderson, Craig A., Arlin J. Benjamin Jr., and Bruce B. Bartholow. 1999. "Does the Gun Pull the Trigger? Automatic Priming Effects of Weapon Pictures and Weapon Names." *Psychological Science* 9 (4): 308–314.

Anderson, Phil. 2011. "Ex-Military Lining Up for Police Jobs." *The Capital-Journal*, August 14. Available online at: http://cjonline.com/news/2011-08-14/ex-military-lining-police-jobs.

Andreas, Peter. 2003. "Redrawing the Line: Borders and Security in the Twenty-first Century." *International Security* 28 (2): 78–111.

The Anti-Imperialist League. 1899. *Soldiers' Letters: Being Materials for the History of a War of Criminal Aggression*. Boston: Rockwell and Churchill Press.

AntiWar.com. 2006. "Abu Ghraib Abuse Photos." AntiWar.com, February 17. Available online at http://www.antiwar.com/news/?articleid=8560.

Apuzzo, Matt. 2014. "War Gear Flows to Police Departments." *The New York Times*, June 8. Available online at https://www.nytimes.com/2014/06/09/us/war-gear-flows-to-police-departments.html?mcubz=1.

Aron, Raymond. 1974. *The Imperial Republic: The United States and the World, 1945–1973*. Upper Saddle River, NJ: Prentice Hall.

Associated Press. 2015. "VA Department of Corrections Wants to Hire More Vets." November 10. Available online at https://www.correctionsone.com/veterans/articles/41422187-Va-Department-of-Corrections-wants-to-hire-more-vets.

Atwood, Margaret. 2015. "We Are Double-Plus Unfree." *The Guardian*, September 18. Available online at http://www.theguardian.com/books/2015/sep/18/margaret-atwood-we-are-double-plus-unfree?CMP=share_btn_tw.

Axelrod , Jim, and Emily Rand. 2016. "Investigation Reveals CENTCOM General Delayed Intel on ISIS Fight Meant for the President." CBS News, September 22. Available online at http://www.cbsnews.com/news/did-a-centcom-general-delay-intelligence-meant-for-the-president.

Bacevich, Andrew. 2002. *American Empire: The Realities and Consequences of U.S. Diplomacy*. Cambridge: Harvard University Press.

———. 2005. *The New American Militarism*. New York: Oxford University Press.

———. 2010. *Washington Rules: America's Path to Permanent War*. New York: Metropolitan Books.

———. 2013. *Breach of Trust: How Americans Failed Their Soldiers and Their Country*. New York: Picador.

———. 2014. "Torture Report Highlights Consequences of Permanent War." *The Boston Globe*, December 9. Available online at http://www.bostonglobe.com/opinion/2014/12/09/torture-report-highlights-consequences-permanent-war/MdEpEx2ilVexZuECsJ88TN/story.html.

———. 2016. *America's War for the Greater Middle East*. New York: Random House.

Bagehot, Walter. 1963. *The English Constitution*. Ithaca, NY: Cornell University Press.

Bailey, Ronald. 2011. "How Scared of Terrorism Should You Be?" Reason.com, September 6. Available online at https://reason.com/archives/2011/09/06/how-scared-of-terrorism-should.

Baldwin, James D. 1960. "Smedley D. Butler and Prohibition Enforcement in Philadelphia, 1924–1925. *Pennsylvania Magazine of History and Biography* 84 (3): 352–368.

Balko, Radley. 2006. *Overkill: The Rise of Paramilitary Police Raids in America*. Washington, DC: Cato Institute. Available online at http://www.cato.org/sites/cato.org/files/pubs/pdf/balko_whitepaper_2006.pdf.

———. 2012. "Police 'Tank' Purchase Riles New Hampshire Town." *The Huff-*

ington Post, February 16. Available online at http://www.huffingtonpost.
com/2012/02/16/police-tank-purchase-new-hampshire_n_1279983.html.

———. 2013a. *Rise of the Warrior Cop: The Militarization of America's Police Forces*. New York: PublicAffairs.

———. 2013b. "What Cop T-Shirts Tell Us About Police Culture." *The Huffington Post*, June 21. Available online at http://www.huffingtonpost.com/2013/06/21/what-cop-tshirts-tell-us-_n_3479017.html.

———. 2014. "Botched Paramilitary Police Raids." Available online at http://www.cato.org/raidmap.

Ball, James, and Spencer Ackerman. 2013. "NSA Loophole Allows Warrantless Search for US Citizens' Emails and Phone Calls." *The Guardian*, August 9. Available online at http://www.theguardian.com/world/2013/aug/09/nsa-loophole-warrantless-searches-email-calls.

Bamford, James. 1983. *The Puzzle Palace: A Report on America's Most Secret Agency*. New York: Penguin Books.

———. 2008. *The Shadow Factory: The Ultra-Secret NSA from 9/11 to the Eavesdropping of America*. New York: Anchor Books.

———. 2013. "Five Myths About the National Security Agency." *The Washington Post*, June 21. Available online at http://www.washingtonpost.com/opinions/five-myths-about-the-national-security-agency/2013/06/21/438e0c4a-d37f-11e2-b05f-3ea3f0e7bb5a_story.html.

———. 2016. "Every Move You Make." *Foreign Policy*, September 7. Available online at http://foreignpolicy.com/2016/09/07/every-move-you-make-obama-nsa-security-surveillance-spying-intelligence-snowden.

———. 2017. "The Multibillion-Dollar Spy Agency You Haven't Heard Of." *Foreign Policy*, March 20. Available online at http://foreignpolicy.com/2017/03/20/the-multibillion-dollar-u-s-spy-agency-you-havent-heard-of-trump.

Barder, Alexander D. 2015. *Empire Within: International Hierarchy and Its Imperial Laboratories of Governance*. New York: Routledge.

Barnett, Ron, and Paul Alongi. 2011. "Critics Knock No-Knock Police Raids." *USA Today*, February 13. Available online at http://usatoday30.usatoday.com/news/nation/2011-02-14-noknock14_ST_N.htm.

Bates, Adam. 2017. *Stingray: A New Frontier in Police Surveillance* (Policy Analysis No. 809). Washington, DC: Cato Institute.

Baum, Dan. 1996. *Smoke and Mirrors: The War on Drugs and the Politics of Failure*. New York: Little, Brown.

BBC News. 1998. "Murder in the Name of War—My Lai." July 20. Available online at http://news.bbc.co.uk/2/hi/asia-pacific/64344.stm.

Becker, Gary S., and Kevin M. Murphy. 2013. "Have We Lost the War on Drugs?" *The Wall Street Journal*, January 4. Available online at http://online.wsj.com/article/SB10001424127887324374004578217682305605070.html.

Bennett, Brian. 2011. "Police Employ Predator Drone Spy Planes on Home Front."

Los Angeles Times, Dec. 10, 2011. Available online at: http://www.latimes. com/news/nationworld/nation/la-na-drone-arrest20111211,0,72624,full.story

———. 2014. "Border Patrol's Use of Deadly Force Criticized in Report." *The Los Angeles Times*, February 27. Available online at http://articles.latimes. com/2014/feb/27/nation/la-na-border-killings-20140227.

Bennett, Brian, and Joel Rubin. 2013. "Drones Are Taking to the Skies in the U.S." *The Los Angeles Times*, February 15. Available online at http://articles.latimes. com/2013/feb/15/nation/la-na-domestic-drones-20130216.

Bennett, Charles. 2010. "Legendary Lawman August Vollmer." *Officer*, May 27. Available online at http://www.officer.com/article/10232661/ legendary-lawman-august-vollmer.

Bennett, James. 2006. *Homeland Security Scams*. Piscataway, NJ: Transaction.

Berkowitz, Leonard, and Anthony LePage. 1967. "Weapons as Aggression-Eliciting Stimuli." *Journal of Personality and Social Psychology*, 7 (2): 202–207.

Beschloss, Michael. 2003. *Our Documents: 100 Milestone Documents from the National Archives*. New York: Oxford University Press.

Bilmes, Linda J., and Michael D. Intriligator. 2013. "How Many Wars Is the US Fighting Today?" *Peace Economics, Peace Science, and Public Policy* 19 (1): 8–16.

Bilmes, Linda J., and Joseph E. Stiglitz. 2008. *The Three Trillion Dollar War: The Tue Cost of the Iraq Conflict*. New York: W.W. Norton

Bjelopera, Jerome P. 2013. "American Jihadist Terrorism: Combating a Complex Threat." Congressional Research Service, Washington, DC. Available online at https://fas.org/sgp/crs/terror/R41416.pdf.

Blaker, James R. 2007. *Transforming Military Force: The Legacy of Arthur Ce-browski*. Westport, CT: Preager Security International.

Bloom, Sandra. 2004. "Neither Liberty Nor Safety: The Impact of Fear on Indi-viduals, Institutions, and Society, Part I." *Psychotherapy and Politics International* 2 (2): 78–98.

Bodin, Jean. 1955. *Six Books of the Commonwealth*. Trans. M. J. Tooley. Ox-ford, UK: Basil Blackwell.

Boettke, Peter J., Christopher J. Coyne, and Abigail R. Hall. 2013. "Keep Off the Grass: The Economics of Prohibition and U.S. Drug Policy." *Oregon Law Review* 91 (4): 1069–1096.

Boot, Max. 2002. *The Savage Wars of Peace: Small Wars and the Rise of Ameri-can Power*. New York: Basic Books.

Booth, William. 2011. "More Predator Drones Fly U.S.-Mexico Border." *The Washington Post*, December 21. Available online at http://www.washing-tonpost.com/world/more-predator-drones-fly-us-mexico-border/2011/12/01/ gIQANSZz8O_story.html.

Bouie, Jamelle. 2014. "The Militarization of the Police." *Slate*, August 13. Avail-able online at http://www.slate.com/articles/news_and_politics/politics/2014/08/ police_in_ferguson_military_weapons_threaten_protesters.html.

Bourne, Randolph S. 1964. "The State." In *War and the Intellectuals: Collected Essays, 1915–1919*, ed. Carl Resek, 65–106. New York: Harper & Row.

Bove, Vincenzo, and Evelina Gavrilova. 2017. "Police Officer on the Frontline or Soldier? The Effect of Police Militarization on Crime." *American Economic Journal: Economic Policy* 9 (3): 1–18.

Brennan, Geoffrey, and James M. Buchanan. 1985. *The Reason of Rules: Constitutional Political Economy*. Cambridge, UK: Cambridge University Press.

Brennan, John. 2012. "The Efficacy and Ethics of U.S. Counterterrorism Strategy." Available online at http://www.wilsoncenter.org/event/ the-efficacy-and-ethics-us-counterterrorism- strategy.

Brenner, Michael. 2014."Ur Imperialism." *Huffington Post*, February 15. Available online at http://www.huffingtonpost.com/michael-brenner/ur-imperialism_b_4453714.html.

Brinkley, Joel. 1992. "Bush and Yeltsin Declare Formal End to Cold War; Agree to Exchange Visits; U.S. Looking for New Course as Superpower Conflict Ends." *The New York Times*, February 2. Available online at http://www.ny-times.com/1992/02/02/world/bush-yeltsin-declare-formal-end-cold-war-agree-exchange-visits-us-looking-for.html?pagewanted=1.

Brown, J. Willard. 1974. *The Signal Corps, U.S.A. in the War of the Rebellion*. New York: Arno Press.

Brownell Committee. 1952. *Brownell Committee Report*. Available online at https://www.nsa.gov/about/cryptologic_heritage/60th/interactive_timeline/ Content/preNSA/documents/19520613_PreNSA_Doc_3201737_Brownell.pdf.

Brzezinski, Zbigniew. 2007. "Terrorized by the 'War on Terror'," *The Washington Post*, March 25. Available online at http://www.washingtonpost.com/wp-dyn/ content/article/2007/03/23/AR2007032301613.html.

Buchanan, James M. 1975. *The Limits of Liberty: Between Anarchy and Leviathan*. Chicago: Public Choice.

———. 2005. "Afraid to Be Free: Dependency as Desideratum." *Public Choice* 124: 19–31.

Burns, Thomas L. 1990. *The Origins of the National Security Agency: 1940–1952*. Fort Meade, MD: National Security Agency, Center for Cryptologic History. Available online at http://www2.gwu.edu/~nsarchiv/NSAEBB/NSAEBB278/02. PDF.

Burton, Lynsi. 2014. "WTO Riots in Seattle: 15 Years Ago." *Seattle Pi*, November 29. Available online at http://www.seattlepi.com/local/article/WTO-riots-in-Seattle-15-years-ago-5915088.php.

California v. Ciraolo, 476 U.S. 207, no. 84-1513. 1986. Available online at https:// scholar.google.com/scholar_case?case=13894501388713609672&q=Californ ia+v.+Ciraolo&hl=en&as_sdt=40006&as_vis=1.

Callahan, Maureen. 2014. "Behind the Secret Plan to Bring Nazi Scientists to US." *The New York Post*, February 1. Available online at http://nypost. com/2014/02/01/behind-the-secret-plan-to-smuggle-nazi-scientists-to-america.

Carlson, Michael, Amy Marcus-Newhall, and Norman Miller. 1990. "Effects of Situational Aggression Cues: A Quantitative Review." *Journal of Personality and Social Psychology* 58 (4): 622–633.

Carpenter, Ted Galen, and Malou Innocent. 2015. *Perilous Partners: The Benefits and Pitfalls of America's Alliances with Authoritarian Regimes*. Washington, DC: Cato Institute.

Carte, Gene. 1980. "August Vollmer and the Origins of Police Professionalism." *Mimeo*. Available online at https://www.ncjrs.gov/pdffiles1/Digitization/68880NCJRS.pdf.

Carte, Gene, et al. 1983. "August Vollmer: Pioneer in Police Professionalism: Oral History Transcript and Related Material, 1972–1983." Available online at https://archive.org/details/augustvollmer02vollrich.

Cebrowski, Arthur K., and John J. Garstka. 1998. "Network-Centric Warfare: Its Origin and Future." *U.S. Naval Institute Proceedings* 124 (1/1, 139): 28–35.

Central Intelligence Agency. 2007a. "Intelligence in the War of Independence: Organization of Intelligence." Available online at https://www.cia.gov/library/publications/intelligence-history/intelligence/orgintell.html.

———. 2007b. "Intelligence in the Civil War." Available online at https://www.cia.gov/library/publications/intelligence-history/civil-war/Intel_in_the_CW1.pdf.

Chapman, Terrence L., and Dan Reiter. 2004. "The United Nations Security Council and the Rally 'Round the Flag Effect." *The Journal of Conflict Resolution* 48 (6): 886–909.

Cherny, Robert W. 2008. "Anticommunist Networks and Labor: The Pacific Coast in the 1930s." In *Labor's Cold War: Legal Politics in a Global Context*, ed. Shelton Stromquist, 17–48. Champaign: University of Illinois Press.

Citizens for Responsibility and Ethics in Washington. 2013. *Strategic Maneuvers: The Revolving Door from the Pentagon to the Private Sector*. Washington, DC: Citizens for Responsibility and Ethics in Washington. Available online at http://www.citizensforethics.org/pages/strategic-maneuvers-generals-defense-department-revolving-door.

Clarke, Richard A., Michael J. Morell, Geoffrey R. Stone, Cass R. Sunstein, and Peter Swire. 2014. *The NSA Report: Liberty and Security in a Changing World*. Princeton, NJ: Princeton University Press.

Clinton, Paul. 2010. "Daryl Gates and the Origins of LAPD SWAT." *Police*, April 16. Available online at http://www.policemag.com/blog/swat/story/2010/04/daryl-gates-and-the-origins-of-lapd-swat.aspx.

Coakley, Robert W. 2011. *The Role in Federal Police Forces in Domestic Disorders: 1789–1878*. Washington, DC: Center of Military History, United States Army.

Coates, Ken, ed. 1971. *Prevent the Silence: Reports from the Sessions of the International War Crimes Tribunal*. London: Allen Lane.

Coburn, Tom. 2015. *A Review of the Department of Homeland Security's Mission and Performance*. Available online at https://www.hsgac.senate.gov/download/?id=B92B8382-DBCE-403C-A08A-727F89C2BC9B.

Cockburn, Alexander, and Jeffrey St. Clair. 1999. *Whiteout: The CIA, Drugs and the Press*. New York: Verso Press.

Cogan, Jacob Katz. 2006. "Noncompliance and the International Rule of Law." *Yale Journal of International Law* 31: 189–210.

Cohen, Eliot A. 2016. *The Big Stick: The Limits of Soft Power & the Necessity of Military Force.* New York: Basic Books.

Cole, David. 2008. "No Reason to Believe: Radical Skepticism, Emergency Power, and Constitutional Constraint." *University of Chicago Law Review* 75: 1329–1364.

———. 2016. *Engines of Liberty: The Power of Citizen Activists to Make Constitutional Law.* New York: Basic Books.

Cole, David, and James X. Dempsey. 2006. *Terrorism and the Constitution: Sacrificing Civil Liberties in the Name of National Security.* New York: The New Press.

Cole, David, and Jules Lobel. 2009. *Less Safe, Less Free: Why America Is Losing the War on Terror.* New York: The New Press.

Coleman, Michael. 2014a. "Mission Creep: Homeland Security a 'Runaway Train'." *Albuquerque Journal*, April 27. Available online at http://www.abqjournal.com/390438/news/homeland-security-a-runaway-train.html.

———. 2014b. "Mission Creep: NM Footprint Grows: 'We've Up-Armored'," *Albuquerque Journal*, April 28. Available online at http://www.abqjournal.com/390807/news/nm-footprint-grows-weve-uparmored.html.

Collins, Dave. 2017. "Connecticut Considers Weaponizing Drones." Associated Press, March 30. Available online at http://www.fox5ny.com/news/244994462-story.

Collins, John M. 1991. *America's Small Wars: Lessons for the Future.* New York: Brassey's.

Conroy, John. 2005. "Tools of Torture." *The Chicago Reader*, February 3. Available online at http://www.chicagoreader.com/chicago/tools-of-torture/Content?oid=917876.

Constantino, Renato. 1975. *The Philippines: A Past Revisited.* Quezon City: Tala Publications.

Cooper, Helene. 2016. "Military Officials Distorted ISIS Intelligence, Congressional Panel Says." *The New York Times*, August 11. Available online at http://www.nytimes.com/2016/08/12/us/politics/isis-centcom-intelligence.html?_r=0.

Corwin, Edward S. 1947. *Total War and the Constitution.* New York: Alfred Knopf.

Cowen, Tyler. 2009. "Does Technology Drive the Growth of Government?" *Mimeo.* Available online at http://www.bcaplan.com/Cowentech.pdf.

Coyne, Christopher J. 2008. *After War: The Political Economy of Exporting Democracy.* Stanford, CA: Stanford University Press.

———. 2013. *Doing Bad by Doing Good: Why Humanitarian Action Fails.* Stanford, CA: Stanford University Press.

———. 2015. "Lobotomizing the Defense Brain." *Review of Austrian Economics* 28 (4): 371–396.

Coyne, Christopher J., and Rachel L. Coyne. 2013. "The Political Economy of Human Rights Scandals." *Homo Oeconomicus* 30 (4): 101–126.

Coyne, Christopher J., and Abigail R. Hall. 2017. "The Drone Paradox: Fighting Mechanized Terror with Mechanized Terror." Mimeo. Available online at https://papers.ssrn.com/sol3/papers.cfm?abstract_id=2815135.

Coyne, Christopher J., and David S. Lucas. 2016. "Economists Have No Defense: A Critical Review of National Defense in Economics Textbooks." *The Journal of Private Enterprise* 31 (4): 65–83.

Coyne, Christopher J., and Rachel L. Mathers. 2010. "The Fatal Conceit of Foreign Intervention." *Advances in Austrian Economics* 14: 227–252.

Coyne, Christopher J., Courtney Michaluk, and Rachel Reese. 2016. "Unproductive Entrepreneurship in U.S. Military Contracting." *Journal of Entrepreneurhsip and Public Policy* 5 (2): 221–239.

Cradle of Aviation. 2016. "Curtiss-Sperry Aerial Torpedo." Available online at http://www.cradleofaviation.org/history/permanent_exhibits/world_war_i/curtiss_sperry_aerial_torpedo.html.

Cullather, Nick. 2006. *Secret History: The CIA's Classified Account of Its Operations in Guatemala, 1952–1954.* Stanford, CA: Stanford University Press.

Customs and Border Protections Today. 2004. "Unmanned Aerial Vehicles Support Border Security." Available online at http://www.cbp.gov/xp/CustomsToday/2004/Aug/other/aerial_vehicles.xml.

Dawson, John W., and John J. Seater. 2013. "Federal Regulation and Aggregate Economic Growth." *Journal of Economic Growth* 18 (2): 137–177.

Defense Logistics Agency. 2015. "Law Enforcement Support Office." Available online at http://www.dispositionservices.dla.mil/leso/Pages/1033ProgramFAQs.aspx#q1.

Delehanty, Casey, Jack Mewhirter, Ryan Welch, and Jason Wilks. 2017. "Militarization and Police Violence: The Case of the 1033 Program." *Research & Politics* 4 (2), open access journal: http://journals.sagepub.com/doi/pdf/10.1177/2053168017712885.

Denson, John V. 1999. *The Costs of War.* Piscataway, NJ: Transaction.

Devins, Neal. 2003. "Congress, Civil Liberties, and the War on Terror." *William & Mary Bill of Rights Journal* 11 (3): 1139–1154.

Dignity Institute. 2015. "FAQ: How Many Countries Have Ratified the UN Convention Against Torture?" Available online at https://dignityinstitute.org/resources/faq/about-torture/faq-how-many-countries-have-ratified-the-un-convention-against-torture.

Domanick, Joe. 2010. "Daryl Gates' Downfall." *The LA Times,* April 18. Available online at http://articles.latimes.com/2010/apr/18/opinion/la-oe-domanick18-2010apr18.

Donovan, James A. 1970. *Militarism, U.S.A.* New York: Charles Scribner's Sons.

Donnelly, Mark P., and Daniel Diehl. 2011. *The Big Book of Pain: Torture & Punishment Through History.* Stroud, Gloucestershire, England: The History Press.

Dorsen, Norman. 1989. "Foreign Affairs and Civil Liberties." *The American Journal of International Law* 83 (4): 840–850.

Douglas, William O. 1987. *The Douglas Letters: Selections from the Private Papers of Justice William O. Douglas.* Ed. Melvin I. Urofsky. Bethesda, MD: Adler & Adler.

Dow Chemical Co. v. United States, 476 U.S. 277, no. 841259. 1986. Available online at https://scholar.google.com/scholar_case?case=2807189437219807369&q=Dow+Chemical+Co.+v.+United+States&hl=en&as_sdt=40006&as_vis=1.

Dudley, Susan, and Melinda Warren. 2014. "Economic Forms of Regulation on the Rise: An Analysis of the U.S. Budget for Fiscal Year 2014 and 2015." Washington, DC: Weidenbaum Center at Washington University and Regulatory Studies Center, George Washington University. Available online at https://wc.wustl.edu/files/wc/imce/2015_regulators_budget_1.pdf.

Dudziak, Mary L. 2012. *War Time: An Idea, Its History, Its Consequences*. New York: Oxford University Press.

Dugan, Andrew. 2014. "A Retrospective Look at How Americans View Torture." *Gallup*, December 10. Available online at http://www.gallup.com/opinion/polling-matters/180008/retrospective-look-americans-view-torture.aspx.

Duncan, Thomas K., and Christopher J. Coyne. 2013a. "The Overlooked Costs of the Permanent War Economy." *The Review of Austrian Economics* 26 (4): 413–431.

———. 2013b. "The Origins of the Permanent War Economy." *The Independent Review: A Journal of Political Economy* 18 (2): 219–240.

———. 2015a. "The Revolving Door and the Entrenchment of the Permanent War Economy." *Peace Economics, Peace Science and Public Policy* 21 (3): 391–413.

———. 2015b. "The Political Economy of Foreign Intervention." In *The Oxford Handbook on Austrian Economics*, ed. Peter J. Boettke and Christopher J. Coyne, 678–697. New York: Oxford University Press.

Dunlap, Charles J. Jr. 1994. "Welcome to the Junta: The Erosion of Civilian Control of the U.S. Military." *Wake Forest Law Review* 29 (2): 341–392.

Dunne, J. Paul. 1995. "The Defense Industrial Base." In *Handbook of Defense Economics, Volume 1*, ed. Keith Hartley and Todd Sandler, 399–430. New York: Elsevier Science B.V.

Dvorak, Kimberly. 2012. "Homeland Security Increasingly Lending Drones to Local Police." *The Washington Times*, December 10. Available online at http://www.washingtontimes.com/news/2012/dec/10/homeland-security-increasingly-loaning-drones-to-l.

Dye, Thomas R. 1975. *Understanding Public Policy*. Upper Saddle River, NJ: Prentice Hall.

———. 2001. *Top Down Policymaking*. New York: Chatham House.

———. 2014. *Who's Running America? The Obama Reign*. New York: Routledge.

The Economist. 2014. "Why the Sheriff Should Follow the Law." May 23rd. Available online at http://www.economist.com/blogs/democracyinamerica/2014/05/america-and-international-law.

Eddington, Patrick G. 2015. "How the F.B.I. Can Detain, Render and Threaten Without Risk." *The New York Times*, November 3. Available online at http://www.nytimes.com/2015/11/03/opinion/how-the-fbi-can-detain-render-and-threaten-without-risk.html?_r=2.

Edel, Charles N. 2014. *Nation Builder: John Quincy Adams and the Grand Strategy of the Republic*. Cambridge: Harvard University Press.

Edwards-Levy, Ariel. 2014. "Americans Are Divided on Use of Torture, But Fewer Support Some of the Harshest Tactics. *The Huffington Post*, December 12. Available online at http://www.huffingtonpost.com/2014/12/12/torture-report-poll_n_6316126.html.

Ekirch Jr., Arthur A. 1956 [2010]. *The Civilian and the Military: A History of the American Antimilitarist Tradition*. Oakland, CA: Independent Institute.

Eland, Ivan. 2013. "Warfare State to Welfare State: Conflict Causes Government to Expand at Home." *The Independent Review: A Journal of Political Economy* 18 (2): 189–218.

Electronic Frontier Foundation. 2012. "Who Is Flying Unmanned Aircraft in the U.S.?" Available online at https://www.eff.org/press/releases/who-flying-unmanned-aircraft-us.

———. 2014. "All of the EFF's Transparency Litigation in One, Shiny InFOIAgraphic." Available online at https://www.eff.org/deeplinks/2014/03/effs-infoiagraphic.

———. 2015. "Drone Flights in the U.S." Available online at https://www.eff.org/foia/faa-drone-authorizations.

———. 2016a. "Arlington Police Department Drone Records." Available online at https://www.eff.org/document/arlington-police-department.

———. 2016b. "DOJ/Queen Anne County Sheriff's Drone Records." Available online at https://www.eff.org/document/doj-queen-anne-county-sheriffs-office.

———. 2016c. "Gadsden, Alabama Police Department Drone Records." Available online at https://www.eff.org/document/gadsden-alabama-police-dept.

———. 2016d. "Ogden, Utah Police Department Drone Records." Available online at https://www.eff.org/document/ogden-police-department-utah.

Electronic Privacy Information Center. n.d. "Foreign Intelligence Surveillance Act Court Orders 1979–2012." Available online at http://epic.org/privacy/wiretap/stats/fisa_stats.html.

Ellickson, Robert C. 1987. "A Critique of Economic and Sociological Theories of Social Control." *Journal of Legal Studies* 16: 67–99.

———. 1991. *Order Without Law: How Neighbors Settle Disputes*. Cambridge, MA: Harvard University Press.

Epstein, Edward Jay. 2007. "Opening Up the CIA." *The Wall Street Journal*, July 14. Available online at http://www.wsj.com/news/articles/SB118436115647966211.

Epstein, Jennifer. 2010. "Eric Holder Warns of Homegrown Terror." *Politico*. Available online at http://www.politico.com/news/stories/1210/46662.html.

Esman, Milton J. 2013. *The Emerging American Garrison State*. New York: Palgrave Macmillan.

Fair, Eric. 2016. *Consequence: A Memoir*. New York: Henry Holt.

Fang, Marina. 2015. "Nearly 90 Percent of People Killed in Recent Drone Strikes Were Not the Intended Target." *The Huffington Post*, October 20. Available online at http://www.huffingtonpost.com/entry/civilian-deaths-drone-strikes_us_561fafe2e4b028dd7ea6c4ff.

Fe Caces, M., and Terry S. Zobeck. 2001. "Youth Drug Use and the National Youth Anti-Drug Media Campaign." Washington, DC: Office of National Drug Control Policy. Available online at https://www.ncjrs.gov/ondcppubs/publications/pdf/report_to_congress.pdf.

Fenn, Peter. 2015. "'No Place to Hide'." *U.S. News & World Report*, June 3. Available online at http://www.usnews.com/opinion/blogs/peter-fenn/2015/06/03/nsa-fbi-spying-excesses-underscore-need-for-a-new-church-committee.

Ferguson, Niall. 2003. *Empire: The Rise and Demise of British World Order and the Lessons for Global Power.* New York: Basic Books.

———. 2004. *Colossus: The Price of America's Empire.* New York: Penguin Press.

Ferguson, Niall, and Moritz Schularick. 2006. "The Empire Effect: The Determinants of Country Risk in the First Age of Globalization, 1880–1913." *Journal of Economic History* 66 (2): 283–312.

Fernández, Belén. 2014. "The Creeping Expansion of the Border Patrol." *Al Jazeera America*, May 7. Available online at http://america.aljazeera.com/opinions/2014/5/border-patrol-immigrationmilitarizationhomelandsecurity.html.

Fettweis, Christopher J. 2013. *The Pathologies of Power: Fear, Honor, Glory, and Hubris in U.S. Foreign Policy.* Cambridge, MA: Cambridge University Press.

Finnegan, John Patrick. 1998. *Military Intelligence.* Washington, DC: U.S. Army Center of Military History.

Fisher v. State, 145 Miss. 116. 1926. Available online at https://casetext.com/case/fisher-v-state-286.

Flood, Sara, Miriam King, Steven Ruggles, and J. Robert Warren. 2015. "Integrated Public Use Microdata Series, Current Population Survey: Version 4.0 Dataset." Available online at https://cps.ipums.org/cps.

Florida Department of Corrections. 2015. "Florida Department of Corrections Honors America's Veterans." Available online at http://www.dc.state.fl.us/secretary/press/2015/11-10-Veterans.html.

Florida v. Riley, 488 U.S. 445, no. 87-764. 1989. Available online at https://scholar.google.com/scholar_case?case=15702097135289839333&q=Florida+v.+Riley&hl=en&as_sdt=40006&as_vis=1.

Fox News. 2014. "Predator Drone Helps Convict North Dakota Farmer in First Case of Its Kind." January 28. Available online at http://www.foxnews.com/us/2014/01/28/first-american-gets-prison-with-assistance-predator-drone.

Friedberg, Aaron L. 1992. "Why Didn't the United States Become a Garrison State?" *International Security* 16 (4): 109–142.

Friedersdorf, Conor. 2012. "How Team Obama Justifies the Killing of a 16-Year-Old American." *The Atlantic*, October 24. Available online at http://www.theatlantic.com/politics/archive/2012/10/how-team-obama-justifies-the-killing-of-a-16-year-old-american/264028.

———. 2016. "The Rapid Rise of Federal Surveillance Drones Over America." *The*

Atlantic, March 10. Available online at http://www.theatlantic.com/politics/archive/2016/03/the-rapid-rise-of-federal-surveillance-drones-over-america/473136.

Friedman, Barry. 2017. *Unwarranted: Policing Without Permission*. New York: Farrar, Straus and Giroux.

Frontline. 2013. "Weapons: Drones (RPVs)." Available online at http://www.pbs.org/wgbh/pages/frontline/gulf/weapons/drones.html.

Froomkin, Dan. 2015. "The Computers Are Listening: How the NSA Converts Spoken Words into Searchable Text." *The Intercept*, May 5. Available online at https://firstlook.org/theintercept/2015/05/05/nsa-speech-recognition-snowden-searchable-text.

Fuller, Lon L. 1964. *The Morality of Law*. New Haven: Yale University Press.

Fulton, Sandra. 2014. "Police Hunger for Drones May Be Growing, but So Are Privacy Concerns." The American Civil Liberties Union, January 16. Available online at https://www.aclu.org/blog/national-security/police-hunger-drones-may-be-growing-so-are-privacy-concerns.

Garrett, Garet. 1953. *The People's Pottage*. Caldwell, ID: Caxton.

Garrett, Thomas A.. and Russell M. Rhine. 2006. "On the Size and Growth of Government." *Federal Reserve Bank of St. Louis Review* 88 (1): 13–30.

Gates, Daryl. 1992. *Chief: My Life in the LAPD*. New York: Bantam.

Gellman, Barton. 2013. "Edward Snowden, After Months of NSA Revelations, Says His Mission's Accomplished." *The Washington Post*, December 23. Available online at http://www.washingtonpost.com/world/national-security/edward-snowden-after-months-of-nsa-revelations-says-his-missions-accomplished/2013/12/23/49fc36de-6c1c-11e3-a523-fe73f0ff6b8d_story.html.

Gellman, Barton, and Ashkan Soltani. 2013. "NSA Infiltrates Links to Yahoo, Google Data Centers Worldwide, Snowden Documents Say." *The Washington Post*, October 30. Available online at http://www.washingtonpost.com/world/national-security/nsa-infiltrates-links-to-yahoo-google-data-centers-worldwide-snowden-documents-say/2013/10/30/e51d661e-4166-11e3-8b74-d89d714ca4dd_story.html.

Gellman, Barton, Julie Tate, and Ashkan Soltani. 2014. "In NSA-Intercepted Data, Those Not Targeted Far Outnumber Foreigners Who Are." *The Washington Post*, July 5. Available online at https://www.washingtonpost.com/world/national-security/in-nsa-intercepted-data-those-not-targeted-far-outnumber-the-foreigners-who-are/2014/07/05/8139adf8-045a-11e4-8572-4b1b969b6322_story.html.

Gentry, Curt. 1991. *J. Edgar Hoover: The Man and His Secrets*. New York: W.W. Norton.

Gertler, Jeremiah. 2012. "U.S. Unmanned Aerial Systems." Congressional Research Service. Washington, DC Available online at: https://www.fas.org/sgp/crs/natsec/R42136.pdf.

Giblin, Matthew J. 2017. *Leadership and Management in Police Organizations*. Los Angeles: Sage.

Gibson, Jacob. 2011. "The American Military-Industrial Complex: WWI, WWII, the Cold

War, and Beyond." *The Examiner*. July 21. Available online at http://www.examiner.com/article/the-american-military-industrial-complex-wwi-wwii-the-cold-war-and-beyond.

Gilbert, G. M. 1995. *Nuremberg Diary*. Boston: De Capo Press.

Gimbel, John. 1990. *Science, Technology, and Reparations: Exploitation and Plunder in Postwar Germany*. Stanford, CA: Stanford University Press.

Glain, Stephen. 2011. *State vs. Defense: The Battle to Define America's Empire*. New York: Crown Publishers.

Glaser, John. 2013. "Obama Administration: Yes, We Can Kill Americans on US Soil." *Anti-War*, March 5. Available online at http://antiwar.com/blog/2013/03/05/obama-administration-yes-we-can-kill-americans-on-us-soil.

Glenn, Jason E. 2006. "The Birth of the Crack Baby and the History That 'Myths' Make." *Mimeo*, available online at https://biblio.csusm.edu/sites/default/files/reserves/birth_of_the_crack_baby_and_the_history_that_myths_make.pdf.

Glennon, Michael J. 2015. *National Security and Double Government*. New York: Oxford University Press.

Goldston, Michael. 1990. "Special Project Conclusion Reports: The Burge Investigation." Chicago Police Department Office of Professional Standards. Available online at http://peopleslawoffice.com/wp-content/uploads/2012/02/Goldston-Report-with-11.2.90-Coversheet.pdf.

Goldwater, Barry. 1973. "War Without Declaration: A Chronological List of 199 U.S. Military Hostilities Abroad Without a Declaration of War, 1798–1972." *Congressional Record*, 119, July 20, S14174-S14183.

Gonzales, Alberto. 2002. "Decision Re Application of the Geneva Convention on Prisoners of War to the Conflict with Al Qaeda and the Taliban." January 22. Available online at http://www2.gwu.edu/~nsarchiv/NSAEBB/NSAEBB127/02.01.25.pdf.

Goodman, Melvin A. 2013. *National Insecurity: The Cost of American Militarism*. San Francisco: City Lights Books.

Gordon, Scott. 2002. *Controlling the State: Constitutionalism from Ancient Athens to Today*. Cambridge, MA: Harvard University Press.

Gorner, Jeremy. 2015. "Former Chicago Police Cmdr. Jon Burge Released from Home Confinement." *The Chicago Tribune*, February 13. Available online at http://www.chicagotribune.com/news/local/breaking/chi-jon-burge-police-torture-released-20150213-story.html.

Gottfried, Paul Edward. 1999. *After Liberalism: Mass Democracy in the Managerial State*. Princeton, NJ: Princeton University Press.

Granick, Jennifer Stisa. 2017. *American Spies: Modern Surveillance, Why You Should Care, and What to Do About It*. Cambridge, MA: Cambridge University Press.

Greenberg, David. 2003. "Fallout Can Be Fun: How Cold War Civil-Defense Programs Became Farce." *Slate*, February 20. Available online at http://www.slate.com/articles/news_and_politics/history_lesson/2003/02/fallout_can_be_fun.html.

Greenwald, Glenn. 2009. *Drug Decriminalization in Portugal: Lessons for Creating Fair and Successful Drug Policies.*" Washington, DC: Cato Institute.

———. 2013a. "NSA Collecting Phone Records of Millions of Verizon Customers Daily." *The Guardian*, June 6. Available online at http://www.theguardian.com/world/2013/jun/06/nsa-phone-records-verizon-court-order.

———. 2013b. "XKeystroke: NSA Tool Collects 'Nearly Everything a User Does in the Internet'." *The Guardian*, July 31. Available online at http://www.theguardian.com/world/2013/jul/31/nsa-top-secret-program-online-data?CMP=share_btn_fb.

———. 2014a. *No Place to Hide: Edward Snowden, the NSA, and the U.S. Surveillance State.* New York: Metropolitan Books.

———. 2014b. "Congress Is Irrelevant on Mass Surveillance. Here's What Matters Instead." *The Intercept*, November 19. Available online at https://theintercept.com/2014/11/19/irrelevance-u-s-congress-stopping-nsas-mass-surveillance.

———. 2015. "For Terrorist Fearmongers, It's Always the Scariest Time Ever." *The Intercept*, June 2. Available online at https://theintercept.com/2015/06/02/fear-mongers-always-scariest-time-ever.

Greenwald, Glenn, and Ewen MacAskill. 2013. "NSA Prism Program Taps into Our Data of Apple, Google and Others." *The Guardian*, June 7. Available online at http://www.theguardian.com/world/2013/jun/06/us-tech-giants-nsa-data.

Gregory, Derek. 2011. "The Everywhere War." *The Geographical Journal* 177 (3): 238–250.

Greve, Michael S. 2012. *The Upside-Down Constitution.* Cambridge, MA: Harvard University Press.

Grigg, William N. 2015. "Flash Bang Reply." Available online at http://www.scribd.com/doc/265760507/Flash-Bang-Reply.

Grigsby, Hugh Blair, ed. 1890. *History of the Virginia Federal Convention of 1788*, vol. 1. Richmond, VA: Virginia Historical Society.

Guevara, Sulpicio, ed. 2005. "The Laws of the First Philippine Republic (the Laws of the Malolos) 1898–1899." Available online at http://quod.lib.umich.edu/p/philamer/aab1246.0001.001/122?rgn=full+text;view=image.

Gusterson, Hugh. 2016. *Drone: Remote Control Warfare.* Cambridge, MA: MIT Press.

Hagedorn, Ann. 2007. *Savage Peace: Hope and Fear in America, 1919.* New York: Simon & Schuster.

Hall, Abigail R. 2015. "Drones: Public Interest, Public Choice, and the Expansion of Unmanned Aerial Vehicles." *Peace Economics, Peace Science, and Public Policy* 21 (2): 273–300.

Hall, Abigail R., and Christopher J. Coyne. 2013. "The Militarization of U.S. Domestic Policing." *Independent Review* 7 (4): 485–504.

Halperin, Alex. 2013. "Radley Balko: "Once a Town Gets a SWAT Team You Want to Use It." *Salon*, July 13. Available online at http://www.salon.com/2013/07/13/radley_balko_once_a_town_gets_a_swat_team_you_want_to_use_it.

Halperin, Morton H., Jerry J. Berman, Robert L. Borosage, and Christine M.

Marwick. 1976. *The Lawless State: Crimes of the U.S. Intelligence Agencies.* New York: Penguin Books.

Halpern, Tomas, and Anthony Martinez. 2013. "Congressman Calls for Review of CBP Policies Following Allegation of Vaginal and Rectal Probe of U.S. Citizen." *Newspaper Tree*, December 21. Available online at http://newspapertree.com/ articles/2013/12/21/congressman-calls-for-review-of-cbp-policies-following-allegations-of-vaginal-and-rectal-probe-of-us-citizen.

Hananel, Sam. 2015. "Appeals Court Says American Can't Sue FBI Over Abuse Claims." *The Boston Globe*, October 24. Available online at https://www. bostonglobe.com/news/nation/2015/10/23/appeals-court-says-american-can-sue-fbi-over-abuse-claims/vGk60So2YNWb5v2r2HkoCI/story.html.

Hand, Learned. 1960. *The Spirit of Liberty: Papers and Addresses of Learned Hand*, ed. Irving Dilliard. New York: Alfred A. Knopf.

Hardin, Russell. 1999. *Liberalism, Constitutionalism, and Democracy.* New York: Oxford University Press.

Harris, Matthew C., Jinseong Park, Donald J. Bruce, and Matthew N. Murray. 2017. "Peacekeeping Force: Effects of Providing Tactical Equipment to Local Law Enforcement." *American Economic Journal: Economic Policy* 9 (3): 291–313.

Hastings, Deborah. 2014. "Family of Toddler Severely Injured During Botched Ga. Drug Raid Faces $1 Million in Medical Bills: Interview." *NY Daily News*, December 18. Available online at http://www.nydailynews.com/news/national/ family-1m-medical-bills-tot-burned-swat-raid-article-1.2050396.

Hayek, F. A. 1960. *The Constitution of Liberty.* Chicago: University of Chicago Press.
———. 1973. *Law, Legislation, and Liberty, Volume 1: Rules and Order.* Chicago: University of Chicago Press.
———. 1981. *Law, Legislation, and Liberty, Volume 3: The Political Order of a Free People.* Chicago: University of Chicago Press.

Hazlitt, Henry. 1946 [1979]. *Economics in One Lesson.* New York: Three Rivers.

Heath, Brad. 2015. "The U.S. Secretly Tracked Billions of Calls for Decades." *USA Today*, April 8. Available online at http://www.usatoday.com/story/ news/2015/04/07/dea-bulk-telephone-surveillance-operation/70808616.

Hedges, Chris. 2002. *War Is a Force That Gives Us Meaning.* New York: PublicAffairs.

Helms, Richard. 2003. *A Look Over My Shoulder: A Life in the Central Intelligence Agency.* New York: Random House.

Hemenway, David, Mary Vriniotis, and Matthew Miller. 2006. "Is an Armed Society a Polite Society? Guns and Road Rage." *Accident Analysis and Prevention* 38 (4): 687–695.

Herman, Susan N. 2011. *Taking Liberties: The War on Terror and the Erosion of American Democracy.* New York: Oxford University Press.

Hersh, Seymour M. 1974. "Huge C.I.A. Operation Reported in U.S. Against Antiwar Forces, Other Dissidents in Nixon Years." *The New York Times*, December 22, p. 1.
———. 2007. "The General's Report: How Antonio Taguba, Who Investigated

the Abu Ghraib Scandal, Became One of Its Casualties. *The New Yorker*, June 25. Available online at http://www.newyorker.com/magazine/2007/06/25/the-generals-report.

Higgs, Robert. 1987. *Crisis and Leviathan: Critical Episodes in the Growth of American Government*. New York: Oxford University Press.

———. 1991. "Eighteen Problematic Propositions in the Analysis of the Growth of Government." *The Review of Austrian Economics* 5 (1): 3–40.

———. 2004. *Against Leviathan: Government Power and a Free Society*. Oakland, CA: Independent Institute.

———. 2006. *Depression, War, and Cold War: Studies in Political Economy*. New York: Oxford University Press.

———. 2007a. *Neither Liberty Nor Safety: Fear, Ideology, and the Growth of Government*. Oakland, CA: Independent Institute.

———. 2007b. "Military-Economic Fascism: How Business Corrupts Government, and Vice Versa." *The Independent Review* 12 (2): 299–316.

———. 2008a. "Underappreciated Aspects of the Ratchet Effect." *The Beacon*, December 16. Available online at http://blog.independent.org/2008/12/16/underappreciated-aspects-of-the-ratchet-effect.

———. 2008b. "Government Growth." *The Concise Encyclopedia of Economics*. Library of Economics and Liberty. Available online at http://www.econlib.org/library/Enc/GovernmentGrowth.html.

———. 2008c. "The Complex Course of Ideological Change." *American Journal of Economics & Sociology* 67 (4): 547–565.

———. 2012. *Delusions of Power: New Explorations of State, War, and Economy*. Oakland, CA: Independent Institute.

History. 2008. "This Day in History: Cardinal Mindszenty of Hungary Sentenced." Available online at http://www.history.com/this-day-in-history/cardinal-mindszenty-of-hungary-sentenced.

Hochschild, Adam. 1999. *King Leopold's Ghost: A Story of Greed, Terror, and Heroism in Colonial Africa*. New York: Houghton Mifflin.

Hodgson, Godfrey. 1990. *The Colonel: The Life and Wars of Henry Stimson 1867–1950*. New York: Alfred A. Knopf.

Hoffman, David H., et al. 2015. "Report to the Special Committee of the Board of Directors of the American Psychological Association: Independent Review Relating to APA Ethics Guidelines, National Security Interrogations, and Torture." American Psychological Association. Available online at https://www.apa.org/independent-review/APA-FINAL-Report-7.2.15.pdf.

Hogan, Michael J. 1998. *A Cross of Iron: Harry S. Truman and the National Security State 1945–1954*. New York: Cambridge University Press.

Holpuch, Amanda. 2014. "Oakland Pays $4.5m to Scott Olsen, Veteran Injured in Occupy Protest." *The Guardian*, March 21. Available online at http://www.theguardian.com/world/2014/mar/21/city-of-oakland-pays-4-million-veteran-occupy.

Holzman, Michael Howard. 2008. *James Jesus Angleton, the CIA, and the Craft of Counterintelligence*. Amherst, MA: University of Massachusetts Press.

Hooper, Troy. 2012. "Operation Midnight Climax: How the CIA Dosed S.F. Citizens with LSD." *SF Weekly*, March 14. Available online at http://www.sfweekly.com/sanfrancisco/operation-midnight-climax-how-the-cia-dosed-sf-citizens-with-lsd/Content?oid=2184385.

Horsey, David. 2012. "Lie About EPA Spy Drones Thrives in Right-Wing Blogosphere." *The Los Angeles Times*, June 19. Available online at http://www.latimes.com/opinion/topoftheticket/la-na-tt-epa-spy-drones-20120619-story.html.

Hovland, Carl Iver, Irving Lester Janis, and Harold H. Kelley 1953. *Communication and Persuasion*. New Haven, CT: Yale University Press, 1953.

Hume, David. 1963. *Essays: Moral, Political, Literary*. New York: Oxford University Press.

Hummel, Jeffrey Rogers. 2012. *War Is The Health of the State: The Impact of Military Defense on the History of the United States*. Unpublished manuscript.

Ikenberry, G. John. 2012. *Liberal Leviathan: The Origins, Crisis, and Transformation of the American World Order*. Princeton, NJ: Princeton University Press.

Ingram, David. 2013. "How Drones Are Used for Domestic Surveillance." *The Christian Science Monitor*, June 19. Available online at http://www.csmonitor.com/USA/Latest-News-Wires/2013/0619/How-drones-are-used-for-domestic-surveillance.

International Association of Chiefs of Police. 2009. "Employing Returning Combat Veterans as Law Enforcement Officers." September. Available online at http://www.theiacp.org/portals/0/pdfs/IACPReturningCombatVeteransFINAL2009-09-15.pdf.

Inquisitr. 2014. "Georgia SWAT Team That Disfigured Baby Bou Bou's Face with a Flash Grenade Will Not Be Charged." October 7. Available online at http://www.inquisitr.com/1524103/georgia-swat-team-that-disfigured-baby-boo-boos-face-with-a-flash-grenade-will-not-be-charged.

Jacobsen, Annie. 2014. *Operation Paperclip: The Secret Intelligence Program That Brought Nazi Scientists to America*. New York: Little, Brown.

Jacoby, Henry. 1973. *The Bureaucratization of the World*. Los Angeles: University of California Press.

Jefferson, Thomas.1854a. *The Writings of Thomas Jefferson, Volume VI*. Washington, DC: Taylor and Maury.

———. 1854b. *The Writings of Thomas Jefferson, Volume VII*. Washington, DC: Taylor and Maury.

Johnson, Chalmers. 2000. *Blowback: The Costs and Consequences of American Empire*. New York: Henry Holt.

———. 2004. *The Sorrows of Empire: Militarism, Secrecy, and the End of the Republic*. New York: Metropolitan Books.

Joseph, George. 2017. "Cellphone Spy Tools Have Flooded Local Police Departments." Citylab, February 8. Available online: http://www.citylab.com/crime/2017/02/cellphone-spy-tools-have-flooded-local-police-departments/512543.

Judicial Watch. 2016. "Cartels Help Terrorists in Mexico Get to U.S. to Explore Targets; ISIS Militant Shaykh Mahmood Omar Khabir Among Them." April 26. Available online at http://www.judicialwatch.org/blog/2016/04/cartels-help-terrorists-in-mexico-get-to-u-s-to-explore-targets-isis-militant-shaykh-mahmood-omar-khabir-among-them.

Kahn, David. 1996. *Codebreakers: The Comprehensive History of Secret Communication from Ancient Times to the Internet.* New York: Scribner.

Kane, Tim. 2014. "The Good Country." *Commentary.* December. Available online at http://www.commentarymagazine.com/article/the-good-country.

Karlstrom, Eric T. 2012. "Mind Control: History and Applications." Available online at http://911nwo.com/?p=2160.

Katz, Howie. 2012. "The True Story Behind the Founding of SWAT." *Pacovilla*, October 13. Available online at http://www.pacovilla.com/the-true-story-behind-the-founding-of-swat.

Keck, Margaret E., and Kathryn Sikkink. 1998. *Activists Beyond Borders: Advocacy Networks in International Politics.* Cornell, NY: Cornell University Press.

Keisling, Jason, and Lauren Galik. 2014. "War on the Streets: How SWAT Has Become Larger and More Invasive." *Reason*, August 25. Available online at http://reason.com/blog/2014/08/25/war-on-the-streets.

Kinzer, Stephen. 2003. *All the Shah's Men: An American Coup and the Roots of Middle East Terror.* New York: John Wiley & Sons.

———. 2006. *Overthrow: America's Century of Regime Change from Hawaii to Iraq.* New York: Times Books.

———. 2015a. "The World of Threats to the US Is an Illusion." *The Boston Globe*, April 12. Available online at https://www.bostonglobe.com/opinion/editorials/2015/04/11/have-seen-enemies-and-they-weak/Cho9J5Bf9jxIkH-KIZvnVTJ/story.html.

———. 2015b. "The United States of Fear and Panic." *The Boston Globe*, December 23. Available online at https://www.bostonglobe.com/opinion/2015/12/23/the-united-states-fear-and-panic/o3DvdxI1nUw45Z2Lza9aLM/story.html.

———. 2017. *The True Flag: Theodore Roosevelt, Mark Twain, and the Birth of American Empire.* New York: Henry Holt.

Koebler, Jason. 2014. "North Dakota Man Sentenced to Jail in Controversial Drone-Arrest Case." *US News and World Report,* January 15. Available online at http://www.usnews.com/news/articles/2014/01/15/north-dakota-man-sentenced-to-jail-in-controversial-drone-arrest-case.

Koh, Harold H. 1997. "Why Do Nations Obey International Law?" *Yale Law Journal* 106 (9): 2599–2659.

Kopstein, Joshua. 2013. "FBI Admits It Uses Surveillance Drones Over U.S. Soil." *The Verge*, June 19. Available online at http://www.theverge.com/2013/6/19/4445362/fbi-admits-it-uses-surveillance-drones-over-us-soil.

Kramer, Paul. 2008. "The Water Cure: Debating Torture and Counterinsurgency—a

Century Ago." *The New Yorker*, February 25. Available online at http://www. newyorker.com/magazine/2008/02/25/the-water-cure.

Kraska, Peter G. 2001. *Militarizing the American Criminal Justice System: The Changing Roles of the Armed Forces and the Police*. Boston: Northwestern University Press.

———. 2007. "Militarization and Policing—Its Relevance to 21st Century Police." *Policing* 1 (4): 501–513.

Krasner, Stephen D. 1972. "Are Bureaucrats Important? (Or Allison Wonderland)." *Foreign Policy* 7: 159–179.

Kreps, Sarah. 2016. *Drones: What Everyone Needs to Know*. New York: Oxford University Press.

Krisch, Nico. 2003. "Weak as Constraint, Strong as Tool: The Place of International Law in U.S. Foreign Policy." In *Unilateralism and U.S. Foreign Policy: International Perspectives*, ed. David M. Malone and Yeun Foong Khong, 41–70. Boulder, CO: Lynne Rienner.

Kuzmarov, Jeremy. 2011. "The Militarization of American Police Has Long Historical Roots." *History News Network*, November 28. Available online at http://historynewsnetwork.org/article/143228.

———. 2012. *Modernizing Repression: Police Training and Nation-Building in the American Century*. Amherst: University of Massachusetts Press.

Lal, Deepak. 2004. *In Praise of Empires*. New York: Palgrave Macmillan.

Landau, Elizabeth. 2009. "Torture's Psychological Impact 'Often Worse' than Physical." *Central News Network*, May 22. Available online at http://www. cnn.com/2009/HEALTH/05/22/torture.health.effects/index.html?iref=24hours.

Lasby, Clarence G. 1971. *Project Paperclip: German Scientists and the Cold War*. New York: Atheneum.

Leary, William M., ed. 1984. "Report of the Special Study Group (Doolittle Committee) on the Covert Activities of the Central Intelligence Agency, 30 September 1954 (excerpts)." In *The Central Intelligence Agency, History and Documents*. Tuscaloosa, AL: The University of Alabama Press.

Lee, Martin A., and Bruce Shlain. 1985. *Acid Dreams: The Complete Social History of LSD: The CIA, the Sixties, and Beyond*. New York: Grove Press.

Lee, Micah, Glenn Greenwald, and Morgan Marquis-Boire. 2015. "Behind the Curtain: A Look at the Inner Workings of NSA's Xkeystroke." *The Intercept*, July 2. Available online at https://firstlook.org/theintercept/2015/07/02/look-under-hood-xkeyscore.

Lee, Trymaine. 2015. "Obama to Ban Military Weapons Sent to Local Police Departments." MSNBC, May 18. Available online at http://www.msnbc.com/msnbc/obama-ban-military-weapons-sent-local-police-departments.

Leeson, Peter T., and Christopher J. Coyne. 2012. "Conflict-Inhibiting Norms." In *Oxford Handbook of the Economics of Peace and Conflict*, ed. Stergios Skaperdas and Michelle Garfinkel, 840–860. New York: Oxford University Press.

Leo, Richard A. 2004. "The Third Degree and the Origins of Psychological Interrogation in the United States." In *Interrogations, Confessions, and Entrapment*, ed. G. Daniel Lassiter.New York: Kluwer Academic/Plenum.

———. 2008. *Police Interrogations and American Justice*. Cambridge, MA: Harvard University Press.

Lewy, Guenter. 1980. *America in Vietnam*. New York: Oxford University Press.

Lian, Bradley, and John R. O'Neal. 1993. "Presidents, the Use of Military Force, and Public Opinion." *Journal of Conflict Resolution* 37 (2): 277–300.

Linfield, Michael. 1990. *Freedom Under Fire: U.S. Civil Liberties in Times of War*. Boston: South End Press.

Loeb, Saul. 2014. "Perry Calls for Drones on Border to Stop Terrorist Crossing." *Newsmax*, August 22. Available online at http://www.newsmax.com/Newsfront/Rick-Perry-border-ISIS-drones/2014/08/22/id/590374.

Lofgren, Mike. 2016. *The Deep State: The Fall of the Constitution and the Rise of a Shadow Government*. New York: Penguin Books.

Los Angeles Police Department. 2014. "History of S.W.A.T." Available online at http://www.lapdonline.org/metropolitan_division/content_basic_view/849.

Lynn, Alison, and Matt Gutman. 2014. "Family of Toddler Injured by SWAT 'Grenade' Faces $1M in Medical Bills." *ABC News*, December 18. Available online at http://abcnews.go.com/US/family-toddler-injured-swat-grenade-faces-1m-medical/story?id=27671521.

Lynn, Brian McAllister. 1989. *The U.S. Army and Counterinsurgency in the Philippine War*, 1899–1902. Charlotte: University of North Carolina Press.

Lyon, Verne. 1990. "Domestic Surveillance: The History of Operation CHAOS." *Covert Action Information Bulleting*, Summer. Available online at http://www.serendipity.li/cia/lyon.html.

MacArthur, Douglas. 1965. *A Soldier Speaks: Public Papers and Speeches of General of the Army Douglas MacArthur*. New York: Frederick A. Praeger.

Madison, James. 1865. "Political Observations, April 20, 1795." In *Letters and Other Writings of James Madison*, vol. 4, 485–505. Philadelphia: J.B. Lippincott.

Mannix, Daniel P. 2014. *The History of Torture*. Lake Oswego, OR: eNet Press.

Marquis-Boire, Morgan, Glenn Greenwald, and Micah Lee. 2015. "XKeyscore: NSA's Google for the World's Private Communications." *The Intercept*, July 1. Available online at https://firstlook.org/theintercept/2015/07/01/nsas-google-worlds-private-communications.

Marthews, Alex, and Catherine E. Tucker. 2015. "Government Surveillance and Internet Search Behavior." *Mimeo*. Available online at http://papers.ssrn.com/sol3/papers.cfm?abstract_id=2412564.

Mazzetti, Mark. 2013. *The Way of the Knife: The CIA, a Secret Army, and a War at the Ends of the Earth*. New York: Penguin Press.

May, Earnest R. 1990. "Cold War and Defense." In *The Cold War and Defense*, ed. Keith Neilson and Ronald G. Haycock, 7–74. New York: Praeger.

McCarthy, Daniel. 2014. "Why Liberalism Means Empire." *The American Con-*

servative, July 16. Available online at http://www.theamericanconservative. com/articles/why-liberalism-means-empire.

McCartney, James. 2015. *America's War Machine: Vested Interests, Endless Conflicts*. New York: Thomas Dunne.

McCoy, Alfred W. 2006. *A Question of Torture: CIA Interrogation, From the Cold War to the War on Terror*. New York: Metropolitan Books.

———. 2009. *Policing America's Empire: The United States, the Philippines, and the Rise of the Surveillance State*. Madison: The University of Wisconsin Press.

———. 2015. "The Real American Exceptionalism: From Torture to Drone Assassination; How Washington Gave Itself a Global Get-Out-of-Jail-Free Card." TomDispatch.com, February 24. Available online at http://www.tomdispatch. com/blog/175960.

———. 2017. *In the Shadows of the American Century: The Rise and Decline of US Global Power*. Chicago: Haymarket Books.

McFarland, Matt. 2015. "Drone Operators Assist in Search and Rescue Efforts After Devastating Floods in Texas." *The Washington Post*, May 29. Available online at https://www.washingtonpost.com/news/innovations/wp/2015/05/29/ drone-operators-assist-search-and-rescue-efforts-after-devastating-floods-in-texas.

McLaughlin, Elliot C., Martin Savidge, and Devon M Sayers. 2014. "SWAT Team Threatened After Grenade Injures Toddler in Drug Raid." CNN, May 31. Available online at http://www.cnn.com/2014/05/30/us/ georgia-toddler-injured-stun-grenade-drug-raid.

McLaughlin, Jenna. 2015. "CIA Torture Tactics Reemerge in New York Prison." *The Intercept*, August 12. Available online at https://theintercept.com/2015/08/12/ cia-torture-tactics-reemerge-new-york-prison.

Mearsheimer, John J. 1994-1995. "The False Promise of International Institutions." *International Security* 19 (3): 5–49.

Michel, Arthur Holland. 2013. "Drones in Bosnia." Center for the Study of the Drone. Available online at http://dronecenter.bard.edu/drones-in-bosnia.

Militia Act of May 2, 1792. Chapter 28, § 2. Second Congress, Session I. Available online at http://www.constitution.org/mil/mil_act_1792.htm.

Miller, Claire Cain. 2013. "Secret Court Ruling Put Tech Companies in Data Bind." *The New York Times*, June 13. Available online at http://www.nytimes. com/2013/06/14/technology/secret-court-ruling-put-tech-companies-in-data-bind.html?pagewanted=all&_r=0.

Miller, Stuart Creighton. 1982. *Benevolent Assimilation: The American Conquest of the Philippines, 1899–1903*. New Haven, CT: Yale University Press.

Millett, Richard L. 2010. "Searching for Stability: The U.S. Development of Constabulary Forces in Latin America and the Philippines." Occasional Paper 30, Combat Studies Institute Press, Fort Leavenworth, Kansas. Available online at www.dtic.mil/get-tr-doc/pdf?AD=ADA519630.

Mills, C. Wright. 1956. *The Power Elite*. New York: Oxford University Press.

Miron, Jeffrey A. 2003. "The Effect of Drug Prohibition on Drug Prices: Evidence from the Markets for Cocaine and Heroin." NBER Working Paper No. 9689. Available online at http://www.nber.org/papers/w9689.pdf?new_window=1.

Miron, Jeffrey A., and Jeffrey Zwiebel. 1995. "The Economic Case Against Drug Prohibition." *Journal of Economic Perspectives* 9 (4): 175–192.

Misencik, Paul R. 2013. *The Original American Spies: Seven Covert Agents of the Revolutionary War.* Jefferson, NC: McFarland.

Missouri Department of Public Safety. 2012. Department of Defense Excess Property Program. Available online at http://www.dps.mo.gov/dir/programs/cjle/dod.asp.

Mitchell, William C., and Randy T. Simmons. 1990. "Public Choice and the Judiciary: Introductory Notes." *Brigham Young University Law Review* 3: 729–744.

Mitchener, Kris James, and Marc Weidenmier. 2005. "Empire, Public Goods, and the Roosevelt Corollary." *The Journal of Economic History* 65 (3): 658–692.

Mizokami, Kyle. 2017. "The Predator Drone Is Going Into Retirement." *Popular Mechanics*, March 1. Available online at http://www.popularmechanics.com/military/news/a25439/predator-drone-retirement.

Moore, Mark H. 1977. *Buy and Bust: The Effective Regulation of an Illicit Market in Heroin.* Lexington, MA: Lexington Books.

Morsink, Johannes. 2000. *The Universal Declaration of Human Rights: Origins, Drafting, and Intent.* Philadelphia: University of Pennsylvania Press.

Mueller, John. 1970. "Presidential Popularity from Truman to Johnson." *American Political Science Review* 64 (1): 18–34.

———. 2006. "Is There Still a Terrorist Threat? The Myth of the Omnipresent Enemy." *Foreign Affairs* 85 (5): 2–8.

———. 2009. *Overblown: How Politicians and the Terrorism Industry Inflate National Security Threats and Why We Believe Them.* New York: Free Press.

Mueller, John, and Mark G. Stewart. 2011. *Terror, Security, and Money: Balancing the Risks, Benefits, and Costs of Homeland Security.* New York: Oxford University Press.

———. 2016. *Chasing Ghosts: The Policing of Terrorism.* New York: Oxford University Press.

Murphy, Frank. 1943. "Concurring, Kiyoshi Hirabayashi v. United States, 320 U.S. 81, 113." Available online at http://caselaw.findlaw.com/us-supreme-court/320/81.html.

Nagy, John A. 2011. *Spies in the Continental Capital: Espionage Across Pennsylvania During the American Revolution.* Yardley, PA: Westholme.

National Association of Destroyer Veterans. 1998. "USS Ault." Available online at http://www.destroyers.org/histories/h-dd-698.htm.

National Commission on Law Observance and Enforcement. 1931. *Report on Lawlessness in Law Enforcement.* Washington, DC: United States Government Printing Office.

National Security Archives. 2000. "The Secret CIA History of the Iran Coup, 1953." Available online at http://www2.gwu.edu/~nsarchiv/NSAEBB/NSAEBB28/index.html.

National Security Council Intelligence Directive No. 12. 1950. "Avoidance of Publicity Concerning the Intelligence Agencies of the U.S. Government." Available online at http://fas.org/irp/offdocs/nscid12.htm.

Neu, Charles E. 1987. "The Rise of the National Security Bureaucracy." In *The New American State: Bureaucracies and Policies Since World War II*, ed. Louis Galambos, 85–108. Baltimore, MD: Johns Hopkins University Press.

Newcome, Laurence R. 2004. *Unmanned Aviation: A Brief History of Unmanned Aerial Vehicles*. Reston, VA: American Institute of Aeronautics and Astronautics.

Newport, Frank. 2015. "Half in U.S. Continue to Say Gov't Is an Immediate Threat." Gallup.com, September 21. Available online at http://www.gallup.com/poll/185720/half-continue-say-gov-immediate-threat.aspx.

Niskanen, William A. 1971. *Bureaucracy and Representative Government*. Chicago: Aldine Atherton.

———. 1975. "Bureaucrats and Politicians." *Journal of Law and Economics* 18 (3) 617–643.

———. 2001. "Bureaucracy." In *The Elgar Companion to Public Choice*, ed. W. F. Shughart II and L. Razzolini, 258–270. Cheltenham, UK: Edward Elgar.

Obama, Barack. 2013. "Speech on U.S. Drone and Counterterror Policy." May 23. Available online at http://www.nytimes.com/2013/05/24/us/politics/transcript-of-obamas-speech-on-drone-policy.html.

———. 2014. "Remarks by the President After Meeting with Elected Officials, Community and Faith Leaders, and Law Enforcement Officials on How Communities and Law Enforcement Can Work Together to Build Trust to Strengthen Neighborhoods Across the Country." December 1. Available online at https://www.whitehouse.gov/the-press-office/2014/12/01/remarks-president-after-meeting-elected-officials-community-and-faith-le.

Office of the Assistant Attorney General. 2010. "Memorandum for the Attorney General Re: Applicability of Federal Criminal Laws and the Constitution to Contemplated Lethal Operations Against Shaykh al-Aulaqi." Available online at https://www.washingtonpost.com/r/2010-2019/WashingtonPost/2014/06/23/National-Security/Graphics/memodrones.pdf?tid=a_inl.

Official Gazette. 1938. "Commonwealth Acy No. 343." First National Assembly, Fourth Special Session. Available online at http://www.gov.ph/1938/06/23/commonwealth-act-no-343.

Olson, Mancur. 1965. *The Logic of Collective Action: Public Goods and the Theory of Groups*. Cambridge, MA: Harvard University Press.

Operation Border Star. 2014. "Operation Border Star Participants." Available online at http://www.dps.texas.gov/PublicInformation/OpBorStarParticipants.pdf.

Oppenheimer, Franz. 1972. *The State: Its History and Development Viewed Sociologically*. New York: Arno Press.

Ostrom, Vincent. 1991. *The Meaning of American Federalism: Constituting a Self-Governing Society*. San Francisco: ICS Press.

Otterman, Michael. 2007. *American Torture: From the Cold War to Abu Ghraib and Beyond*. Victoria, Australia: Melbourne University Press.

Padgett, Time. 2009. "Drones Join the War Against Drugs." *Time*, June 8. Available online at http://content.time.com/time/nation/article/0,8599,1903305,00.html.

Page, Benjamin I., and Robert Y. Shapiro. 1992. *The Rational Public: Fifty Years of Trends in Americans' Policy Preferences*. Chicago: University of Chicago Press.

Pallitto, Robert M. 2011. *Torture and State Violence in the United States*. Baltimore: The Johns Hopkins University Press.

Paul, Rand. 2014. "We Must Demilitarize the Police." *Time*, August 14. Available online at http://time.com/3111474/rand-paul-ferguson-police.

Paulsen, Michael Stokes. 2009. "The Constitutional Power to Interpret International Law." *The Yale Law Journal*: 1762–1842.

Peacock, Alan T., and Jack Wiseman. 1961. *The Growth of Public Expenditure in the United Kingdom*. Princeton, NJ: Princeton University Press.

Peltzman, Sam. 1980. "The Growth of Government," *Journal of Law and Economics* 23 (2): 209–87.

Pen America. 2013. "Chilling Effects: NSA Surveillance Drives U.S. Writers to Self-Censor." November 12. Available online at http://www.pen.org/sites/default/files/2014-08-01_Full%20Report_Chilling%20Effects%20w%20Color%20cover-UPDATED.pdf.

Penney, Jonathon W. 2016. "Chilling Effects: Online Surveillance and Wikipedia Use." *Berkeley Technology Law Journal*, 31 (1): 117–182.

Pennsylvania Department of Corrections. 2016. "DOC Employment." Available online at http://www.cor.pa.gov/Employment/Pages/default.aspx#VeteransPreference.

People's Law Office. 2014. "118 Documented Burge Area 2 and 3 Torture Victims 1972–1991." Available online at http://peopleslawoffice.com/wp-content/uploads/2014/01/1.6.14.-Documented-TortureSurvivorsunderBurge.pdf.

Perlroth, Nicole, Jeff Larson, and Scott Shane. 2013. "N.S.A. Able to Foil Basic Safeguards of Privacy on Web." *The New York Times*, September 5. Available online at http://www.nytimes.com/2013/09/06/us/nsa-foils-much-internet-encryption.html?pagewanted=all&_r=0.

Perry, Rick. 2008. "Texas Securing Our Nation's Border." Office of the Governor Rick Perry. Available online at http://governor.state.tx.us/news/editorial/10224.

Peterson, Gary. 2013. "From Military to Police Force: A Natural Transition?" *San Jose Mercury News*, August 18. Available online at http://www.mercurynews.com/breaking-news/ci_23886231/from-military-police-force-natural-transition.

Physicians for Social Responsibility, Physicians for Global Survival, and Physicians for the Prevention of Nuclear War. 2015. *Body Count: Casualty Figures after 10 Years of the War on Terror*. Washington, DC Available online at http://www.psr.org/assets/pdfs/body-count.pdf.

Pierson, Paul. 2004. *Politics in Time: History, Institutions, and Social Analysis*. Princeton, NJ: Princeton University Press.

Plaw, Avery, Matthew S. Fricker, and Carlos R. Colon. 2015. *The Drone Debate:*

A Primer on the U.S. Use of Unmanned Aircraft Outside Conventional Battle-fields. Lanham, MD: Roman & Littlefield.

Poitras, Laura, Marcel Rosenbach, and Holger Stark. 2014. "'A' for Angela: GCHQ and NSA Targeted Private German Companies and Merkel." *Spiegel International Online*, March 29. Available online at http://www.spiegel.de/international/germany/gchq-and-nsa-targeted-private-german-companies-a-961444.html.

Polsby, Nelson. 1964. *Congress and Presidency*. Upper Saddle River, NJ: Prentice Hall.

Porter, Bruce D. 1994. *War and the Rise of the State: The Military Foundations of Modern Politics*. New York: Free Press.

Posen, Barry R. 2014. *Restraint: A New Foundation for U.S. Grand Strategy*. Ithaca, NY: Cornell University Press.

Posner, Eric A. 2009. "International Law: Governments Respect International Law Only When It Suits Their National Interests. Don't Expect That to Change Any Time Soon." *Foreign Policy*, September 17. Available online at http://foreignpolicy.com/2009/09/17/think-again-international-law.

Posner, Eric A., and Adrian Vermeule. 2007. *Terror in the Balance: Security, Liberty, and the Courts*. New York: Oxford University Press.

Powers, Thomas 2004. *Intelligence Wars: American Secret History from Hitler to Al-Qaeda*. New York: New York Review of Books.

Preble, Christopher A. 2009. *The Power Problem: How American Military Dominance Makes Us Less Safe, Less Prosperous, and Less Free*. Ithaca, NY: Cornell University Press.

Prevost, Richard. 2010. "Water Cure: U.S. Policy and Practice in the Philippine Insurrection." Virginia State Bar. Available online at http://www.vsb.org/docs/sections/military/water.pdf.

Price, Byron. 1945. *Report on the Office of Censorship*. Washington, DC: U.S. Government Printing Offices.

Priest, Dana, and William M. Arkin. 2010. "A Hidden World, Growing Beyond Control." *The Washington Post*, July 19. Available online at http://projects.washingtonpost.com/top-secret-america/articles/a-hidden-world-growing-beyond-control.

——. 2011. *Top Secret America: The Rise of the New American Security State*. New York: Little, Brown.

Radack, Jesselyn. 2014. "Why Edward Snowden Wouldn't Get a Fair Trial." *Wall Street Journal*, January 21. Available online at http://www.wsj.com/articles/SB10001424052702303595404579318884005698684.

Rahall, Karena. 2015. "The Green to Blue Pipeline: Defense Contractors and the Police Industrial Complex." *Cardozo Law Review* 36 (5): 1–52.

Ramirez, Eugene. 2003. "Origins of SWAT." *Police Magazine*, May 1. Published online at http://www.policemag.com/channel/swat/articles/2003/05/point-of-law.aspx.

Raustiala, Kal. 2009. *Does the Constitution Follow the Flag? The Evolution of Territoriality in American Law*. New York: Oxford University Press.

Redford, Audrey, and Benjamin Powell. 2016. "Dynamics of Intervention in the War on Drugs: The Build-Up to the Harrison Act of 1914." *The Independent Review: A Journal of Political Economy* 20 (4): 509–530.

Reel, Monte. 2016. "Secret Cameras Record Baltimore's Every Move from Above." Bloomberg.com, August 23. Available online at https://www.bloomberg.com/features/2016-baltimore-secret-surveillance.

Reese, Shawn. 2013. *Defining Homeland Security: Analysis and Congressional Consideration.* Washington, DC: Congressional Research Services.

Rehnquist, William H. 1998. *All the Laws but One: Civil Liberties in Wartime.* New York: Vintage.

Rejali, Darius. 2007. *Torture and Democracy.* Princeton, NJ: Princeton University Press.

Remsberg, Charles. 2013. "Warrior Mindset: 8 Elements of Tactical Performance." *PoliceOne*, June 5. Available online at http://www.policeone.com/Officer-Safety/articles/6261735-Warrior-mindset-8-elements-of-tactical-performance.

Reppetto, Thomas. 2010. *American Police: A History, 1845–1945.* New York: Enigma.

Resignato, Andrew. J. 2000. "Violent Crime: A Function of Drug Use or Drug Enforcement?" *Applied Economics* 32: 681–688.

Rezvani, Arezou, Jessica Pupovac, David Eads, and Tyler Fisher. 2014. "MRAPs and Bayonets: What We Know About the Pentagon's 1033 Program." NPR.org, September 2. Available online at http://www.npr.org/2014/09/02/342494225/mraps-and-bayonets-what-we-know-about-the-pentagons-1033-program.

Richman, Sheldon. 2014. "A Foreign Policy for Knaves." Reason.com, October 12. Available online at https://reason.com/archives/2014/10/12/a-foreign-policy-for-knaves.

Risen, James. 2000. "Secrets of History: The C.I.A. in Iran—A Special Report; How a Plot Convulsed Iran in '53 (and in '79)." *The New York Times*, April 16.

———. 2014. *Pay Any Price: Greed, Power, and Endless War.* New York: Houghton Mifflin Harcourt.

———. 2015. "Outside Psychologists Shielded U.S. Torture Program, Report Finds." *The New York Times*, July 10. Available online at http://www.nytimes.com/2015/07/11/us/psychologists-shielded-us-torture-program-report-finds.html?_r=1.

Risen, James, and Eric Lichtblau 2005. "Bush Lets U.S. Spy on Callers Without Courts." *The New York Times*, December 16. Available online at http://www.nytimes.com/2005/12/16/politics/16program.html?ex=1292389200&en=e32070e08c623ac1&ei=5089&_r=1&.

Robin, Corey. 2004. *Fear: The History of a Political Idea.* New York: Oxford University Press.

Robison, Jennifer. 2002. "Decades of Drug Use: Data from the '60s and '70s." July 2. Available online at http://www.gallup.com/poll/6331/Decades-Drug-Use-Data-From-60s-70s.aspx.

Roosevelt, Kermit Jr. 1979. *Countercoup: The Struggle for Control of Iran*. New York: McGraw-Hill.

Root, Hilton. 2008. *Alliance Curse: How American Lost the Third World*. Washington, DC: Brookings Institution Press.

Roper Center Public Opinion Archives. 1991. "A Half-Century's Polling on the USSR and Communism." *The Public Perspective*, November/December: 25–34.

Rose, Alexander. 2007. *Washington's Spies: The Story of America's First Spy Ring*. New York: Bantem Dell.

Ross, Colin A. 2006. *The CIA Doctors: Human Rights Violations by American Psychiatrists*. Richardson, TX: Manitou Communications.

Rossiter, Clinton. 2009. *Constitutional Dictatorship: Crisis Government in the Modern Democracies*. New Jersey: Transaction.

Roth, Mitchell. 2000. "A Century of Criminal Justice." *Crime and Justice International* 16 (36). Available online at http://www.cjimagazine.com/archives/cji4cf1.html?id=216.

Ruppert, Madison. 2011. "The Pentagon's 1033 Program: Giving Free Military Equipment to Police Departments Around the U.S." Activist Post, December 6. Available online at http://www.activistpost.com/2011/12/pentagons-1033-program-giving-free.html.

Russell, Bertrand. 1943. *An Outline on Rubbish: A Hilarious Catalogue of Organized and Individual Stupidity*. Girard, KS: Haldeman-Julius Publications.

Saad, Lydia. 2002. "Americans Greatly Comfortable with Patriot Act: Few Believe It Goes Too Far in Restricting Civil Liberties. *Gallup*, March 2. Available online at http://www.gallup.com/poll/5113/latest-summary-american-public-opinion-war-terrorism.aspx.

Sack, Kevin. 2017. "Door-Busting Drug Raids Leave a Trail of Blood." *The New York Times*, March 18. Available online at https://www.nytimes.com/interactive/2017/03/18/us/forced-entry-warrant-drug-raid.html?_r=1.

Saiya, Nilay, and Anthony Scime. 2015. "Explaining Religious Terrorism: A Data-Mined Analysis." *Conflict Management and Peace Studies* 32 (5): 487–512.

Sauer, Tom. 2005. *Nuclear Inertia: US Nuclear Weapons Policy After the Cold War*. London: I.B. Tauris.

Savage, Charlie. 2016. "Obama Administration Set to Expand Sharing of Data That N.S.A. Intercepts." *The New York Times*, February 25. Available online at http://www.nytimes.com/2016/02/26/us/politics/obama-administration-set-to-expand-sharing-of-data-that-nsa-intercepts.html?_r=0.

———. 2017. "N.S.A. Gets More Latitude to Share Intercepted Communications." *The New York Times*, January 12. Available online at https://www.nytimes.com/2017/01/12/us/politics/nsa-gets-more-latitude-to-share-intercepted-communications.html?_r=1.

Savage, Charlie, and Laura Poitras. 2014. "How a Court Secretly Evolved, Extending U.S. Spies' Reach." *The New York Times*, March 11. Available online at http://www.nytimes.com/2014/03/12/us/how-a-courts-secret-evolution-extended-spies-reach.html?mwrsm=Email.

Scahill, Jeremy. 2013. *Dirty Wars: The World Is a Battlefield*. New York: Nation Books.

———. 2016. *The Assassination Complex: Inside the Government's Secret Drone Warfare Program*. New York: Simon & Schuster.

Schann, Joan Neuhaus, and Jessica Phillips. 2011. "Analyzing the Islamic Extremist Phenomenon in the United States: A Study of Recent Activity." The James A. Baker III Institute for Public Policy at Rice University. Available online at http://bakerinstitute.org/files/760.

Schwarz, Frederick A. O., and Aziz Z. Huq. 2008. *Unchecked and Unbalanced: Presidential Power in a Time of Terror*. New York: New Press.

Schwirtz, Michael, and Michael Winerip. 2015. "After 2 Killers Fled, New York Prisoners Say, Beatings Were Next." *The New York Times*, August 11. Available online at http://www.nytimes.com/2015/08/12/nyregion/after-2-killers-fled-new-york-prisoners-say-beatings-were-next.html?_r=1.

Serle, Jack. 2015. "Almost 2,500 Now Killed by Covert US Drone Strikes Since Obama Inauguration Six Years Ago: The Bureau's Report for January 2015." *The Bureau of Investigative Journalism*, February 2. Available online at https://www.thebureauinvestigates.com/2015/02/02/almost-2500-killed-covert-us-drone-strikes-obama-inauguration.

Seybolt, Taylor B. 2008. *Humanitarian Military Intervention: The Conditions for Success and Failure*. New York: Oxford University Press.

Shakespeare, William. 1823. *The Dramatic Works of William Shakespeare*. Chiswick, UK: C. Whittingham.

Shane, Scott. 2015. "Hometown Extremists Tied to Deadlier Tolls Than Jihadists in the U.S. Since 9/11." *The New York Times*, June 24. Available online at http://www.nytimes.com/2015/06/25/us/tally-of-attacks-in-us-challenges-perceptions-of-top-terror-threat.html?_r=1.

Sharp, Gene. 2012. *The Politics of Nonviolent Action, Part One: Power and Struggle*. Boston: Porter Sargent.

Sheets, Connor Adams. 2014. "What Are 'Rectal Feeding,' 'Rectal Hydration'? Doctors Call CIA Tactics Torture." *International Business Times*, December 12. Available online at http://www.ibtimes.com/what-are-rectal-feeding-rectal-hydration-doctors-call-cia-tactics-torture-1751952.

Shelsby, Ted. 1991. *The Baltimore Sun*, March 2. Available online at http://articles.baltimoresun.com/1991-03-02/business/1991061100_1_rpv-aai-drones.

Sherry, Michael S. 1997. *In the Shadow of War: The United States Since the 1930s*. New Haven, CT: Yale University Press.

Shoup, General David M. 1969. "The New American Militarism." *The Atlantic* 223 (4): 51–56.

Simon, Herbert A. 1997. *Administrative Behavior*, 4th ed. New York: Free Press.

Singer, P. W. 2009. *Wired for War: The Robotics Revolution and Conflict in the 21st Century*. New York: Penguin Books.

Slahi, Mohamedou Ould. 2015. *Guantanamo Diary*. New York: Little, Brown.

Smith, Adam. [1776] 1937. *An Inquiry into the Nature and Cause of the Wealth of Nations*. New York: Modern Library.

Solove, Daniel J. 2013. *Nothing to Hide: The False Tradeoff Between Privacy and Security*. New Haven, CT: Yale University Press.

Sparrow, Bartholomew H. 2006. *The Insular Cases and the Emergence of American Empire*.Lawrence: University of Kansas Press.

Springer, Paul. 2013. *Military Robots and Drones*. Santa Barbara, CA: ABC-CLIO.

State v. Nagle, 23 Ohio St. 3d 185. 1986. Available online at https://casetext.com/case/state-v-nagle-5.

Stimson, Henry Lewis, and McGeorge Bundy. 1971. *On Active Service in Peace and War*. New York: Hippocrene.

Storey, Moorfield, and Marcial P. Lichauco. 1977. *The Conquest of the Philippines by the United States: 1898–1925*. Manchester, NH: Ayer.

Storr, Virgil Henry. 2013. *Understanding the Culture of Markets*. New York: Routledge.

Subra, Baptiste, Dominique Muller, Laurent Bègue, Brad J. Bushman, and Florian Delmas. 2010. "Effects of Alcohol and Weapon Cues on Aggressive Thoughts and Behaviors." *Personality and Social Psychology Bulletin* 36 (8): 1052–1057.

Sulick, Michael J. 2012. *Spying in America: Espionage from the Revolutionary War to the Dawn of the Cold War*. Washington, DC: Georgetown University Press.

Sullum, Jacob. 2014. "A Drug-War Horror: Raid Puts Toddler in Coma." *The New York Post*, June 3. Available online at http://nypost.com/2014/06/03/a-drug-war-horror-raid-puts-toddler-in-coma.

Sumner, William Graham. 1934. *Essays of William Graham Sumner*, ed. Albert G. Keller and Maurice R. Davie. New Haven, CT: Yale University Press.

Svendsen, Lars. 2008. *A Philosophy of Fear*. London: Reaktion.

Sweeney, Michael S. 2001. *Secrets of Victory: The Office of Censorship and the American Press and Radio in World War II*. Chapel Hill, NC: University of North Carolina Press.

Sykes, Alan O. 2013. "The Inaugural Robert A. Kindler Professorship of Law Lecture: When Is International Law Useful?" *NYU Journal of International Law & Politics* 45 (3): 787–814.

Taguba, Antonio. 2004. "Article 15-6 Investigation of the 800th Military Police Brigade." Available online at http://www.npr.org/iraq/2004/prison_abuse_report.pdf.

Taylor, Adam. 2015. "The U.S. Keeps Killing Americans in Drone Strikes, Mostly by Accident." *The Washington Post*, April 23. Available online at https://www.washingtonpost.com/news/worldviews/wp/2015/04/23/the-u-s-keeps-killing-americans-in-drone-strikes-mostly-by-accident.

Taylor, G. Flint. 2015. "The Chicago Police Torture Scandal: A Legal and Political History." *CUNY Law Review* 17: 329–381.

Teller, Henry M. 1902. "The Problem in the Philippines." Available online at https://play.google.com/books/reader?id=UoxAAAAMAAJ&printsec=frontc over&output=reader&hl=en&pg=GBS.PA3.

Theohary, Catherine A. 2016. "Conventional Arms Transfers to Developing Nations, 2007–2015." Congressional Research Service, Washington, DC Available online at https://fas.org/sgp/crs/weapons/R44716.pdf.

Thomas, Norman. 1918. "Justice to War's Heretics." *The Nation*, November 9: 547–549.

Thornton, Mark. 1991. *The Economics of Prohibition*. Salt Lake City: University of Utah Press.

Thrall, A. Trevor, and Jane K. Cramer. 2009. *American Foreign Policy and the Politics of Fear: Threat Inflation Since 9/11*. New York: Routledge.

Timberlake, James H. 1963. *Prohibition and the Progressive Movement: 1900–1920*. Cambridge, MA: Harvard University Press.

Tirman, John. 2011. *The Deaths of Others: The Fate of Civilians in America's Wars*. New York: Oxford University Press.

———. 2015. "The Human Cost of War and How to Assess the Damage." *Foreign Affairs*, October 8. Available online at https://www.foreignaffairs.com/articles/middle-east/2015-10-08/human-cost-war.

Tocqueville, Alexis de. 1840. *Democracy in America. Part the Second, The Social Influence of Democracy*, trans. Henry Reeve. New York: J. & H. G. Langley.

Torreon, Barbara Salazar. 2016. "Instances of Use of United States Forces Abroad, 1798–2016." Congressional Research Service, Washington, DC Available online at https://fas.org/sgp/crs/natsec/R42738.pdf.

Towne, Stephen E. 2015. *Surveillance and Spies in the Civil War: Exposing Confederate Conspiracies in America's Heartland*. Athens: Ohio University Press.

Tucker, Patrick. 2017. "Look for Military Drones to Begin Replacing Police Helicopters by 2025." *Defense One*, August 28. Available online at http://www.defenseone.com/technology/2017/08/look-military-drones-replace-police-helicopters-2025/140588.Tullock, Gordon. ([1965] 2005). "The Politics of Bureaucracy." In *The Selected Works of Gordon Tullock: Vol. 6. Bureaucracy*, ed. C. Rowley, 13–235. Indianapolis: Liberty Fund.

Turner, Charles W., John F. Layton, and Lynn S. Simons. 1975. "Naturalistic Studies of Aggressive Behavior: Aggressive Stimuli, Victim Visibility, and Horn Honking." *Journal of Personality and Social Psychology* 31 (6): 1098–1107.

Turse, Nick. 2008. *The Complex: How the Military Invades Our Everyday Lives*. New York: Metropolitan Books.

———. 2015. "The Golden Age of Black Ops: Special Ops Missions Already in 105 Countries in 2015." TomDispatch.com, January 20. Available online at http://www.tomdispatch.com/blog/175945.

Turse, Nick, and Deborah Nelson. 2006. "Civilian Killings Went Unpunished."

The Times, August 6. Available online at http://www.genocidewatch.org/images/Vietnam6Aug06CivilianKillingsWentUnpunishedDeclassifiedPapersShowU.S.AtrocitiesWentFarBeyondMyLai.pdf.

Twain, Mark. 1972a. "Glances of History (suppressed)," in *Mark Twain's Fables of Man, Volume 7*, ed. John S. Tuckey, 391–393 Berkeley, CA: University of California Press.

———. 1972b. "Outlines of History (suppressed)," in *Mark Twain's Fables of Man, Volume 7*, ed. John S. Tuckey, 395–396. Berkeley, CA: University of California Press.

———. 1992. *Mark Twain's Weapons of Satire: Anti-Imperialist Writings on the Philippine American War*, ed. Jim Zwik. Syracuse, NY: Syracuse University Press.

United Nations General Assembly. 1984. "Convention Against Torture and Other Cruel, Inhuman, or Degrading Treatment or Punishment." Available online at http://www.un.org/documents/ga/res/39/a39r046.htm.

United Nations Human Rights Council. 2015. "Report of the Commission of Inquiry on Human Rights in Eritrea" (Advance Edited Version). Available online at http://www.ohchr.org/EN/HRBodies/HRC/CoIEritrea/Pages/Report-CoIEritrea.aspx.

United States Army Field Manual 7-10. 1962. Washington, DC: Department of the Army. Available online at http://www.survivalebooks.com/free%20manuals/1962%20US%20Army%20Vietnam%20War%20Rifle%20Company%20Infantry%20&%20Airborne%20Battle%20Groups%20326p.pdf.

USAICoE History Office. 2013. "Army Security Agency Established, 15 September 1945." Available online at http://www.army.mil/article/110544.

U.S. Army. n.d. "Ralph Van Deman: Doctor, Lawyer, Intelligence Chief." Masters of Intelligence Art Series. Available online at http://huachuca.army.mil/files/History_MVAND.PDF.

U. S. Army Signal Corps. 1919. *Report of The Chief Signal Officer to the Secretary of War*. Washington, DC: Government Printing Office.

U.S. Bureau of Justice Statistics. 1994. *Sourcebook of Criminal Justice Statistics*. Available online at http://www.albany.edu/sourcebook/pdf/sb1994/sb1994-section2.pdf.

———. 2003. *Sourcebook of Criminal Justice Statistics*. Available online at http://www.albany.edu/sourcebook/archive.html.

U.S. Department of Defense. 2014. "Base Structure Report—Fiscal Year 2014 Baseline." Available online at http://www.acq.osd.mil/eie/Downloads/BSI/Base%20Structure%20Report%20FY14.pdf.

———. 2017. "U.S. Department of Defense Budget for Fiscal Year 2018, Financial Summary Tables." Available online at http://comptroller.defense.gov/Portals/45/documents/defbudget/FY2018/FY2018_Financial_Summary_Tables.pdf.

U.S. Department of Homeland Security. 2012. *Department of Homeland Security Strategic Plan*. Available online at www.dhs.gov/x/library/assets/dhs-strategic-plan-fy-2012- 2016.pdf.

U.S. Department of Justice, Office of the Inspector General. 2007. "A Review of the Federal Bureau of Investigation's Use of National Security Letters." March. Available online at https://oig.justice.gov/special/s0703b/final.pdf.

U.S. Department of State. 1967. "Armed Actions Taken by the United States Without a Declaration of War, 1789–1967." Research Project 806A. Historical Studies Division, Bureau of Public Affairs, Washington, DC

U.S. Department of State, Office of the Historian. 2015. "The Philippine-American War, 1899–1902." Available online at https://history.state.gov/milestones/1899-1913/war.

U.S. Department of the Army. 1970. "Report of the Department of the Army Review of the Preliminary Investigations into the My Lai Incident." Available online at http://www.loc.gov/rr/frd/Military_Law/pdf/RDAR-Vol-I.pdf.

U.S. Federal Bureau of Investigation. 2012. "Terrorism." Available online at http://www.fbi.gov/about-us/investigate/terrorism/terrorism_jttfs.

U.S. General Services Administration. 2012. "1122 Program Equipment and Supplies Catalog." Available online at https://dps.georgia.gov/sites/dps.georgia.gov/files/related_files/document/1122_Catalog.pdf.

———. 2014. "1122 Program Equipment and Supplies Catalog." Available online at http://www.gsa.gov/portal/mediaId/186487/fileName/1122_Catalog-Feb2014Finalv2.action.

———. 2015. "1122 Program." Available online at http://www.gsa.gov/portal/content/202569?utm_source=FAS&utm_medium=print.

U.S. House of Representatives Joint Task Force on U.S. Central Command Intelligence Analysis. 2016. "Initial Findings of the U.S. House of Representatives Joint Task Force on U.S. Central Command Intelligence Analysis." August 10. Available online at http://intelligence.house.gov/uploadedfiles/house_jtf_on_centcom_intelligence_initial_report.pdf.

U.S. Senate Permanent Subcommittee on Investigations. 2012. "Federal Support for and Involvement in State and Local Fusion Centers." Available online at https://www.hsgac.senate.gov/subcommittees/investigations/media/investigative-report-criticizes-counterterrorism-reporting-waste-at-state-and-local-intelligence-fusion-centers.

U.S. Senate Select Committee on Intelligence. 2014. "Committee Study of the Central Intelligence Agency's Detention and Interrogation Program." Washington, DC: U.S. Senate. Available online at http://i2.cdn.turner.com/cnn/2014/images/12/09/sscistudy1.pdf.

U.S. Senate Select Committee on Intelligence, Subcommittee on Health and Scientific Research of the Committee on Human Resources. 1977. "Project MKULTRA, The CIA's Program of Research in Behavior Modification." Washington, DC: U.S. Senate. Available online at https://web.archive.org/web/20071128230208/http://www.arts.rpi.edu/~pellr/lansberry/mkultra.pdf.

U.S. Senate Select Committee to Study Governmental Operations with Respect to

Intelligence Activities. 1976. *Intelligence Activities and the Rights of Americans, Book II.* Washington, DC: U.S. Government Printing Office.

U.S. War Department. 1914. *Regulations Governing Commercial Radio Service Between Ship and Shore Stations, United States Army*, Manual No. 2-A. Washington DC: War Department.

Vagts, Alfred. 1937. *A History of Militarism: Romance and Realities of a Profession.* New York: W.W. Norton.

Valentine, Douglas. 1990. *The Phoenix Program: America's Use of Terror in Vietnam.* New York: William Morrow.

———. 2004. "ABCs of American Interrogation Methods." *Counterpunch,* May 15. Available online at http://www.counterpunch.org/2004/05/15/abcs-of-american-interrogation-methods.

van Vark, Caspar. 2015. "Drones Set to Give Global Farming a Makeover." *The Guardian*, December 26. Available online at http://www.theguardian.com/global-development/2015/dec/26/drones-farming-crop-problems-uavs.

Vibes, John. 2014. "DOD 1033 Program Requires Police to Use Military Gear Within One Year or Return It." *Free Thought Project*, August 27. Available online at http://thefreethoughtproject.com/police-required-military-gear-year-return.

Vignarajah, Krishanti. 2010. "The Political Roots of Judicial Legitimacy: Explaining the Enduring Validity of the *Insular Cases*." *The University of Chicago Law Review* 77 (3): 781–845.

Vile, John R. 2005. *The Constitutional Convention of 1787: A Comprehensive Encyclopedia of America's Founding.* Santa Barbara, CA: ABC-CLIO.

Vine, David. 2015. *Base Nation: How U.S. Military Bases Abroad Harm America and the World.* New York: Metropolitan Books.

Vladeck, Stephen I. 2004. "Emergency Powers and the Militia Acts." *Yale Law Journal* 114: 149–194.

Waddell, Kaveh. 2015. "Who Is Spying on US Cellphones? Lawmakers Demand an Answer." *Defense One*, November 9. Available online at http://www.defenseone.com/technology/2015/11/who-spying-us-cellphones-lawmakers-demand-answer/123527.

Wallsten, Peter, Carol D. Leonnig, and Alice Crites. 2013. "For Secretive Surveillance Court, Rare Scrutiny in Wake of NSA Leaks." *The Washington Post*, June 22. Available online at http://www.washingtonpost.com/politics/for-secretive-surveillance-court-rare-scrutiny-in-wake-of-nsa-leaks/2013/06/22/df9eaae6-d9fa-11e2-a016-92547bf094cc_story.html.

Wagner, Laura. 2015. "North Dakota Legalizes Armed Police Drones." NPR, August 27. Available online at http://www.npr.org/sections/thetwo-way/2015/08/27/435301160/north-dakota-legalizes-armed-police-drones.

Wagner, Richard E. 2014. "American Federalism: How Well Does It Support Liberty?" Mercatus Center, available online at http://mercatus.org/sites/default/files/Wagner_Federalism_v2.pdf.

Walton, Reggie. 2013. "2013-07-29 Letter of FISA Court President Reggie B. Walton to the Chairman of the U.S. Senate Judiciary Committee Patrick J. Leahy

About Certain Operations of the FISA Court." Available online at http://www.leahy.senate.gov/download/honorable-patrick-j-leahy.

Washington, George. 1796. "Washington's Farewell Address 1796." Published online as part of Yale University's The Avalon Project: Documents in Law, History and Diplomacy, http://avalon.law.yale.edu/18th_century/washing.asp.

Weber, Max. 1958. "Politics as Vocation." In *Max Weber: Essays in Sociology*, trans. Hans Heinrich Gerth and C. Wright Mills, 77–128. New York: Oxford University Press.

Weiner, Tim. 2007. *Legacy of Ashes: The History of the CIA*. New York: Anchor Books.

Weingast, Barry. 1995. "The Economic Role of Political Institutions: Market-Preserving Federalism and Economic Development." *Journal of Law, Economics, and Organization* 11 (1): 1–31.

Wessler, Nathan Fred. 2014. "Trickle Down Surveillance." *Al Jazeera America*, June 12. Available online at http://america.aljazeera.com/opinions/2014/7/surveillance-lawenforcementnsastringray3.html.

White, John. 1998. "Seeing Red: The Cold War and American Public Opinion." Paper presented at the Power of Free Inquiry and Cold War International History Conference Program. Available online at http://www.archives.gov/research/foreign-policy/cold-war/conference/conference-program.html.

Whitehead, John. 2013. *A Government of Wolves: The Emerging American Police State*. New York: Select Books.

———. 2015. *Battlefield America: The War on the American People*. New York: Select Books.

White House Office of the Press Secretary. 2014. "Press Conference by the President." August 1. Available online at https://www.whitehouse.gov/the-press-office/2014/08/01/press-conference-president.

Whitlock, Craig. 2014. "White House Plans to Require Federal Agencies to Provide Details About Drones." *The Washington Post*, September 26. Available online at https://www.washingtonpost.com/world/national-security/white-house-plans-to-require-federal-agencies-to-provide-details-about-drones/2014/09/26/5f55ac24-4581-11e4-b47c-f5889e061e5f_story.html.

Whittington, Keith E. 2009. "Constitutional Constraints in Politics." In *The Supreme Court and the Idea of Constitutionalism*, ed. Steven Kautz, Arthur Melzer, Jerry Weinberger, and M. Richard Zinman, 221–234. Philadelphia: University of Pennsylvania Press.

Whittle, Richard. 2014. *Predator: The Secret Origins of the Drone Revolution*. New York: Henry Holt.

Willers, Jack Conrad. 1977. "A Philosophic Perspective of Bureaucracy." *Peabody Journal of Education* 55 (1): 45–50.

Wills, Garry. 2010. *Bomb Power: The Modern Presidency and the National Security State*. New York: Penguin Books.

Wilson, O. W. 1953. "August Vollmer." *Journal of Criminal Law and Criminology* 44 (1): 91–103.

Wilson Woodrow. 1918. *Selected Addresses and Public Papers of Woodrow Wilson*, ed. Albert Bushnell Hart. New York: Boni & Liveright.

Woo, Elaine, and Eric Malnic. 2010. "Daryl F. Gates Dies at 83; Innovative but Controversial Chief of the LAPD." *Los Angeles Times,* April 17. Available online at http://www.latimes.com/local/obituaries/la-me-daryl-gates17-2010apr17-story.html#axzz2tQ9zsOFA.

Work, Bob. 2015. "The Third U.S. Offset Strategy and Its Implications for Partners and Allies." U.S. Department of Defense, January 28. Available online at http://www.defense.gov/News/Speeches/Speech-View/Article/606641/the-third-us-offset-strategy-and-its-implications-for-partners-and-allies.

Yardley, Herbert O. 1931. *The American Black Chamber.* Annapolis, MD: U.S. Naval Institute.

Yoo, John, and Robert J. Delahunty. 2002. "Memorandum Regarding Application of Treaties and Laws to al Qaeda and Taliban Detainees." January 9. Available online at http://www2.gwu.edu/~nsarchiv/NSAEBB/NSAEBB127/02.01.09.pdf.

Zimbardo, Philip. 2007. *The Lucifer Effect: Understanding How Good People Turn Evil.* New York: Random House.

Zimmerman, Dwight Jon. 2010. "Marine Force Recon in Vietnam and the Killer Kane Operations." *Defense Media Network,* July 8. Available online at http://www.defensemedianetwork.com/stories/marine-force-recon-in-vietnam-and-the-killer-kane-operations.

Index

CPSIA information can be obtained
at www.ICGtesting.com
Printed in the USA
LVHW041349260722
724431LV00003B/194